Jeannette Rankin

AMERICA'S CONSCIENCE

JEANNETTE RANKIN, *by Mary Theresa Mimnaugh, pen and ink, circa 1980*

Aug 4, 2003

For Maru,
A story of
Montana's first
RINO!
T

Jeannette Rankin

AMERICA'S CONSCIENCE

BY Norma Smith

FOREWORD BY Joan Hoff
INTRODUCTION BY Kathryn Anderson

MONTANA
HISTORICAL
SOCIETY
PRESS

Helena

The publication of this book was supported by a grant
from the Montana History Foundation.

MF
MONTANA HISTORY
F O U N D A T I O N

BOOK DESIGN Arrow Graphics, Missoula
TYPESET IN New Baskerville

PRINTED IN CANADA

A portion of chapter seven, "First Congresswoman: Pacifist," appeared
in a slightly different version as "The Woman Who Said No to War:
A Day in the Life of Jeannette Rankin," *Ms. Magazine*, March 1986.

02 03 04 05 06 07 08 09 10   11 10 9 8 7 6 5 4 3 2 1

ISBN 0–917298–79–9

LIBRARY OF CONGRESS CATALOGING-IN-PUBLICATION DATA

Smith, Norma, 1913–2001.
  Jeannette Rankin, America's conscience / by Norma Smith ; foreword by
Joan Hoff ; introduction by Kathryn Anderson.
    p. cm.
Includes bibliographical references and index.
ISBN 0–917298–79–9 (alk. paper)
    1. Rankin, Jeannette, 1880–1973. 2. Pacifists—United States—Biography.
3. Legislators—United States—Biography.   4. Feminists—United States—
Biography.   I. Title.

HQ1413.R36 S65   2002
328.73'092—dc21   2002003321

Contents

Illustrations

Foreword

IT IS A GREAT PLEASURE to see Norma Smith's biography of Jeannette Rankin finally published, and my heartfelt thanks goes to the staff at the Montana Historical Society who edited this final version. I corresponded with Smith from the mid-1970s to the mid-1980s as she struggled to revise her manuscript and find a publisher. During this time we exchanged research notes and other material about Rankin, visited by phone and in person, tried to locate missing Rankin papers from a resident of Great Falls who had obtained them when Jeannette's brother Wellington closed his law office in Helena, collaborated on several video projects about Rankin, and in general critiqued each other's work about this remarkable congresswoman from Montana.

As a personal friend of Jeannette Rankin, Smith was filled with invaluable anecdotes and insights into the life and times of the only person to vote against both world wars. Her comments on a talk I gave at the 1977 Montana History Conference on the importance of Rankin's foreign policy views for post-Vietnam American diplomacy helped me revise an article I later wrote in 1980 for *Montana The Magazine of Western History*. Likewise, her comments about an encyclopedia article I was writing clarified my views about Rankin's problematic relationship with both the early-twentieth-century woman's movement and the "second wave" feminists of the 1960s and 1970s.

According to Smith, Rankin did not "consider it appropriate" to comment publicly on the Equal Rights Amendment, which had been introduced in Congress in 1923 but not officially approved and sent to the states for passage until the year 1972—a year before Rankin died. While Rankin's association in the 1920s with the faction of the woman's movement opposed to the ERA may have reflected her views, "I believe she was sympathetic [to the ERA]," Smith wrote me in 1984, "but of course she thought any other issues subordinate to that of peace." Smith further thought that Rankin "was rather ambivalent toward the woman's movement in the 60's. She felt that many of them were upper-middle-class women who were too much interested in their own egos, money, and status. She was rather disagreeable to some of them. On their part, too, they behaved rather badly, treating her like a treasured antique suitable to put on the shelf and admire, as many young people treat the elderly, who they suppose are incapable of understanding the issues of today. I myself saw instance[s] of this. . . . So there was some friction between JR and some of the women's [movement] leaders."

We also often discussed Rankin's personality and her memories and interviews toward the end of her life. While I initially thought that Rankin's "desire for the limelight knew no bounds," Smith correctly noted that "she always put bounds, those of the cause, on her vanity, sacrificing herself frequently. She certainly had her fair share, perhaps more, of vanity and love of flattery; but this trait is fairly common in public figures, for obvious reasons." Smith also realized that because Rankin "had been interviewed all her life, and knew how to put her best foot forward," toward the end of her life she simply began to forget details and so performed less well in public. Unfortunately, in the late 1960s she was frequently interviewed and frequently her memory failed her. As a result, Smith relied less on these interviews than other biographers.

Smith had an abiding faith in the importance of Jeannette Rankin's contributions to pacifism and feminism, and she understood better than anyone else who has written about Rankin that her commitment to the cause of peace and equality grew steadily throughout her long life. Beginning in the teens as a participant in the progressive, peace, and suffrage movements, Jeannette Rankin served her country for over fifty years, in the words of one admirer, as a "gallant warrior for peace and justice."

In May 1985 the State of Montana donated a statue of Jeannette Rankin to the National Statuary Hall Collection for display in the Capitol in Washington, D.C. The other Montanan so honored is, of course, Charles M. Russell, the noted western artist. Some may think it odd that Montanans have chosen an artist and a pacifist to represent their state, but the choice makes more sense when one recalls the records of Montana senators Thomas J. Walsh, Burton K. Wheeler, Lee Metcalf, and Mike Mansfield. Although none of these men were committed pacifists in the Rankin tradition, they were all, like Rankin, rebels and reformers and, on occasion, opposed war.

The Rankin statue at the Capitol honors the contributions of this singular twentieth-century woman even as it disguises how controversial she was during her lifetime. Smith's biography extends our understanding of both the controversy Rankin generated and the contributions that she made because of it. This long-overdue book is a testament to both Smith's and Rankin's perseverance. I am grateful for both. I only wish that Norma were alive to appreciate its publication as much as I do.

JOAN HOFF
Research Professor of History
Montana State University, Bozeman

Introduction

JEANNETTE RANKIN—suffragist, congresswoman, and peace activist—
began sharing her life story with Norma Smith in 1963. Inspired
by Rankin's unwavering crusade for social justice and peace, Smith
(1913–2001) wrote this biography in the 1970s, tracing Rankin's
history from her girlhood in Missoula, Montana, through her
work on woman's suffrage, to her historic antiwar votes in both 1917
and 1942 and her lifelong opposition to war. As Smith proceeded,
growing interest in women's issues and antiwar sentiment confirmed
her commitment to the project's historical significance. As another
generation struggles with issues of national security and human
rights, the Montana Historical Society Press offers this posthumous
publication of Smith's richly detailed story: *Jeannette Rankin,
America's Conscience.*

In the same year that Rankin and Smith began their conversations,
Betty Friedan published *The Feminine Mystique* and a commission
appointed by President John F. Kennedy issued its comprehensive
report on the Status of Women. As the conversations continued in
roughly sixteen interviews over the next eight years (between 1963
and 1971), the civil rights and antiwar movements gained momentum, state and federal legislation began to erode gender inequities,
and the women's liberation movement struggled to articulate the
political dimensions of personal life. In January 1968 women calling
themselves the Jeannette Rankin Brigade protested in Washington,
D.C., against the Vietnam War. By the time Rankin and Smith finished their conversations, the National Women's Political Caucus
had emerged as a bipartisan effort to claim a greater role for
women in national politics. Both Smith's questions and Rankin's

memories, then, were constructed amid intensifying interest and rapid change in women's roles.

Norma Smith was a journalist with an eye for a good story. Her training in history—she received her master's degree from Montana State College, Bozeman, in 1961—also heightened her appreciation for the importance of context. In researching this biography, she investigated individuals, groups, and organizations with whom Jeannette Rankin had contact and the places where she lived and worked. She combed local and national archives for details about the specific economic and political events shaping Rankin's choices and experiences and explored the sources of her ideas and ideals. Unfortunately, Rankin paid so little attention to collecting and preserving her materials that many essential supporting documents and papers have been lost or destroyed. Scholars familiar with the surviving materials know that they leave many questions unanswered.[1] One of the strengths of Smith's biography is that her special access to Rankin, her family, and friends enabled her to fill some of the gaps with new and illuminating details.

At a time when contemporary events and advancing age prompted Jeannette Rankin to reflect on and share her ideas about both women and peace, she and Smith enjoyed a special relationship. Smith's daughter Celia observed that her mother probably felt as close to Jeannette Rankin as to any of her friends. Her daughter Ellen added that their mother did not form friendships easily and may have had a particular affinity for the prickly side of Rankin's personality. Although a generation apart in age, they held many views in common. Like Rankin, Smith was a pacifist and women's rights advocate. As their conversations continued during the late sixties, their opposition to America's involvement in Vietnam developed similarly, as did their disapproval of some of the women's liberation movement's strategies and tactics. According to her daughters, when Smith reports Jeannette Rankin's criticisms of the women's movement, she could have been speaking for herself.[2]

1. Jeannette Rankin papers, Schlesinger Library, Radcliffe College, Cambridge, Mass. Additional materials, including Norma Smith's notes and research materials, are available in the Merrill G. Burlingame Special Collections, Montana State University Library, Bozeman (hereafter MSU).
2. Celia O'Connor, telephone conversation with Kathryn Anderson, August 24, 2001; Ellen Payton, telephone conversation with Kathryn Anderson, September 3, 2001.

While many interviewers have acknowledged Rankin's gracious cooperation with their inquiries, she seemed particularly open to Smith, offering hospitality to her and her daughter on several long weekends in Georgia and Montana. Rankin shared personal letters that she may not have revealed to others—one so meaningful that she carried it around in her purse until it disintegrated—and that Smith chose out of respect for Rankin's privacy not to explore in her book.[3] Rankin seemed to have trusted Smith. In the interviews that emerged from their relationship, Smith gained information and perspective from which she conveys an engaging sense of Rankin's persona. The result is a loving account, though not uncritical. Smith balanced her close relationship with sufficient distance to capture many of the complexities and contradictions in Rankin's personality and positions. However, since no tape recordings or interview transcripts are available, we must read Smith's interpretation of their content and meaning with attention to the particular conditions under which Smith tapped Rankin's memory. The choice to ask, or not ask, certain questions, combined with gaps in the historical record, means that many aspects of Rankin's life remain enigmatic.

The Montana Historical Society Press has edited Smith's manuscript nearly thirty years after its completion to clarify details, dates, and language while remaining faithful to the author's voice and meaning. Unable to complete and refine Smith's working footnotes, they have substituted an essay on sources to clarify the extent of Smith's research. Although not an ideal solution, it allows this important work to be made available to a wider audience.[4] Joan Hoff [Wilson] alerted readers to Smith's "more thorough" biography in her essay on Jeannette Rankin in *Notable American Women* in 1980. Its publication here is a welcome contribution. It offers new insights to those familiar with Rankin's life and an inspiring story for those encountering Rankin for the first time.

Smith meant to write a substantive but popular biography. In addition to interviewing Rankin, she consulted other accounts of Rankin's life and political career (see Essay on Sources) and familiarized herself with contemporary scholarship in women's history. With some prodding, she explored Rankin's relationships

3. Celia O'Connor, August 24, 2001.
4. Smith's original manuscript, with working notes, is available at MSU.

with women friends and colleagues. But she did not intend to enter the conversations evolving in academic conferences and publications about women's changing roles, women and politics, or women in the West. In fact she thought that situating Rankin's life in the context of women's history would narrow its significance and scope. While Smith makes a convincing case that peace and governmental reform became more important to Rankin than women's issues, examining her life in relation to recent scholarship in the history of women and politics enriches our understanding of both.

In the nearly forty years that separate this publication from Smith's first thoughts about a Rankin biography, scholarly interest in women, western women, and political women has blossomed into a mature discipline with contested issues of its own. The story of women as political actors has always been one of the central themes in women's history, but the narrative has become more complex with greater attention to the ways in which women's experiences differ depending on their race, ethnicity, and class. Historians and political scientists have challenged traditional definitions of politics that excluded women. With a broader conceptualization of political behavior, we have begun to document women's political activities long before the suffrage movement, long before they could legally vote in any kind of election, and long before the first woman was elected to Congress. In fact the story begins before European contact in North America.[5]

Born in 1880, Jeannette Rankin came of age during a transition period for both women's roles and American politics. Her life exemplifies the contributions of women of a certain race and class who participated in social reform, woman suffrage, and electoral politics in the early twentieth century and beyond. Her lifelong activism on behalf of peace and governmental reform demonstrates the legacies of a woman's political culture rooted in the nineteenth century that manifested itself more clearly in lobbying and organizing than in voting and holding office. As the first woman and only suffragist elected to Congress, Rankin's place in

---

5. Glenna Matthews, *The Rise of Public Woman: Woman's Power and Woman's Place in the United States, 1630–1970* (New York, 1992). For a discussion of how Europeans influenced gender relationships as they sought to reproduce familiar patriarchal institutions in their relationships with tribes, see Laura F. Klein and Lillian A. Ackerman, eds., *Women and Power in Native North America* (Norman, Okla., 1995).

scholarly narratives of this period is assured. While the opportunity to vote against both world wars ensured her prominence, Rankin's activities as a lobbyist before, during, and after her terms in Congress and her lifelong efforts for peace and governmental reform established her enduring significance.

Rankin's life in politics began, according to Smith, when she studied social theory and policy at the New York School of Philanthropy and gained access to a national network of thinkers and activists. Reform activity gave Rankin a sense of purpose in early adulthood that she had not found in school or work. Contact with like-minded reformers inspired her to begin forming an analysis of the social problems she had witnessed and to develop strategies for addressing them. But social reform in the abstract was one thing; implementing it was another. She discovered that social work did not particularly suit her when she worked in Spokane and Seattle. Smith reports Rankin's painful memories of a highly reputed program's inability to meet the basic needs of the children for whom it was responsible. Smith also hints at Rankin's dissatisfaction with the gender division of labor: women cared for the children while men made policy. Disillusioned with social work, Rankin sought a niche where she could feel both comfortable and effective.

While a student at the University of Washington, Rankin became involved in the state's suffrage movement in the final months of its successful campaign in 1910. She was beginning to understand that social problems required political as well as philanthropic responses, but the timing of her shift from social work to suffrage resulted from opportunity as much as ideology. Some of her contemporaries viewed suffrage primarily as a means to achieve their reform goals, but Rankin was also committed to achieving equal rights for women. Regarded from the end of her political career, one can see the integral relationship between reform and suffrage more clearly. The ideals and social awareness that she gained in reform activities and the political speaking, organizing, and campaigning skills she gained in the suffrage movement combined to launch her lifelong commitment to social and political change that involved women in central roles.

Rankin's success as a speaker and organizer in the Washington state campaign caught the attention of national suffrage leaders and gave her meaningful work at a time when few options were available, even for educated, middle-class white women. An able but relatively unknown westerner, she managed to maneuver between competing strategies for state and national suffrage. As a field secretary for the National American Woman Suffrage Association (NAWSA) from 1913 to 1915, Rankin organized in fifteen states, including the successful Montana campaign in 1914. She also cooperated with Alice Paul, the indomitable leader of the National Woman's Party (NWP) and mobilized Montana delegations for Paul's campaign for a federal amendment. Rankin used the collective pronoun "we" when referring to NAWSA,[6] but she told Smith about her lifelong friendship with Alice Paul and her gratitude for NWP members who supported her votes against war.

Smith's story emphasizes Rankin's independence from both national suffrage organizations when coordinating the final push for a referendum on suffrage in Montana. The commitment to grass roots democracy that would guide her later work for governmental reform was apparent in her preference for effective workers over prominent community women. A fellow Montanan, Smith captures some of the East-West tensions underlying Rankin's disagreement with NAWSA leaders over tactics. Her portrait of a strong-willed leader with a temper, and a fierce commitment to grass roots methods, contributes valuable insights into some of Rankin's contradictions. Smith explains how Rankin, seemingly oblivious to the first twenty years of suffrage activities in Montana, became committed to the cause while studying in New York.[7]

Scholarship on Montana suffrage undertaken after Smith completed her research includes historian Paula Petrik's analysis of population and employment patterns as the state's economy shifted from urban mining to agriculture. Petrik argued that successive generations of women adapted differently to these changing conditions and constructed distinct arguments for their enfranchisement. Rankin belonged to what Petrik defined as the

---

6. "Jeannette Rankin: Activist for World Peace, Women's Rights, and Democratic Government." Transcript of oral history interviews conducted June and August 1972 by Malca Chall (hereafter Chall interview), Regional Oral History Office, Bancroft Library, University of California, Berkeley (hereafter ROHO).

7. Although Smith focuses on Rankin's leadership in the final, triumphant years of the Montana suffrage campaign, she also acknowledges Doris Buck Ward's more comprehensive exploration of Montana's quarter-century struggle. See Doris Buck Ward, "The Winning of Woman Suffrage in Montana" (master's thesis, Montana State University, Bozeman, 1974).

third cohort, comprised of predominantly young women, both married and unmarried, who had some experience with paid employment. Their success depended on the cumulative efforts of preceding generations and a progressive climate more receptive to their increased political participation. They crafted appeals to immigrant laborers while, on other occasions, they resorted to the implication that voting women would preserve, or at least not undermine, the interests of white and native born men.[8] According to Petrik, male voters in the rural and mining communities of eastern Montana responded to the argument that women voters would mitigate foreign influence and supported suffrage in sufficient numbers by 1914 to counteract the lack of a majority in western urban communities. Thus, in the end, suffrage arguments succeeded in Montana on conservative grounds.

Understanding the elitist, racist, and nativist rhetoric that came to dominate the late stages of the suffrage movement is a compelling issue for contemporary scholars.[9] Here, Rankin's experience was typical for women of her race and class. As the election approached, Montana suffragists including Rankin relied increasingly on claims that voting women would improve society and less on the argument that women deserved enfranchisement as a right. Building on recent feminist scholarship on rhetoric, Sara Hayden analyzed Rankin's skill at exploiting ambiguities in western concepts of domesticity as she adapted both her arguments and her style to particular audiences.[10] Smith, for her part, acknowledges the conservatism of much of Rankin's suffrage rhetoric while reporting

---

8. Paula Petrik, *No Step Backward: Women and Family on the Rocky Mountain Mining Frontier, Helena, Montana, 1865–1900* (Helena, Mont., 1987), 115, 131.

9. Aileen S. Kraditor, *The Ideas of the Woman Suffrage Movement: 1890–1920* (New York, 1971); Evelyn Brooks Higginbotham, "In Politics to Stay: Black Women Leaders and Party Politics in the 1920s," in *Women, Politics, and Change*, Louise A. Tilly and Patricia Gurin, eds. (New York, 1990), 199–220; and Rosalyn Terborg-Penn, *African American Women in the Struggle for the Vote, 1850–1920* (Bloomington, Ind., 1998).

10. Sara Hayden, "Negotiating Femininity and Power in the Early Twentieth-Century West: Domestic Ideology and Feminine Style in Jeannette Rankin's Suffrage Rhetoric," *Communication Studies,* 50 (Summer 1999), 83–102. According to Hayden, Rankin used a bold, empowering style with abstract language and logical arguments, stressing ways in which the vote might benefit women when she spoke to female audiences. To mixed audiences or when appealing specifically to male voters, Rankin employed a feminine style, characterized by inductive reasoning, personal examples, and suggestions instead of demands. In these instances, in a style appropriate to her subordinate position in relation to those who had the power to determine her right to vote, she emphasized ways in which women might use the vote to benefit men.

that, in hindsight, Rankin viewed particularly the anti-immigrant arguments as inappropriate.

Jeannette Rankin said she "ran for woman suffrage and got elected to Congress," implying a logical connection between suffrage and electoral politics.[11] However, her experience was neither inevitable nor typical. Her election followed a history of strained relationships between suffragists and political parties. As historian Paula Baker has explained, women and men inhabited distinct political cultures in the nineteenth century. Political parties united men, especially white men, around a common identity that depended, in part, on excluding women.[12] Their reluctance to extend voting rights meant that suffragists endured many disappointments in their attempts to gain recognition in party platforms. Not until male voters in all of the western states had enfranchised women did major parties grudgingly include suffrage planks in 1916. Even then, they refrained from endorsing a federal amendment, calling instead on states to give women the vote. Carrie Chapman Catt represented the sentiment of many suffragists in 1917: "Many of us have deep and abiding distrust of all political parties; they have tricked us so often that our doubts are natural."[13] As a founder and leader of the League of Women Voters, Catt urged women to join political parties after 1920, but she and other suffrage leaders tended to maintain their distance.

Rankin's late entry into the suffrage campaign may have spared her some of the bitterness that longtime advocates felt toward political parties, but other factors contributed to her unique relationship to party politics, none more pivotal than her relationship with her brother Wellington. A progressive Republican and prominent Montana lawyer, Wellington's political credentials freed her to claim or abandon a party identity as it suited her needs. While she worked as a field secretary for NAWSA, Wellington monitored the political situation in Montana and offered timely support and advice during the Montana suffrage campaign. When she began

---

11. Jeannette Rankin, interview with Katrina Rebecca Cheek, November 14, 1968, reprinted as appendix in Cheek, "The Rhetoric and Revolt of Jeannette Rankin" (master's thesis, University of Georgia, 1969), 164.

12. Paula Baker, "The Domestication of Politics: Women and American Political Society, 1780–1920," *American Historical Review*, 89 (June 1984), 620–47.

13. M. G. Peck, *Carrie Chapman Catt: A Biography* (New York, 1944), 283. Quoted in Kristi Andersen, *After Suffrage: Women in Partisan and Electoral Politics before the New Deal* (Chicago, 1996), 78.

getting conflicting responses to the idea of running for Congress in 1916, Wellington responded: "You run and I'll elect you."

Wellington's advice on local issues no doubt contributed to her success in 1916, but she did not hesitate to ignore him when they disagreed. Claiming concern for her political future, Wellington exerted considerable pressure on her to cast "a man's vote" for war, for which, Rankin confided to Smith, he felt "a little ashamed" decades later. Wellington's collaboration with longtime friends, Democrats Burton K. Wheeler and Sam Ford, created the political vacuum in Montana politics that enabled Rankin to win a second seat in Congress in 1940. With her help, he came close to winning an election himself in 1942, losing by only 1,100 votes. They supported each other in midcentury in spite of their increasingly divergent views and lifestyles. He was more conservative, she more radical; he lived as the wealthy man he was, she chose to live simply. A full understanding of the personal and political implications of Rankin's relationship with her brother may still elude us, but Smith's portrayal of their relationship provides intriguing details.

Rankin ran for Congress as a Republican, the party of her father and brother, but the phrase she repeated to Smith many times is revealing: "I was never a Republican. I ran on the Republican ticket." Among suffragists who claimed a partisan identity, most chose the Republican Party because it was more friendly to women's issues. According to historian Melanie Gustafson, women related to parties differently than men; they tended to place principle above party loyalty and readily embraced nonpartisan activities.[14] Certainly, this was true in Rankin's case. Although nominally a Republican, Rankin ran a nonpartisan campaign in 1916. The peculiarities of the race, in which all candidates ran for two at-large positions, allowed her to propose a winning and relatively nonpartisan slogan: "Vote for your local candidate and vote for Jeannette Rankin." In 1918, when the Republican Party failed to nominate her for the senate, she ran as a candidate for the National Party.

---

14. Melanie Gustafson, "Partisan and Nonpartisan: The Political Career of Judith Ellen Foster, 1881–1910," in *We Have Come to Stay: American Women and Political Parties, 1880–1960,* Melanie Gustafson, Kristie Miller, and Elisabeth Israels Perry, eds. (Albuquerque, N.M., 1999), 1–12. On women in the Republican party, see Jo Freeman, *A Room at a Time: How Women Entered Party Politics* (Lanham, Md., 2000), ix, 42; and Melanie Gustafson, *Women and the Republican Party, 1854–1924* (Urbana, Ill., 2001).

While many contemporaries in the suffrage movement considered Rankin's success in 1916 a triumph for all women, her election typifies neither the political experience of suffragists nor the experience of women in politics. In Nevada Anne Martin, like Rankin, led a successful suffrage campaign in 1914. Also like Rankin, after a few years of working for suffrage at the national level, Martin decided that running for office was the "next step." In spite of considerable support from both Nevada suffragists and colleagues in the National Woman's Party, her campaigns for the United States Senate in 1918 and again in 1920 gained only 20 percent of the vote.[15]

Although seasoned suffrage organizers failed to elect Anne Martin, election returns support Rankin's claim that Montana suffragists were responsible for her success.[16] All but one of the counties that had supported suffrage in 1914 also supported Rankin in 1916. The margin of victory, however, came from thirteen counties that had opposed suffrage, supporting Smith's point that family political connections were critical. Seeking political office as the next step distinguished Rankin and Martin from other suffragists. Election to national office placed Rankin in a class by herself.[17]

The prospect of a woman in the halls of Congress created a whole new conversation about the role of women in politics. Before Rankin's historic victory, women had been elected to local and state office, even in non-suffrage states, but primarily in positions related to governing the public schools.[18] Thus, Montana's election of May Trumper as State Superintendent of Public Instruction in 1916 was not news. Neither was the election of Emma A. Ingalls and Maggie Smith Hathaway, who won seats to the Montana House

---

15. On Martin's campaigns, see Kathryn Anderson, "Practical Political Equality: Anne Martin's Senatorial Campaigns in Nevada, 1918 and 1920 (Ph.D. diss., University of Washington, Seattle, 1978).

16. Mary Murphy argues that Good Government Clubs, founded "to preserve the momentum of the suffrage campaign," had a role in electing all four women in 1916 and in the success of several pieces of legislation of interest to women in the subsequent legislature. *Mining Cultures: Men, Women, and Leisure in Butte, 1914–1941* (Urbana, Ill., 1997), 153.

17. Ellis Waldron and Paul B. Wilson, *Atlas of Montana Elections, 1889–1976* (Missoula, Mont., 1978), 54–69. For a comparison of Rankin and Martin, see Kathryn Anderson, "Steps to Political Equality: Woman Suffrage and Electoral Politics in the Lives of Emily Newell Blair, Anne Henrietta Martin, and Jeannette Rankin," *Frontiers*, 28 (November 1997), 101–21.

18. Andersen, *After Suffrage*, 113.

of Representatives in 1916, twenty years after Martha Hughes Cannon became the first woman state legislator in Utah in 1896.[19] Rankin's election was definitely newsworthy. It was also distinctive, compared to the women who followed her in national office, because she "ran for woman suffrage" and included issues in her platform such as an eight-hour day, prohibition, and child welfare. In other words, she "ran as a woman."[20] In contrast Alice Robertson, an Oklahoman who became the first woman to serve in Congress after the Nineteenth Amendment granting woman's suffrage passed in 1920, opposed suffrage and voted against issues supported by organized women during her term. Nominated by her party in a district it expected to lose, Robertson's experience was more typical than Rankin's. Even more typical were the women who inherited elective office; two-thirds of the first generation of women to serve in Congress after suffrage were widows of former representatives. "Such a congresswoman struck party leaders as a useful surrogate until a male heir apparent could be designated."[21]

Unlike most of the women who would follow her in Congress in the next few decades, Rankin championed women's causes during her term, notably the federal suffrage amendment and a bill to reduce maternal and infant mortality. The Rankin-Robinson bill (cosponsored with Senator Joseph Robinson) would have provided direct health care for mothers and babies, more authority for the Children's Bureau, and more than twice the funding of the Sheppard-Towner Maternity and Infancy Protection Act that passed in 1921 a few years after Rankin's term had ended.[22]

As a cosponsor of the more ambitious bill and a lobbyist for the bill that eventually passed, Rankin's activities exemplified women's political options in this transitional period. Her arguments and political style reflected the suffrage and reform traditions from which she came. To minimize the potential role conflict

---

19. Glenna Matthews, *The Rise of Public Woman*, 174.
20. Linda Witt, Karen M. Paget, and Glenna Matthews, *Running as a Woman: Gender and Power in American Politics* (New York, 1994), 31.
21. Ibid.
22. Molly Ladd-Taylor, " 'My Work Came Out of Agony and Grief': Mothers and the Making of the Sheppard-Towner Act," in *Mothers of a New World: Maternalist Politics and the Origins of Welfare State*, Seth Koven and Sonya Michel, eds. (New York, 1993), 328–29; Nancy Cott, *The Grounding of Modern Feminism* (New Haven, Conn., 1987), 98; and J. Stanley Lemons, *The Woman Citizen: Social Feminism in the 1920s* (Urbana, Ill., 1973), chap. 6 on the importance of the Sheppard-Towner Act. The bill expired in 1927 and was extended for an additional two years.

between "woman" and "political activist," she and other women legitimized their public role by claiming to act on behalf of others, not themselves. Assuming that responsibility for children and the home fell primarily to women, they sought to create or reform social institutions to support women's traditional role. Historians have developed the concept of "maternalism" to describe this combination of assumptions and activities.[23] As a politician, Rankin had the opportunity to introduce legislation but lacked the power to see it into law. As a lobbyist for the Sheppard-Towner bill, she could articulate her ideals while experienced politicians worked on the compromises necessary to achieve a bill that could pass.

Regardless of her stand on women's issues, Rankin could not escape the consequences of the fact that most people considered "woman politician" a contradiction in terms. Campaigning for suffrage had introduced her to the conflicting roles women faced as advocates in the political arena. As Rankin's niece Mackey Brown described it: "They had to call on influential citizens like perfect little ladies, and at the same time nerve themselves up to rather brazen 'unladylike' behavior."[24] Moreover, for both candidates and officeholders, gaining equitable treatment from the press was, and continues to be, a challenge. Even coverage of Rankin's vote against World War I focused on her appearance and demeanor more than her convictions. She tempered her strong commitment to women's issues with attention to tastefully appropriate apparel, which Smith describes in detail, but she could not prevent the press from focusing on her gender rather than her issues.

With few models and facing much resistance, Rankin and her contemporaries tried a variety of strategies to define for themselves what it meant to be a woman in politics. Wyoming's Nellie Tayloe Ross became the first woman governor in 1924 when she was elected to complete her deceased husband's term. A politician's wife who celebrated her commitment to domesticity and distanced herself from suffragists and women's issues, she became a leader

---

23. On the legacies of maternalism, see Kathryn Kish Sklar, "The Historical Foundations of Women's Power in the Creation of the American Welfare State, 1830–1930," in *Mothers of a New World*, 43–93.

24. Mackey Brown, "Montana's First Woman Politician—A Recollection of Jeannette Rankin Campaigning," *Montana Business Quarterly* (Autumn 1971), 24, quoted in Witt, *Running as a Woman*, 56.

in the Democratic Party who learned to mobilize women. As historian Virginia Scharff explained, "throughout this remarkable career, Ross faced the double bind of insisting that sex was no handicap for a politician while assuring her constituency that politics did not 'unsex' any woman."[25] Belle Moskowitz never ran for office but exerted considerable influence behind the scenes as aide and strategist for Alfred E. Smith, Democratic governor of New York and unsuccessful candidate for president in 1928. Less well known than either Rankin or Ross, Moskowitz was arguably the most powerful woman in politics in the 1920s. One group of scholars has argued that Rankin's high visibility and Moskowitz's behind-the-scenes power represented "the limits of what was possible for women in the immediate aftermath of suffrage."[26]

To accommodate the political activities of Rankin and her contemporaries before and after 1920, a generation of scholars has devoted considerable energy to finding the appropriate place for the Nineteenth Amendment in the narrative of American history and politics. Historian Nancy Cott argued that excessive focus on ratification of a federal suffrage amendment "obscures the similarities in women's political behavior before and after it and the relation of that behavior to broader political and social context."[27] As Smith's account demonstrates, the form and substance of Rankin's activities before 1920 continued for the rest of her life. Although election to Congress gave her greater visibility, her story is not atypical. Yet the idea that 1920 served as a "great divide" in women's history has been particularly difficult to dispel.

Historians have ignored women in their studies of politics before 1920 if they equated political activity with voting and holding office. Women themselves did not think of their activities as political if they understood the partisan world as male and public and their world as female and private. Yet the clubs and voluntary associations women joined in the nineteenth century played a role in building their communities. Certainly, the political culture

---

25. Virginia Scharff, "Feminism, Femininity, and Power: Nellie Tayloe Ross and the Woman Politician's Dilemma," *Frontiers*, 25 (1995), 88.

26. Witt, *Running as a Woman*, 32–33. On Moskowitz, see Elizabeth Israels Perry, *Belle Moskowitz: Feminine Politics and the Exercise of Power in the Age of Alfred E. Smith* (New York, 1987).

27. Nancy Cott, "Across the Great Divide: Women in Politics Before and After 1920," in *Women, Politics, and Change*, 154.

reflected in their voluntary activities and partisan work at the turn of the century remained distinct from male political culture, and women masked the political nature of their activities by describing them in domestic terms like "social housekeeping." But significant changes were occurring in both political parties and gender roles. According to political scientist Jo Freeman, "elections became less an act of male solidarity and more of a civic duty" in the party system that evolved between Progressivism and the New Deal.[28] This created an opportunity for women to move into new arenas of political activity and to think of themselves in new ways as political actors.

While woman suffrage may have marked an end to a separate women's political culture, we have come to appreciate the legacies of that culture as women joined men in political parties and interest groups. Both major parties escalated their outreach to women after 1920, notably through women's divisions and women's partisan clubs rather than by offering women positions of power. As in the labor force, argued Paula Baker, women "gained a substantial presence as the work was becoming less skilled, more stratified, and except at the very top, less important."[29] Although their impact may not have been visible in elected and appointed offices or in studies of voting patterns, their presence made a difference for feminists in the sixties, according to Jo Freeman: "if there had not already been many women inside all of our political institutions, this movement would have faced the same closed doors that women discovered in the 1920s."[30]

As women entered parties and other political activities in increasing numbers, they met resistance from male leaders anxious to contain their potential power. In the process, explained political scientist Kristi Andersen, women and men negotiated new gender boundaries in politics that would remain relatively stable until another generation of women challenged them again in the seventies.[31] As interest groups gained ascendance over political machines, the qualities that distinguished women's political culture in the nineteenth century became more familiar

---

28. Freeman, *A Room at a Time*, 22.
29. Paula Baker, "She is the Best Man on the Ward Committee," in *We Have Come to Stay*, 159.
30. Freeman, *A Room at a Time*, 7.
31. Andersen, *After Suffrage*, chap. 6.

in party politics. Michael McGerr noted that increased reliance on education and advertising "represented a partial feminization of male political style," although he stopped short of arguing that women were responsible for the transformation. Suggesting that women's voluntary associations were at the heart of the Progressive movement that led to changing political conditions, Suzanne Lebsock ventured to ask: "Is it possible that interest group politics, the characteristic politics of the twentieth century, was invented mainly by women?" Recent studies of organized women pursuing political goals from within their specific racial and ethnic groups lend credence to the implications of her question.[32]

Interest group politics, not party politics, dominated Rankin's political activities after her historic term in Congress. One of the ironies of Rankin's career is that the first woman elected by a major party was not a party woman. Smith explains Rankin's lack of party loyalty with reference to her personality and her preference for being in charge. Others see Rankin as "heir to an old and honorable tradition of principled, altruistic political service," one that focused on social ideals rather than self-aggrandizement.[33] Certainly, her activities upon leaving Congress echoed the aspects of women's political culture that she had absorbed in the reform and suffrage work that consumed her before 1916. In addition reading Benjamin Kidd's *The Science of Power* when she left office gave her a source of authority for her ideas about social change that she would continue to cite for the rest of her life.

Kidd was an English social theorist at the turn of the century who believed in social progress and sought to explain the mechanisms by which it might evolve. His first book, *Social Evolution* (1894), accepted the inevitability of competition and argued that humanitarian impulses would create conditions under which individuals could compete on equal terms. Whether Rankin read his first book is unclear. She would have disagreed with his idea that humanitarian impulses were rooted in religion, but his theories were consistent with those of the New York School of Philanthropy where she

---

32. Michael McGerr, "Political Style and Women's Power, 1830–1930," *Journal of American History*, 77 (December 1990), 870; Suzanne Lebsock, "Women and American Politics, 1880–1920," in *Women, Politics, and Change*, 58; Elizabeth Salas, "Soledad Chavez Chacon, Adelina Otero-Warren, and Concha Ortiz Y Pino: Three Hispana Politicians in New Mexico Politics, 1920–1940," in *We Have Come to Stay*, 161–73.

33. Witt, *Running as a Woman*, 30.

studied social reform. Her references to Kidd typically alluded to his last book, *The Science of Power* (1918), in which he distinguished between force, as in pressure applied in the present, and power, as in ideals focused on the future.

Kidd's theories appealed to Rankin because he claimed that women, by virtue of their responsibilities for children and the home, were better suited than men to create a positive future through the power of ideals. Although most of Rankin's statements imply a belief in essential differences between women and men, she told an interviewer in 1972 that she had "always thought that it's the same thing in men that changed civilization. The great leaders in thought and in change have been those who have been working for the future."[34]

Smith claims that "as a lobbyist [Rankin] was to spend more time in Congress than some Congressmen." She also quotes journalist Drew Pearson to the effect that Rankin was more effective as a lobbyist than as a congressman. Clearly, lobbying, organizing, and speaking consumed much of Rankin's attention for the remainder of her life. Immediately after leaving Congress, she traveled to Europe with a group of women interested in peace, including Jane Addams, Florence Kelley, and Mary Church Terrell, and returned to lobby for release of political prisoners and prisoners of war. As field secretary for the National Consumers' League, she lobbied for the Sheppard-Towner bill and protective legislation for women and children. In its concern for the ways in which women differed from men, this legislation stood in stark contrast to the Equal Rights Amendment (ERA), introduced in 1923, which focused on the ways in which women and men were similar. Based on Rankin's activities and affiliations in the 1920s, we can assume that she would have opposed the ERA. Smith did not elaborate except to imply that Rankin came to view the ERA as just.

Rankin's lobbying and organizing efforts for social reform in the 1920s turned increasingly to causes for peace, including the Women's International League for Peace and Freedom (WILPF) and the Women's Peace Union. As Joan Hoff argued in a comprehensive analysis of Rankin's pacifist activities, the "no" votes for which she is famous were merely highlights of a life devoted

---

34. Chall interview, ROHO.

to a "sustained and systematic" campaign against war.[35] She launched earnest but unsuccessful peace efforts at the local level in Georgia, her adopted home after her first Congressional term. They included "sunshine" clubs for youth to inculcate "peace habits" and study groups for adults that she eventually nurtured into the Georgia Peace Society. Beginning in 1929, she worked for a decade with the National Council for Prevention of War (NCPW). She supported the League of Nations and World Court with reluctance, according to Hoff, and opposed investing the court with any authority to enforce its rulings. Moreover, she actively lobbied and testified for legislation that would outlaw war and against appropriations for military preparedness.

By the time Rankin decided to run for a second term, Hoff observed, perceptions of the peace movement had changed from that of respectable bipartisan Progressivism to "the bastion of reactionary Republicans." But Rankin lived long enough for her ideas on peace to find a more receptive audience among liberals and activists opposed to the war in Vietnam. As long as she could travel, she continued to speak and lobby for disarmament and for domestic reforms in government and the economy central to her foreign policy ideals. In her conversations with Smith, Rankin disclosed a sense of despair over the lack of progress in her lifetime toward peaceful solutions to international conflict. Yet she acknowledged to Hannah Josephson not long afterward that she realized she was part of a special generation of women who pursued lofty ideals at the beginning of the twentieth century. Joan Hoff argued that "the measure of Jeannette Rankin's life was not the failure of her mission to change American foreign policy, it was the example she set as a great crusader against war."[36]

The measure of Norma Smith's biography is her success in conveying Jeannette Rankin's passion for the crusade. With affection and wit, Norma Smith provides a rich anecdotal account of Rankin's political activities in reform and suffrage, in office, and as an advocate for peace and political reform. While she might be surprised to find that her narrative parallels and complements

---

35. Joan Hoff Wilson, "Jeannette Rankin and American Foreign Policy: Her Lifework as a Pacifist," *Montana The Magazine of Western History*, 30 (Spring 1980), 40.

36. Rankin, interview with Hannah Josephson, April 1972, ROHO; Hoff Wilson, "Jeannette Rankin and American Foreign Policy," 39.

recent scholarship in women's history and politics, Smith related Rankin's story with confidence that its themes would resonate powerfully with future generations. She was right. The courage and persistence with which Rankin faced the obstacles in her path continues to be a source of inspiration to all who share her ideals of peace and social justice.

Preface

In 1961 Montana State College awarded Jeannette Rankin an honorary doctorate. Sitting in the audience waiting for my master's degree in history, I decided to write her biography. I was used to writing because I had a degree in journalism from the University of Idaho and had worked at the Moscow (Idaho) *News-Review*, a small daily newspaper, where I wrote about community affairs. I also knew something about Montana history because I had written my master's thesis on the Butte Miners' Union, a thesis Montana historian Michael P. Malone later called the best account of early unionism in Butte. Finally, I had opportunity: my husband, a biologist, sometimes worked at the Center for Communicable Disease Control in Atlanta, Georgia, and Jeannette Rankin had a winter home in Watkinsville not far away. While in Georgia I introduced myself to Jeannette Rankin as a fellow Montanan, and she agreed to let me interview her, knowing that I planned to write a biography. We soon became friends, and from 1963 to 1971, whenever I was in Georgia, I visited her, driving to her home with my teenage daughter Ellen.

We would spend the weekend with Jeannette, who would feed us breakfast and lunch. I would take us out to dinner in Athens, the home of the University of Georgia. A social worker at heart, she never missed an opportunity to do what she thought would improve someone's life. My daughter recognized this when she told me once on the way to Watkinsville, "you know, I like Jeannette, but she's always trying to teach me something."

This book is born of those weekend conversations—about sixteen in all—which included both formal interviews and less formal discussion, supplemented by frequent correspondence with Jeannette and her companions and primary and secondary source research. I have donated my notes and papers, including the interview and research notes for this book, to the library of Montana State University, Bozeman, along with royalties earned by this book.

Jeannette was very kind to me and supportive of the biography. The story it tells—of the life of a woman who fought for suffrage, voted against both world wars while serving in the United States House of Representatives, and dedicated her life to the cause of peace—was written with her cooperation. Special thanks are due to my niece Karen Longeteig and her husband Hasan Khan, who persisted many years in marketing this manuscript, to my daughters Celia O'Connor, Frances Sherertz, and Ellen Payton, who helped with the revisions, and also to Jeannette Rankin's friend and secretary, Reita Rivers, who helped me with many details after Jeannette Rankin's death.

CHAPTER ONE

Determined Woman

"A 40-HOUR-A-WEEK JOB
ISN'T WORTH DOING."

IN 1916 THE MINERS, cowboys, and housewives of Montana elected a woman, Jeannette Rankin, to the United States Congress. This unprecedented action astounded the country because in most states a woman could not even vote. The capital almost expected a little country girl to come riding into Washington astride a buckskin pony, Winchester at her side, shouting an Indian war whoop. Or she would be a strident man-hating suffragist in dowdy clothes.

She was neither. She spoke well, for she was trained and experienced. She dressed well, for she was an accomplished seamstress. She liked men, and they liked her; she had persuaded many of them to give women the vote. Although she could ride a horse, sidesaddle, she drove a car; three years earlier she had driven over five thousand miles of primitive roads from Montana to Washington, D.C., and back again.

Nor was she a country bumpkin. She had two college degrees. She had traveled the country from New York to California and Florida to Michigan campaigning for woman's suffrage. She had studied social conditions in New Zealand. As a lobbyist she was already familiar with the halls of Congress. She knew the ways of society; she had danced at President Theodore Roosevelt's inaugural ball.

As for the imagined Winchester, this woman from the land of cowboys and Indians never touched a gun; Jeannette Rankin was a pacifist. Acclaimed for her unique feminine achievement of election to Congress, she was almost immediately derided for her "unmanly" vote against the First World War. She was to repeat that vote in the Second World War.

Jeannette Rankin's pacifism, and her feminism too, were natural extensions, she believed, of her deep concern for humanity. She had been a children's social worker; in order to protect children she had entered the woman's suffrage movement, believing that children's protective legislation could only be secured if women had the vote. Her humanitarian impulses also led her to work for reforms that we now take for granted: maternal and infant care programs, equality for minorities, public development of public resources, and election reforms.

Rankin's temperament and training suited her for her career as a crusader. She had, for instance, a talent for meeting new ideas and new situations confident of her ability to improvise solutions to unforeseen problems. Her contemporary, the journalist Walter Lippman, complained that his expensive classical education left him unprepared for the great cultural and technological changes that took place during his lifetime. But Rankin's childhood in the fast-growing town of Missoula, Montana, had trained her to expect change.

Genuinely interested in everyone, no matter his or her nationality, class, or social position, she had a genius—again born of rubbing shoulders in the young community of Missoula, where everyone had come from somewhere else—for accepting people. She also had from childhood the habit of hard work. "A 40-hour-a-week job isn't worth doing," she said. And she was independent. When conscience commanded her to vote an unpopular vote against the war, she did so.

A pragmatist with little interest in or knowledge of classical theories, she saw that the country could produce enough food, enough cloth, enough bricks, enough teachers, and enough doctors to feed, clothe, shelter, educate, and care for every child. Why, then, she wondered, did children still suffer privation? She saw that war after war had been fought in the names of religion, democracy, and idealism. Yet nothing was settled; wars continued. Why, then, did we not beware of holy wars? She saw that women had special interests in children, family, and society to which men were not attending. Why, then, should not women have the vote?

Working for change and living her conscience meant Jeannette had to fight the human desire, born of fear, greed, or apathy that there be no change. She accepted this problem as a challenge. But she never quite accepted the problems within herself. She had to overcome a natural timidity and reserve, frequent bad health, and a very bad temper. Independence sometimes became inflexibility; and uncompromising fixity of purpose sometimes alienated less dedicated people.

While many reformers and pacifists took their strength from religion—such as Quakerism—or from an almost religious faith in socialism, Jeannette never accepted any specific social doctrine. When Jeannette was age eighty-nine, during a public interview before fifteen hundred people, an earnest young minister asked her, "What, Miss Rankin, sustained you in the face of these defeats? How could you keep going?" He knew she was not orthodoxly religious, but he expected some reference to a higher power, to a belief in the essential meaningfulness of the universe, to faith, to something. Jeannette tried to avoid the question, but the man persisted, and, pinned to the wall, she smiled and said, "I don't know. Just stubborn, I guess."

For all the problems it caused her, that stubbornness served Jeannette well. She simply would not allow herself to be defeated. She worked until she was nearly ninety-three years old, through wars, depressions, ridicule, calumny, fatigue, many outright failures, and a few successes for a better life for humanity. Jeannette Rankin was a determined woman.

CHAPTER TWO

A Pioneer Family

"IF YOU CAN TAKE CARE OF JEANNETTE, I CAN TAKE CARE OF THE REST OF THE FAMILY."

JEANNETTE'S PARENTS were both pioneers. Her mother, Olive Pickering, twenty-four years old, husbandless, and bored with New Hampshire, had been persuaded to go to Montana Territory in 1878 by her Uncle Bill Berry. Back home to visit relatives, he had an aura of glamour. After heading west in 1849 during the California gold rush, Berry traveled to the Montana goldfields in the mineral rush of the 1860s, eventually settling in the town of Missoula, where he became sheriff. His stories of cowboys and Indians and miners sounded romantic. He tempted Olive with tales of eligible bachelors and with the prospect of employment. The Missoula school teacher was getting married, and Olive, who had taught school for several years, could take her place.

Olive begged her parents to let her go. There was little future for her in New Hampshire, she felt. Marriageable men were scarce, and the Pickerings, people of moderate standing in New England for more than a hundred years, were already related to almost everyone they knew. Although one ancestor, Timothy Pickering, had been the third United States secretary of state as well as a congressman and senator from Massachusetts, the family fortunes had fallen somewhat since; Olive's father was a farmer who preferred writing articles for newspapers to working on his farm. So Olive conducted a determined campaign, to which her parents finally acquiesced on condition that her sister Mandanna accompany her. Mandanna, who had a fiancé, returned home within a few months, but Olive would not see New Hampshire for thirty-five years.

To allow two young girls to take such a long and potentially dangerous journey, even accompanied by an uncle, the Pickerings must have had a sense of adventure. Two of the great Indian wars had just taken place in Montana, the Sioux War of 1876–77 and the Nez Perce War of 1877. No doubt Uncle Bill assured them that life in Montana was now peaceful. So the girls and Uncle Bill boarded the train and traveled west, watching the landscape roll by at thirty miles an hour. At Corinne, Utah, they took a mule stage north; there were no trains in Montana in 1878. No doubt the girls looked about them curiously; Utah was the land of Mormons, and certainly they had heard that Mormons had several wives. They may also have heard that women in Utah could vote, as could the women of Wyoming Territory, which they had just crossed by train. These two strange lands atop the Rocky Mountains were the only places in the world where women had full voting rights.

The stage bumped north over the black lava of southern Idaho, fording streams and crossing the Snake River by mule ferry. The trip took several days. It was a hard trip and expensive, too, seventy-five dollars one way. Mostly they rode day and night, with occasional overnight accommodations at "road ranches." Women travelers were uncommon enough that they were given the owners' bedroom. Men slept in a common bunkhouse. The road was only a steep, rutted trail that crossed the Continental Divide three times. On one down slope, covered with slippery pine needles, the driver tied a large log against the back wheels to act as a brake. "I laughed and Mannie prayed," Olive remembered later. They passed "freight trains," three or four wagons coupled together, pulled by twelve yoke of oxen, carrying ore to the railroad in Utah and supplies to the mines in Montana, especially Butte City with its silver and copper. They stopped in Butte overnight. Olive had heard lurid stories of the rough mining camps of the West; she wanted to explore, but Mannie made her stay inside.

There was something interesting happening in Butte that summer, something that later would profoundly affect the career of

Olive's as yet unthought-of daughter. It was the organization of the Butte Miners' Union, soon to become the largest local union in the nation and a powerful influence in Montana politics. The miners were striking to maintain their wages of $3.50 a day and could be seen marching around in orderly procession, four hundred men headed by a brass band. They were unarmed, and "nothing but the most courteous language was used by all," said the weekly newspaper. After a lot of rhetoric about the rights of capital and labor, the miners won their strike and organized their union without a shot being fired. Butte was not then the violent town it was later to be after it became a one-company town.

Olive and her companions continued to Missoula, one hundred miles northwest of Butte. In years past road agents frequently had attacked stages along this stretch of road, but here again everything was peaceful. By 1878 the stages had been held up so many times that the stage drivers and shotgun messengers had become, as one traveler characterized it, "leery and harder to hold up than a flock of wild geese." Thus did Olive arrive unharmed into the town of Missoula, a pretty place, with good land, a lovely river, creeks running out of the mountains every mile or so, an abundance of fine timber, grazing land for cattle, and bottomland for hay. Demand at the mines for lumber and cattle and agricultural products was greater than the supply, so Missoula was prosperous and growing. It was twenty-two years old and held a scant three hundred people; in ten years it would grow to thirty-five hundred. Now there were two stores, a bank, a Methodist church, and a school.

Olive and Mandanna boarded with the recently married schoolteacher Emma Dickinson. Her husband, W. O. Dickinson, kept a store, had a strange bald scar on his head, and wore an Indian scalp on his belt. Olive was afraid to ask if he had scalped the Indian himself, but she did learn that he had been scalped once himself and left for dead. Olive got the job teaching school. Asked if she could teach algebra, she said she thought she could teach "as much as is needed." She did not really know any algebra; she thought she could learn. She knew she was not well trained. "I was young and good-looking and dressed well," she explained, "and the school board knew I needed a job, so they gave me one." And, in fact, teachers were in short supply; they kept getting married.

Teaching in Missoula was not so different from teaching in New Hampshire except for the Indians, who wandered by and peeked in the windows. Olive never got used to them. She liked teaching, though, had a feeling for words, a sense of humor, and made puns that delighted the children. At the end of the year, however, the school board had to look for a new teacher, because Olive had married, in August 1879, a tall, handsome, red-bearded, longhaired Scotch-Canadian, John Rankin.

John Rankin had been born in Ontario, Canada, in 1841, the fourth of nine children. He had gone to school through the third grade only, before quitting to become a carpenter's helper. He and a brother worked awhile in Michigan, and then on flatboats on the Missouri River, the main highway into Montana. They saved a little money, and in 1869 boarded their own boat for Fort Benton, Montana, head of Missouri River navigation. After two and a half months on the river, nearing their goal, their boat ran aground in the shallow stream. The brothers picked up their tools and footed it the 120 miles remaining to Fort Benton. They went to Helena, then in the midst of a gold rush, built a mill for crushing ore, and then went west again, across the continental divide to Missoula. They tried some gold prospecting, but there was more profit in supplying the miners. John was a good carpenter and woodsman, and the mines needed timber; the heavy forests of the Bitterroot attracted him. Soon he was making money in the lumber and building business.

He established a small cattle ranch on Grant Creek and built a water-powered sawmill six miles up where the rapid creek tumbled out of the mountain. He built a bridge 250 feet long across the Missoula River, designed and built residential and business buildings, even a church. By 1878 he had been in Montana nine years, had accumulated several thousand dollars in cash, his ranch and sawmill, and extensive lumber interests. Among the most prosperous men in the area, Rankin was something of a loner, who often did not associate with other prominent Missoulians in their numerous business ventures. While he served as a county commissioner for one term, thereafter he took no active interest in politics although nominally he was a Republican.

Personally he seems to have been quiet but well liked. He was peaceful but willing to use his fists if necessary. He had carried a gun during the Nez Perce Indian scare 1877, but Jeannette would remember later that he was critical of the army and its methods with the Indians. He never carried a gun again and would not even allow one on the ranch—unusual behavior in a country where people routinely shot game for meat. Perhaps it was a safety precaution; he had accidentally lost the use of one eye and hearing in one ear from a cannon blast at a community celebration. He enjoyed a good time and could dance a Scottish jig, jumping up and clicking his heels together in the air. When he and Olive were married he was thirty-eight, she twenty-six.

Olive and John Rankin moved into the sturdy frame house on Grant Creek. It was comfortable pioneering. There were trout, deer, and elk. On the ranch there was beef, pork, chickens, fruits, and vegetables. A milk house built over the creek cooled pans of milk waiting to be skimmed. Olive sold cheese, butter, and eggs. It was a good time and place to raise a family. Montana Territory was entering into a period of rapid and peaceful growth. The earliest frontier period was past, the gold rush over, the vigilante days gone. The Nez Perce Indian War and the Battle of the Little Bighorn had occurred only two and three years before, but there were no more disturbances. Two decades later outside financial interests would come to dominate the state in their pursuit of copper profits, severely damaging its political and social climate as they did so. But in western Montana in the 1880s and 1890s, everything seemed possible. People believed in progress, even perfectibility, and they enthusiastically worked to improve their community.

Every year they broke new land, cut new timber, built new residences, schools, and churches, dug new irrigation ditches, and planted new gardens. Neighbors helped one another, learned from one another, profited from the differences in backgrounds, and worked together to organize government, businesses, schools, and churches. It was not paradise, but people thought eventually it might be, and as an example of grass roots participatory democracy, which Jeannette always advocated, it was as good as could be found anywhere.

Early in this era on June 11, 1880, Jeannette was born. John and Olive Rankin were probably relieved, proud, and perhaps a little disappointed: parents often wanted their firstborn to be a boy. Probably the disappointment was not acute; the little girl, whom they named for her Scottish grandmother, was lively, healthy, and bright. Four children followed Jeannette: Philena (who died in childhood), Harriet, Wellington (the only boy), and Mary. Almost every year there was another baby. Then there was

Jeannette sits behind the table in this formal photograph of the Rankin family, taken circa 1895. Pictured (clockwise from Jeannette) are Harriet, Wellington, Olive, Grace, Edna, Mary, and John. Philena, who died at age eight, is represented by the portrait on the table.

a miscarriage, and later two more girls, Grace and Edna, twelve and thirteen years younger than Jeannette. All of the children were strong, lively, and individualistic, with Jeannette probably the liveliest and most individualistic of all. At age ninety she remembered a childhood family outing on which her mother told her father, "If you can take care of Jeannette, I can take care of the rest of the children."

Even as a child she was so strong minded that she often pushed other people's opinions aside and made enemies. But if she was willful and obstinate, she was also sensitive and compassionate. She read Bible stories with tears running down her face and complained of taking calves away from their mothers. Wherever she saw pain, Jeannette tried to do something about it. She insisted on having a wounded horse thrown and tied so she could sew up a bad cut. She made a leather shoe for the family dog, who had lost part of his paw in a trap—and scolded him imperiously when he gnawed it off.

In the mid-1880s John Rankin built the family one of Missoula's finest houses, the first with central heating and hot and cold running water. It had a tub in the bathroom and a cupola on the roof. In the 1890s there was electricity. In the summer, after the snow had melted, the family would move the six miles to the Grant Creek ranch, to a tight little farmhouse lit by coal oil lamps. The children played around the millpond, picked huckleberries, and burrowed in the huge sawdust piles. One pile contained ice, cut in the winter from the pond. They rode horses to fetch the cows, the girls sidesaddle. Both at the ranch and in town friends of their own ages came to parties and suppers. There were dances, sleigh rides, sports, clubs, and literary and musical evenings.

Jeannette wanted to become a nurse. The most notable woman of the times, Florence Nightingale, was a nurse, famous as the "lady with the lamp" in the Crimean War. Compassionate, energetic, and ambitious, she was a natural model for the young Jeannette, but Jeannette's father discouraged her, saying her health was not good enough. There is little evidence as to Jeannette's health. In later years she rarely admitted to illness; as an adult she suffered from tic douloureux, a painful malady characterized by searing, burning, lightning-like jabs in the cheek, without even her closest associates knowing it. As for childhood health, "I may have fainted a few times when I was a child," was all she would say in her old age.

Whatever the state of her health, she was always busy. She helped enlarge a room in the family home, took hammer and nails and built a board sidewalk in front of one of her father's rental houses. Once, when she had teenage friends visiting the family lumber mill, she insisted on showing them how to operate it, pulling the levers so the carriage would place the log properly, then lowering and running the saw that cut the huge logs into boards. She was always interested in mechanical things. In old age she experimented with new ways of housing the poor although, always more interested in the ideas and planning than in the practical details, most of her innovations were unsuccessful.

Religion in the Rankin household was not emphasized. The parents rarely went to church, though the children went with their friends to Presbyterian Sunday school. John Rankin had been raised a Presbyterian, Olive a Congregationalist. Uncle Bill

Berry, much admired because he was a sheriff, was an atheist and did not care who knew it. Discipline was lax. Father "didn't care what we did," Jeannette was to say. "He loved children." Such permissiveness might have lead to trouble with such passionate, energetic children. A hot-tempered and opinionated bunch, they argued a lot, "threw things at one another—a glass of water if nothing else was handy." Perhaps the reason they did not get into more trouble is that they did not have the time. Possibly Jeannette should have said that father did not care what they did as long as they worked.

For they all worked. Though Jeannette had a myriad of household responsibilities, she was familiar with her father's business, too. In emergencies she helped cook in his lumber camp. Harriet kept the business books. Wellington was given business responsibilities and decisions to make, while still in his early teens. The three helped their father run a sixty-five-room hotel he built in the early 1890s—a three-story brick building with electricity, a good dining room, a bath on every floor, and a call-bell system. They could not have been more than ten to fourteen years old.

Jeannette was especially busy with household tasks, for she was the oldest. The oldest girl in a large family often acquires responsibility and develops abilities far ahead of her age. At five, such children make their own beds, dust the living room, stir the gravy, and change the baby. At twelve, they may plan and cook the meals, sew, clean house, and mind the younger children. In Jeannette's generation many such girls became schoolteachers or missionaries; her career was to combine a little of both.

In Jeannette's case her responsibilities were increased by the partial abdication of her parents. John Rankin died in 1904, when Jeannette was twenty-four and Edna only eleven. While he was alive, his business affairs took most of his time; he was often away from home. Additionally, Olive Rankin ceded much of her maternal role to Jeannette even before John's death. Curiously quiet and withdrawn given her youthful adventurous spirit, Olive allowed other people to run her errands and make her decisions. Jeannette and the other children did everything for her, from shopping to taking care of the finances after their father died. A large woman of regal bearing, dressed for company in purple velvet with a Chantilly lace collar, she was treated like royalty. Her son all but bowed when he entered her presence.

It has been suggested that Olive Rankin's surprising passivity and obesity might have been caused by thyroid deficiency, but whatever the cause, the result was that Jeannette became the housewife of the family. She not only baked the bread and sewed the clothes, she also saw to the children's education, health, and manners, becoming quite dictatorial in the process. Her sisters had no choice, for instance, as to what they would wear. Younger sister Edna, who feared Jeannette's quick temper, did not dare complain when Jeannette placed ruffles on her dress that emphasized her fat stomach. (Jeannette realized herself that the dress was unbecoming and replaced the ruffles with a popular Alice blue ribbon sash.) In another instance Jeannette ordered Edna to come into the dining room. There the child saw the family's largest table draped in sheets; a doctor had come to remove her tonsils. "She just told me I was going to have my tonsils out," Edna remembered later, "and I had nothing to say about it."

Responsibility without authority is hard to shoulder. In Jeannette's case, it strengthened her character, and as an adult, she called on that fortitude to stand firm in support of unpopular causes. But as a child her responsibilities made Jeannette irritable and domineering, according to her younger sisters and brother. Never placid, Jeannette's disposition was, in fact, often explosive. As adults her brother and sisters recognized that Jeannette had been imposed upon, but they still resented her attempt to run the family. What made the situation worse was that the other children were all lively, capable, strong-minded people, too.

As they grew older the girls all attended the Montana State University preparatory department in their hometown, the university having been established in 1893, partly through John Rankin's efforts. (In 1965 the school became known as the University of Montana and the land grant college in Bozeman took the name Montana State University.) Harriet later became the university's dean of women, and Mary taught English there. Edna was the first woman to earn a law degree at Montana State University, Missoula; later, she worked all over the world in the birth control movement. Grace, the second youngest and Jeannette's favorite, whom Jeannette called the smartest of the lot, married Thomas Kinney, a Missoula-area lumberman.

Then there was Wellington, a talented, brilliant man. As the only boy in the family, he was set apart; Olive Rankin called him simply "The Boy." Handsome with ingratiating manners, Wellington, unlike Jeannette, had a passion for power and money. He went to Harvard College and Harvard Law School before returning to Montana, where he established a lucrative practice. He would become an enormously successful businessman, rancher, criminal lawyer, multimillionaire, the largest individual landholder in the United States, and a noted eccentric. Extraordinarily eloquent, he mesmerized his audiences whether giving a political speech or addressing a jury. His clients were usually acquitted, though it might take them the rest of their lives and all of their holdings to pay his fee.

Ambitious for political office, Wellington ran seven times but was elected only once: to the position of state attorney general in 1920. In spite of his money, eloquence, and power, he was never popular in Montana. People said his fees were exorbitant and, even worse, his ranches overgrazed. He cut corners. Men from the state penitentiary were paroled to him as hired hands. Lights in the bunkhouse went out at nine o'clock; he did not want the help sitting up all night reading comic books. Jeannette said the convicts were alcoholics, and he took them in to rehabilitate them; some Montanans thought it was just his way of saving money.

Jeannette and Wellington began their adult lives with similar political and social outlooks—liberal, progressive. As they grew older, however, their views diverged. She was to spend her life in self-imposed poverty, working for peace and children's welfare; he was to spend his getting richer. Nevertheless, they remained close. Jeannette said, probably truthfully, that she did not resent the fact that Wellington went to Harvard while she had to settle for the new raw college in her hometown. She adored him; even when both were in their eighties, one could catch overtones of a maternal feeling toward "little brother." He was kind to her and generous with money although not above occasionally ridiculing her in public.

Above all, Wellington always supported Jeannette's career and the woman's suffrage movement; he gave not only money but also time and thought. Nor did his support waver once Jeannette gained a reputation as a radical despite the fact that her radicalism damaged his own political ambitions. Her political confidante, campaign manager, and financial backer, Wellington was vital to Jeannette's career. Nevertheless, when Jeannette seriously disagreed with him, as she did about the wars, she followed her own conscience.

Whence came Jeannette's conscience, her feminism, her compassion, and her determination? Some writers suggest that feminists had unusual fathers, who nourished their daughters' minds and spirits. No doubt Jeannette's father was unusual, but he was not a man of education and public position, like Elizabeth Cady Stanton's father, for instance; he was immersed in his business. Jeannette herself remembered him kindly but did not believe he had any more influence than most fathers did.

He must be credited for his willingness to let his children grow in their own ways; they were not stifled. He must have helped build his children's self-confidence, for he seems to have done them the honor of accepting them for the intelligent, capable, responsible people they were. Apparently he expected much, criticized little. There is at least negative evidence that he gave them an example of integrity: he was not involved in the Montana Improvement Company scandal, in which many other Missoula business leaders were indicted for illegally cutting timber on government lands. Politics and business, the Anaconda Company and the Northern Pacific Railroad, were involved; the scandal became national. The children knew their father was not mixed up in the mess.

It has been suggested that Jeannette's pacifism came from her father, simply because he did not carry a gun. But that was not really unusual; no matter what the legend says, many westerners did not carry guns, especially in that peaceful period. In hindsight it is easy to read too much into family influences. Jeannette herself was to point this out many years later, in regard to Gandhi's son, who was a drunkard. People blamed this on Gandhi, who, in his single-minded concern for the Indian revolution, had treated his son badly. Unwilling to hear anything derogatory about the man she considered a saint, Jeannette said, "Ordinary fathers have drunken sons, too."

Jeannette's mother, although she became an obese and passive woman, still must have kept some of the adventurous spirit that had brought her to Montana at age twenty-four. So Jeannette grew up in an atmosphere of freedom. Her parents did not directly outline a specific mode of behavior. What they imparted to her was the freedom to think and act, faith in her capability, and a sense of personal responsibility, also known as conscience.

CHAPTER THREE

Waiting for Life to Come to Her

"GO. GO. GO.
IT MAKE NO DIFFERENCE WHERE."

IN 1898 JEANNETTE RANKIN walked from home to the university under golden cottonwoods in the fall and between high snowbanks in the winter. She did not stand out among her classmates; if one noticed her at all, it would have been for her straight posture and her abundant hair with its glint of red. Slim and slightly above medium height, she had a fresh, fair complexion, a long, straight nose, a wide mouth, and full upper cheeks over prominent bones. Her eyes were gray-green-blue and, like her father's, oddly set, slanting downward at the outer corners under heavy brows. She made her own clothes in the uniform of the day—a dark wool gored skirt with extra fullness in the back, a wide belt, and a white cotton shirtwaist with leg-of-mutton sleeves—likely purchased for $1.50 from a downtown department store.

Like most college freshmen, Jeannette had no clear vision of the future. And college itself did not really interest her. "It was just the thing to do," she would say later, "and there didn't seem to be anything else, don't you know, so I just went on." The university was only three years old. It had a faculty of thirteen, most with master's degrees, paid salaries ranging from one to two hundred dollars. But it was a hard-working, rapidly growing, forward-looking place. Montana, too, was growing. In the eighteen years since Jeannette's birth, it had acquired railroads and telephones, five times the population, and full state status. Missoula had grown from three hundred to five thousand.

There were also changes in politics. Although Montana was strongly Democratic and had voted for William Jennings Bryan in the 1896 presidential election, the Populists had a large following and socialism was mentioned in respectable circles. The election of the conservative Republican William McKinley was a shock; Montana hated eastern domination and especially the "goldbugs," not only because of the Montana and Idaho silver mines, but because hard money policies favored eastern creditors at the expense of western debtors.

The United States had just finished the war with Spain. In spring 1898 Theodore Roosevelt had resigned his job as assistant secretary of the Navy in Washington, D.C., and ridden with his Rough Riders up San Juan Hill in Cuba. For this, he was rewarded with the governorship of New York, and the United States gained Hawaii, Puerto Rico, the Philippines, Guam, and Wake Island. Nearly everyone was enthusiastic about this "splendid little war," which had lasted only four months—although enthusiasm waned somewhat as the war to free Cuba from foreign domination turned into an imperialistic war to control the Philippines.

Whatever Jeannette thought of it, she would not have said much about it in public, for she was quiet and reserved. Her major professor said she was a "timid girl, who worked hard for what she got." She herself said, fifty years later, "When I decided to make my first speech at school, everyone listened because they'd never heard me speak to anyone before." Likely she exaggerated somewhat.

She expressed herself forcefully, however, when an English teacher asked her to read aloud Tennyson's "The Charge of the Light Brigade":

> Half a league, half a league, half a league onward
> Into the valley of death rode the six hundred.
> Theirs not to reason why, theirs but to do or die.
> Into the valley of death
> Rode the six hundred.

"This is hideous," she said angrily, "I can't read it."

She majored in biology, because she liked the teacher, and wrote a senior thesis on the sizes and distribution of snail shells at various

A biology major, Jeannette, shown here in the lab, wrote her senior thesis on the sizes and distribution of snail shells at various altitudes in the local mountains. She graduated from Montana State University in Missoula in 1902.

altitudes in the local mountains. Years later she complained that college had not taught her to think, and she sympathized with the dropouts of the 1960s. But she was not studious. Probably she enjoyed collecting snail shells, weighing them, and counting the whorls, but she hated writing the thesis. She always said her mind went blank when confronted with a piece of paper.

In 1902 she graduated with a class of eighteen, whose biographies, apparently written by themselves, were printed in the local newspaper, the *Missoulian*, June 1, 1902. They ran ten to thirty lines, telling of school honors and activities and hopes for the future. Jeannette's biography, however, was short: "Jeannette Pickering Rankin: A native Montanan, she was born at Grant Creek, June 11, 1880, and attended the public schools at Missoula until the time of her entrance into the University. Her favorite studies were the sciences."

Fifteen years later, when she was a famous congresswoman, she again summarized her life in brief. Biographical data in the *Congressional Record* was furnished by the congressmen, and as the Butte newspaper, the *Montana American*, reported on February 17, 1918, this biographical data "is so fulsome as to be humorous . . . the log cabin he was born in, his early struggles to get an education, how he studied by the dim candlelight . . . some representatives require a page to tell their story, but lo . . . modest Jeannette had the shortest biography in the book. She told it in five words, to wit, 'Jeannette Rankin, Republican, of Missoula.'" That was Jeannette all her life, very reserved in her private persona and intolerant of nonsense.

Still, despite her reserve, she had friends who loved her dearly. Jeannette considered this combination of friendliness and remoteness a family trait. "We're all gregarious, even if we are loners," she said. She went to the parties that celebrated commencement. She even, along with eighteen other "bachelor maids," gave a "Bal Poudre," with two hundred guests. Held in the Elks' Hall, which the girls decorated with wild syringa, festoons of wide red ribbon, and red lampshades on the lights, the affair boasted "plenty of dancing men," and some "swell gowns." The hostesses powdered their hair and placed beauty patches on "their rosy cheeks or white shoulders," the *Missoulian* reported on May 12, 1902. It was the social event of the season.

Following commencement Jeannette and two other young women took the train to the West Coast to visit relatives. It was her second big trip; at age twelve she had accompanied her father on a visit to his mother in Michigan. Apparently, no one thought it unusual for three unchaperoned young women to travel from city to city. A certain female freedom is evinced also in a baseball game that took place that summer in Missoula, with nearly a thousand watching, between a "bloomered aggregation of female ball tossers" and a male team. The girls played like girls, the *Missoulian* reported, except for two who were experts. Perhaps due to chivalry, the girls won ten to nine, in six innings.

It is easy to guess what Jeannette and her friends talked of that summer: Mary MacLane of Butte and her shocking, best-selling book. The twenty-one-year-old MacLane had published her own diary, the story of a restless renegade, unemployed, friendless, railing at life. She wrote in steamy, profane language of her longings—for freedom, love, happiness, fame, and, most of all, experience—and her frustrating inability to fulfill them. Had she been born a man she would have been able to give vent to her ambitions. As a woman she was forced to live vicariously while she waited for life to come to her.

"Oh, "she wrote, "it is a hard and bitter thing to be a woman." She dreamed of a strong, fascinating man with steely, gray eyes who would carry her away, a devil who would bring her body both pleasure and pain. Calling traditional marriage a "monstrous fraud," she swore she would never wed. "May I never, I say, become that abnormal, merciless animal, that deformed monstrosity—a virtuous woman." Having complained of being trapped in an uncouth Montana town, she found herself freed by the publication of her diary, for within a few months she had earned seventeen thousand dollars in royalties and had left Butte for New York.

The Story of Mary MacLane (1902) was banned in Butte, attacked and ridiculed in Montana newspapers, and surely nearly every young girl read it, even if she had to hide it from her mother. It certainly raised issues for Jeannette to ponder. She, too, felt confined and restless; she, too, had to wait for life to come to her. And, having finished college, she had nothing to do but wait for an acceptable proposal of marriage. Apparently, she had several, all of which she declined.

Why did she never marry? She was not sexless. One colleague who knew Jeannette in her fifties recalled that Jeannette had a passionate nature and emanated a feeling of banked fires. Unlike some of the "old suffs" (suffragists), she said, many of whom didn't have men friends, Jeannette numbered many men, some of them very distinguished, among her friends. She was to receive offers of marriage in her middle and even old age.

Marriage as a career, one might think, would have suited Jeannette. She loved children, understood caring for them, and knew how to sew, cook, and run a home. And although women's options were expanding at the turn of the century, traditional pursuits outside of motherhood remained limited and poorly paid: school teaching, dressmaking, clerking in a store. Possibly Jeannette felt marriage would demand a giving of herself that was impossible; she had a core of privacy that no one breached. Or perhaps Jeannette feared turning into her mother, who had grown passive and fat after her marriage. Some people have theorized that Jeannette never found a man she thought equal to her brother Wellington. Brother and sister were certainly close, but Jeannette always felt more maternal toward her little brother than awed by him. After all, she had helped feed him and changed his diapers.

Whatever the reason, she attended showers and receptions in honor of her friends' weddings, and continued to mark time, busy with small children, sewing, household duties. She did some serious reading on politics and social conditions, but she was bored. "The kid crowd went sleighing," she wrote in her diary. "I went with them, but was real lonesome not to have anything definate to do."

No longer a kid, she had not yet found a place in the adult world. Unprepared for a job, she had rejected the idea of marrying, and she was filled with nervous energy. "Go! Go! Go!" she wrote in her diary. "It makes no difference where just so you go! Go! Go! Remember at the first opportunity go." As historian Ronald Schaffer noted, this was a close paraphrase of the words of that famous apostle of the strenuous life, now the president of the United States, Theodore Roosevelt: "Get action, do things . . . don't fritter away your time; create, act, take a place wherever you are and be somebody."

But there was no place to be somebody. She was forced to fall back on school teaching, although she did not have the right credentials and was annoyed at having to take an examination for a temporary certificate. She passed the test and taught in the one-room school at Grant Creek, but she did not enjoy it. The next year she obtained a job teaching fourth and fifth grades at Whitehall, about 150 miles from Missoula. However, after her temporary certificate ran out, she failed the examination for a new one.

Jeannette left her job and returned to Missoula in December and got a job with Ella Burke, head trimmer of the Golden Rule department store, the most accomplished milliner and seamstress in Missoula, now a city of eight thousand. Jeannette learned professional methods to add to her self-taught sewing skills. She was to fall back on this resource in the future, but for now, this career was short-lived. She quit her job to care for her father, who had contracted Rocky Mountain spotted fever, a disagreeable and often deadly illness characterized by high fever and convulsions. It was fortunate for the rest of the family that she was available to nurse him and assume the family responsibilities (Wellington was at Harvard University), but despite her best effort, John Rankin died on May 3, 1904. Jeannette was ill prepared for the shock.

Wellington, nineteen, came home to run the ranch and liquidate some of their father's business interests. He arranged matters so competently that Olive Rankin and the others hardly had to think of finances. Jeannette had an allowance of seventy-five dollars a month (about what a Butte miner made if he was a good worker), which was more than ample while she was living at home. When Wellington returned to Harvard in the fall, Jeannette's responsibilities at home became greater than ever. She continued to care for the family, but she was restless, too. When Wellington became ill in Cambridge (or Jeannette believed he had), she leapt at the chance to go care for him and persuaded a girlfriend, Jimmie Mills, to travel east with her.

Wellington soon recovered, and the young women had a nice six-month trip. Accompanied by Wellington and other Harvard boys, they took in the sights of Boston. They even thought of enrolling at Massachusetts Institute of Technology, apparently not realizing that MIT did not accept women. The highlight of the winter was a trip to Washington, D.C., to attend the inaugural of President Theodore Roosevelt, the darling of young progressive Republicans like Wellington Rankin. They liked his conservationist ethos and his concern for the disadvantaged. They were hopeful that Roosevelt's "trust-busting" would restore American capitalism to free enterprise. They liked his alliances with successful small businessmen, farmers, and skilled mechanics. His imperialism was not then an issue for many Progressives, some of whom sincerely believed that America had a duty to educate less fortunate peoples in Christianity, civilization, and democracy—to "take up the white man's burden," as Rudyard Kipling's famous poem phrased it.

The Rankin's Missoula friend, Congressman Joseph M. Dixon (who would manage Roosevelt's third party presidential run in 1912) got them tickets for the inaugural ball. Jeannette liked dancing and was good at it. And she enjoyed seeing the women's gowns. The first lady, Edith Carow Roosevelt, wore pale blue brocaded satin, with a low neck and bare arms; as a seamstress, Jeannette was interested in the way the gown draped at the waist, giving fullness without bunching. Then they were invited to stay a few days in New York, in the Waldorf Astoria, by Jimmie's brother Dr. W. P. Mills, a Missoula physician who was in New York taking a refresher course. They looked at the latest fashions and visited the sights.

Although she had a glorious time, Jeannette also saw some sights that tourists were not expected to notice: the suffering of the slum dwellers in Boston and New York. To someone coming from the relative equality of Missoula, it was shocking. Wellington thought so, too. Even the self-centered Mary MacLane of Butte had been shocked at her first sight of the juxtaposition of extreme wealth and grinding poverty in the east. The immigrants who had come to the "golden shore" were crowded into tenements lacking heat, water, and sanitation; they worked for sweat wages in the face of discrimination and police brutality.

On Fifth Avenue, on the other hand, were the rich in their fine carriages, some powered by the traditional horse and some by the new gasoline engine. The clothes in the shop windows were unbelievably expensive and elaborate. Jeannette thought, as she was to repeat many times in the next sixty-nine years, that it is wrong to spend money on luxuries while children go hungry. Jeannette's eyes were opened to unimagined misery, but again she had no place, no power, no way to act. She returned home to Missoula and family duties. Wellington and the older sisters were away; the little girls Grace and Edna were in their early teens. Olive Rankin leaned heavily on Jeannette.

Jeannette did some reading. She even bought herself a copy of *The Long Day, The Story of a New York Working Girl as Told By Herself* (1906). She inscribed her name and the date, August 9, 1906, in her strong, angular handwriting. Somehow this little book, which vividly described a young girl's struggles with jobs and boarding houses, would remain in Jeannette's small library, in its various locations in Montana and Georgia, for the next sixty-seven years.

She took a correspondence course in furniture design. She was creative; she liked planning and designing and working with her hands, and she enjoyed the course. But it was just a time-killing occupation. She became very depressed. She contracted "inflammatory rheumatism." She needed another trip. In 1907 she went to San Francisco to visit an uncle and see the city, just recovering from the fire and earthquake of the year before. Looking around, with eyes opened from her stay in the East, she found poor people nearly as miserable as those in the slums of New York. Instead of resting her inflammatory rheumatism, she went to work in a settlement house in the Italian section of Telegraph Hill.

The settlement house was private charity's answer to the problems of poor immigrants. In 1907 alone more than a million immigrants entered the United States. Handicapped by a lack of money, poor English, and their ignorance of the customs of the country, immigrants faced widespread discrimination. In great demand as poorly paid, unskilled labor, they often lived in overcrowded, unsanitary, and dilapidated neighborhoods, lacked access to medical care, and were the last whites hired for high-paying jobs. Settlement houses such as Hull House in Chicago, the Henry Street Center in New York, and the house on Telegraph Hill where Jeannette worked in San Francisco tried to ameliorate their conditions by holding classes in English, maternal and child health care, and citizenship. They provided day nurseries for working mothers and a safe place for children to play after school. Many of the settlement workers lived in the slums where they worked to better understand the conditions of those they were trying to help.

Jeannette worked with the children, keeping them clean and interested and teaching them letters and skills while their mothers worked or attended classes or political meetings. She also attended meetings herself on wage-and-hour legislation, factory working conditions, and child labor laws. Jeannette had seen the misery of the poor in New York and Boston. In San Francisco she saw people trying to do something about it. She felt a social worker might do even more than a nurse to alleviate and prevent suffering. Impressed with the dedication, motivation, and ability of the professional social workers, she decided to join their ranks. First, though, she needed knowledge and skill. In fall 1908 she boarded the train and went to New York to enroll in a school for social workers, the New York School of Philanthropy. She was twenty-eight years old and no longer was waiting for life to come to her. In the future she would grasp it with her own two hands.

From New York Jeannette wrote her sister Mary, "there is nothing horrid about studying social problems." Mary might find them depressing, but Jeannette believed something could be done. The reason political economy had hitherto been so useless was that the theories of older writers such as Adam Smith and Thomas Malthus did not fit present conditions. Poverty and misery could be eliminated. The benefits of the industrial revolution could be extended to all. Morality, said one of her textbooks, did not consist of austerity and restraint, but in expanding consumption for all.

The New York School of Philanthropy believed "not that the creation of a favorable environment will of itself transform character, but that the normal man, who is now crushed, will under favorable conditions, rise unaided." These were not new ideas to her, Jeannette wrote, but only what she had said to herself "1001 times." Politically, however, these were controversial ideas. Social Darwinists argued an opposing view: that the poor were essentially unfit—which was why they were poor—and that helping them would only worsen the situation by allowing them to produce more unfit children. The Yale economist William Graham Sumner, the leading exponent of this view, said the protection of the "property of men and the honor of women" was all that government should concern itself with. He was against welfare laws, state education, sanitary laws, housing regulations, and labor unions.

But change was in the air. Four hundred thousand people voted the Socialist ticket in 1904; and in 1912 the Socialist candidate for president attracted six percent of the voters. Between 1900 and 1908, union membership rose from a half million to over four million. African Americans met in Niagara Falls, New York, in 1905, to protest lynching, disenfranchisement, and segregation. Six years later some of those same activists founded the National Association for the Advancement of Colored People. Change was coming to the halls of power, too. In 1906 Congress bowed to popular pressure and passed a pure food and drug act and a meat inspection act, and in 1908, after years of declaring wage-and-hour laws unconstitutional, the United States Supreme Court upheld an Oregon law limiting a day's work for women in industry to ten hours.

Books and articles on social questions circulated by the hundreds. Jeannette read Benjamin Kidd, author of *Social Evolution* (1898) and *The Science of Power* (1918), who said people's humanitarian impulses were rational and should be heeded. He argued that women could make a special contribution to society because they were not seeking temporary self-gain. Concerned with their children and their children's children's children, and, therefore, with the future, women could counteract the bad social effect of self-seeking male initiative. Kidd's writings—particularly *The Science of Power*—probably influenced Jeannette more than those of any other person; she was still quoting him sixty years later.

Jeannette read everything she could find on social problems. She read the single-tax advocate Henry George's *Progress and Poverty* (1879), which explained how the progress of the industrial

revolution meant poverty for the masses. She rea\
eries of the lower depths in England in the socialis\
People of the Abyss (1903). Unlike George and Lon\
the School of Philanthropy was not trying to chang\
It believed reform could be accomplished within \
framework. It trained social workers to administer p\
ity and gave broad education in social and race relati\
problems, and criminology. On these subjects, it broug\ _ \n outstanding guest lecturers.

Jeannette was especially impressed with Florence Kelley, so
self-assured and so eloquent. A lawyer active in securing protective labor legislation for women and children, Kelley directed
the National Consumers' League, which worked for industrial
reform through consumer activity. Jeannette and Florence Kelley
would be closely associated in the future. The liberal lawyer and
future Supreme Court justice Louis D. Brandeis spoke on wage-
and-hour laws. His successful defense of the Oregon law had just
established a judicial precedent. Booker T. Washington, an ex-
slave, noted educator, and one of the ablest public speakers of
his time, emphasized the importance of industrial training for
the poor as the first step toward their independence. Judge Ben
Lindsey of Denver, who had helped establish one of the pioneer
juvenile courts and served as its judge, described Colorado's in-
novative methods for dealing with juvenile offenders and the
state's new legislation that held negligent parents and employers
accountable for the children's transgressions.

After the morning lectures came practical work. Jeannette
spent two months visiting the slums with more experienced workers. She wrote her mother:

> I expect to enjoy the work very much. It is in the Jewish and
> Italian district. Just off the Bowery and in the happiest part of
> New York despite the misery. . . . I took the dearest . . . sweetest
> little boy to an orphan society. He was about three years old and
> the mother had two younger. The father is missing. If I had been
> near home I'm sure I would have wanted to keep him. He was so
> full of joy and life. The mother didn't mind losing him. She just
> waved her hand and said "By-by."

The sights, sounds, smells, and tragedies of the Bowery were
certainly different from those of Jeannette's peaceful home in

issoula. Was she trying to reassure her mother about the "happiest part of New York despite the misery," or was she trying to fool herself? Had Jeannette communicated what was happening to the little boy's mother, or had language and cultural barriers created a situation—as too often happened during the Progressive Era—in which a child was permanently removed from his home without the express consent of his parent? Jeannette was certainly capable of such self-deception.

Another project was to visit homes and schools to find children to attend a school for the deaf. She was impressed that in the families of the deaf she found many other disabilities, a syndrome of problems brought on by poverty. She worked for two months in the night police courts, dealing mostly with prostitutes. She was supposed to help young girls, first offenders, find other means of support. Some were sent temporarily to a Florence Crittenden League home. Some needed clothes, shoes, medical or dental care before they could become employable. There was no public source of such help, so Jeannette tried to get it from charitable institutions or private individuals. Often employment was not the answer. Jeannette bitterly remembered finding one prostitute a job in a factory, but the girl lost her fingers in a machine and had to go back to her old profession. It was another proof of the need for legal imposition of factory safety measures.

Jeannette felt devastated by some of these cases. It was hard for her to avoid personal emotional involvement, an unprofessional and unproductive attitude, she was told. In turn, she criticized the attitude of some of the other students, whose detachment suggested to her a lack of commitment. They were mainly interested in getting jobs, she felt, while she was preparing for a career of service. She had an airy disregard for money and would never understand the importance other people attached to a regular paycheck. Too, she felt set apart from the other students, who primarily had attended prestigious women's colleges, by what she thought of as her poor education in a tiny frontier college. She wrote her sisters that there were "such well trained college girls" in her classes that she expected to fail. But her grades were mostly Bs, with a couple of As and a couple of Cs.

Jeannette was too busy and too interested in her work to pay attention to the attractions of New York—museums, theaters, concerts. She did notice some changes. There were taxicabs, much nicer than the steam cars on the elevated. Some people were driving their own Model T Fords, just brought out that year. They cost $850, a year's wages for most people. Manners and morals were declining. The city fathers had found it necessary to pass an ordinance forbidding women to smoke in public.

Jeannette graduated in spring 1909 and took the four-day train trip back to her family and the cool Montana summer. She looked for something to do and began by investigating the Missoula County jail. She had been taught to assess the social health of a community by looking at its jail. She found it overcrowded; jailers often placed prostitutes and lumberjacks in one bullpen. Food and sanitary conditions were bad. She may have been feeling the importance of her new degree because she made the uncharacteristic mistake of talking down to the imprisoned prostitutes. "They laughed at me," she said.

Everybody thought she was wasting her time. Even the judge, J. W. Weber, an old family friend, who first agreed that "something ought to be done," said, "My God, that woman again," when she tried to prod him into action. Her family laughed at her, too. She saw she could do nothing single-handedly, so she encouraged her friends to telephone Judge Weber and other officials and discuss conditions at the jail. Agitation made the officials uncomfortable. "That's just Jeannette Rankin; it's nothing," Edward C. Mulroney, the county attorney, said, but the judge replied, "Then why are all the good women in town telephoning me?"

The jail was improved only temporarily, if at all, but Jeannette learned two important lessons: never talk down to people, no matter what their condition, and enlist citizens at the grass roots to work on a project. This grass roots method was one she was to advocate all her life. She also agitated for a public bathhouse, for the lumberjacks who came to town had no place to clean up but the baths in the better saloons. She collected quite a sum of money, which she had to return when she could not get the project started. People were right in thinking the lumberjacks preferred the saloons.

Next she took the train across the Bitterroot Mountains to Spokane, Washington, to begin her career as a professional children's social worker at the Washington Children's Home Society. Soon she transferred to the society's home in Seattle. This statewide, private, charitable organization cared for needy children temporarily in its own receiving home while it found them adoptive or foster homes. The goal was to eliminate the large and inhumane state orphanages.

The society was proud of its new home in the woods of northeast Seattle. The latest thing in child-care facilities, it had playrooms, schoolrooms, a solarium, nurseries, dormitories, and rooms for matron and caretakers. The offices where the decisions were made, however, were downtown, and staffed by men. Jeannette lived in the home with the children, not really a social worker at all, but a child's nurse. A Washington Children's Home Finder pamphlet of June 1909 described her probable duties: "The third floor is built as a receiving ward for all incoming children. It is the plan to bring the children here and keep them segregated long enough to make a careful study of them in reference to disease or moral taint. The caretaker of this floor has her room so arranged that she may have watchful oversight of the boys on one side and the girls on the other."

Jeannette had expected to be investigating needy cases, helping with the transportation of children, finding them homes with adoptive or foster parents, investigating potential homes. But such work was done by the male members of the staff. To live with the children, to see them come into the home sick and starved, became more painful than she could bear.

The annual report of the children's home told of cases of extreme poverty and suffering:

> Wearing flour sacks crudely made over by their sick mother for clothes, six little sons of Charles Salo, of Black Diamond, who deserted his family nearly a year ago, were yesterday signed over to the Washington Children's Home Society for adoption. Mrs. Salo, trembling from illness and want of nourishment . . . said she wanted to keep them together as long as she could . . . Salo, a laborer, was a hard drinker, and the last time the little family saw him was when, with an oath, he picked up the cookstove, carried it on his back, and sold it to get money to buy liquor. . . .
>
> An inventory of the home found one chair, two beds, and a table.
>
> There were no dishes and not a morsel of food in the house. . . . Elmer, the eldest, 10 years old, picked up coal and bravely tried to take the burden of the family support from the mother.

"I will never forget it, " Jeannette said sixty years later, her eyes darkening with pain. "There wasn't enough money. There were too many children; only a few could be placed. Half of them returned when people changed their minds. They had suffered so much from poverty, were in such ill health, had such bad habits, that nobody wanted them. They came back and wept in my office. All those awfully sad things about the children—I couldn't take it."

In that year, 1909, the society placed 286 children but 113 of these were returned. Thirteen died in the receiving home. And yet this organization was a shining example of child care. Unhappy and dissatisfied, Jeannette disagreed with what was being done but could offer no better solutions of her own. Social work, she realized, was not enough. Preventive reforms were needed: social, economic, and legal reforms. Little Elmer Salo should not have had to suffer for ten years only to be "rescued" so damaged in mind and body that nobody wanted him.

She was disappointed also at the poor use the society made of her training. She had been put to nursing children while men in remote offices made the decisions. Probably, in fact almost surely, she lost her temper. After a few weeks she either quit her job or lost it. With her job went her living quarters. She moved to a boarding house and enrolled at the University of Washington to study economics, political science, and public speaking to prepare herself to work for social legislation. However, securing this legislation, she felt, required that women gain the right to vote. "I saw," she said, "that if we were to have decent laws for children, sanitary jails, safe food supplies, women would have to vote."

She took classes in English composition, municipal government, transportation, and public speaking. Professor Maynard Lee Daggy gave her an "H" for "honors" in oral expression. He was an ex-Chautauqua speaker, a humanist and populist, interested in social affairs. He himself should be given "honors," for he helped this "timid girl" gain the skills she needed to support herself for thirty years and make an unusual mark in the world by her speaking. She would make more than six thousand speeches, formal and extemporaneous, in the next sixty years. She would come to speak on street corners, in Carnegie Hall, in Congress, in hotels, living rooms, kitchens, committee rooms, churches, jails, dance halls, and parks; to labor unions, farmers, businessmen, politicians, women, children, and students; at ladies' teas and to legislatures; in hundreds of cities and countrysides in the United States, Europe, South America, Africa, and Asia.

Jeannette also received a "satisfactory" in composition. She seems not to have finished the other two courses and earned only eight credits for the year. How the energetic woman spent her time outside of class and what she used for money is not entirely known. She no longer had a salary and probably had given up her allowance on getting a job. She could have written home for money, but it would not have been like her. Speculation is that she earned her living as a seamstress—a Jeannette Rankin is listed as a dressmaker in the 1910 Seattle city directory. She had the training and experience and would fall back on this resource six years later. A Seattle newspaper account of 1917, inaccurate in most respects, says she scrubbed floors. Jeannette would not have scorned such a job; she never looked down on menial labor.

In April 1910 she plastered the university district with red and white signs proclaiming votes for women. She had read that she could secure these posters free from the College Equal Suffrage League. She distributed them on her own initiative, even talking a barber into putting one in his shop window. Later, watching from the window of her room across the street, she was amused to see men stop for a surprised look at the poster, then go inside. "The men always thought we were very funny, don't you know," she said, "but we soon learned we could turn their humor to our account." Their laughter was nervous and uneasy, she thought, because in the backs of their minds many men thought woman's suffrage only fair, even though they did not like it. They would laugh first and vote "yes" later. "As for the barber, the poster in his window brought him in a lot of jolly customers." Impressed by Jeannette's motivation, the leader of the College Equal Suffrage League and a lawyer and political science professor at the university, Adella M. Parker, tracked Jeannette down and suggested she work for the upcoming suffrage referendum in the November election. Jeannette agreed to start in the fall, accepting only expenses. This was her start in politics.

CHAPTER FOUR

A Career in the Suffrage Movement

⟋⟍

"I HAVE NOT SLEPT IN
THE SAME BED TWO NIGHTS
IN SUCCESSION . . ."

THE 1910 WOMAN'S suffrage campaign in the State of Washington marked a turning point for both Jeannette and the movement. The timid girl became a persuasive orator, who could speak comfortably in public, even to those who opposed her views. Her self-confidence grew, and her success coincided with—and was nurtured by—the parallel success of the suffrage cause, which had begun to gain momentum. Women had been working for suffrage for over sixty years by 1910, and progress had been slow in coming. But in 1910 suffragists won Washington, followed by victory in California in 1911 and further victories in Arizona, Kansas, and Oregon in 1912. Within ten years the movement would force the adoption of the federal amendment.

Surprisingly, the thirty-year-old Jeannette had become interested in woman's suffrage only a few years earlier, when her supervisor in the New York juvenile court had asked her for help writing a suffrage speech. Researching the subject, Jeannette had been amazed to find that eastern women had been agitating for the vote unsuccessfully since 1848. It is odd that she did not already know this. She had been thirteen when Colorado women secured the vote and sixteen when woman's suffrage passed in Idaho. And in 1892 and 1893 Montana Populists had campaigned with a suffrage plank and had even run a woman, Ella Knowles, a brilliant whirlwind campaigner, for state attorney general. Yet the teenage Jeannette seems not to have noticed. So it was only in 1908 and 1909 that Jeannette read of the selfless struggle of the eastern suffragists. She became so interested and talked so much about it at home that Wellington suggested that woman's suffrage might make her a better career than social work.

When she began her suffrage work in Seattle in early fall 1910 a bit of luck awaited her: she was assigned to work with Minnie J. Reynolds, a former Denver journalist who had been working in New York headquarters. They were a good team; Jeannette knew Seattle and Reynolds was an experienced campaigner—she had worked as the statewide press coordinator in the successful 1893 Colorado campaign. Minnie J., as she was called, became a close friend. More than any other single person she influenced the direction of Jeannette's career. She encouraged Jeannette's commitment to suffrage and introduced her to pacifism. Her convincing arguments stayed with Jeannette for sixty-three years and through two world wars.

Minnie J. was fifty, twenty years older than Jeannette. One of the first newspaperwomen in Colorado, she had gathered Denver news by bicycling from house to house. Well known for her political writings, poetry, and Populist activities, she had run unsuccessfully for the state legislature. During the Colorado suffrage campaign, she successfully secured endorsements for the amendment from 75 percent of the state's newspapers. She then had moved to New York, where she worked for magazines and newspapers and wrote novels and stories about Europe.

As Reynolds explained the situation to Jeannette, the real problem was liquor. Men were afraid women would saddle them with prohibition. The veteran Pacific northwestern suffragist, Abigail Scott Duniway, now aged and infirm in Portland, had seen the problem clearly. She had told the eastern suffrage leaders, until they were tired of listening and dismissed her as a crank, that the temperance connection was killing the suffrage movement. Since women could only win the ballot through men's votes, the suffragists needed to convince men that their liberties would be preserved.

Duniway argued in her autobiographical history of the suffrage movement, *Path Breaking*:

The man who would be ruled by his wife would not be worth corralling in the chimney corner after she had driven him home. . . . [Woman has] made her greatest blunder . . . demanding the ballot, not simply because it is her right . . . but because she expects to reconstruct the genus man. . . . [She] drives nails into the closed coffin lid of her own and other women's liberties.

To say to men "Give us the ballot and we'll put down your whisky" arouses men to say by their votes, "Very well, we won't give you the ballot and that will settle it."

Duniway had complained to suffrage leader Susan B. Anthony about the prohibition tie-up, but Anthony felt that promoting the temperance movement helped secure the adherence of churchwomen, who otherwise were inclined to follow the dicta of the Apostle Paul about not speaking in public. Anthony's organization, the National Woman Suffrage Association and its successor, the National American Woman Suffrage Association (NAWSA), remained committed to temperance; NAWSA president from 1904 to 1915, Dr. Anna Howard Shaw, enthusiastically supported prohibition.

Partly at issue was a longstanding East-West tension. Duniway and other western women resented eastern leaders coming into the West, expecting their expenses to be paid, ordering around local volunteers, running a "hurrah campaign," and frightening the men with the specter of prohibition. The fact that the West was far ahead of the East in the area of woman's rights heightened this resentment. The West had the women voters, better access for women to education, more progressive social legislation, and better laws protecting married women's property rights. But the eastern women, organized and headquartered in New York and ignorant of western conditions, wanted to run the show. California, Oregon, and Washington long since would have granted women the vote, westerners thought, if suffragists had not talked prohibition. On the other hand, eastern women thought Duniway courted failure with her soft-spoken tactics.

The history of woman's suffrage in the State of Washington, however, substantiated Duniway's view. The women of Washington Territory gained the vote in 1883 only to see that right annulled by the territorial supreme court in 1887 at the behest of liquor and gambling interests. The court declared the suffrage law invalid on the grounds of a defective title. So the 1888 legislature passed another law enfranchising women, and again suit was brought. This time the territorial supreme court declared that Congress really meant only men when it gave state legislatures the right to enfranchise whomever they saw fit. No wonder Duniway was bitter about the suffragists' temperance connection. But for the liquor problem, Washington would have come into the union in 1889 as the first state with full woman's suffrage.

In 1909, however, the Washington legislature approved a constitutional amendment to be submitted to the voters in November 1910. The campaign for the referendum began inauspiciously due to fragmentation within the state and national organizations. To lead the campaign, NAWSA hired Emma Smith DeVoe, an Illinois suffragist who had moved with her husband to Tacoma, Washington, in 1906. An able organizer, she had served as the state president of NAWSA since shortly after her arrival in Washington; nonetheless, DeVoe alienated some of the independent western women who regarded her as an "eastern import." Adding to the tension was a dispute between state factions (eastern Washington and western Washington) regarding seating of delegates to the NAWSA national convention held in Seattle in July 1909. NAWSA seated both factions but allowed neither to vote, angering everyone. The result was the creation of dozens of independent groups across the state, many of which refused to affiliate with NAWSA.

In Seattle there was Carrie Hill of the Woman's Christian Temperance Union (WCTU), who had worked for suffrage for thirty years. Of an entirely different background was Nellie Mitchell Fick, a society woman whose beautiful house and elaborate parties were regularly described in the Sunday papers. Dr. Cora Smith Eaton, a physician, opened her own campaign headquarters, responsible only to her, with a paid publicity bureau staffed by men. Adella Parker's Collegiate Equal Suffrage League, where Jeannette had gotten her start, ran its own program. Small towns had completely independent clubs.

In Spokane was the redoubtable May Arkwright Hutton. As a young woman she had cooked in a beanery in the back of a saloon in a north Idaho mining town and later had run a boarding house. She was uneducated and married a man even less so. But the Huttons struck it rich with a silver mine and moved to Spokane, where May Hutton educated herself. She wore colorful, outrageous clothes, used makeup and strong language, and weighed three hundred pounds. Shunned by many of the "respectable" women in the movement, who suspected her of being an ex-prostitute, she remained a suffrage leader in eastern Washington, where she spent money, traded votes, and played politics "like a man."

Such fragmentation should have been a weakness, but perhaps it was a strength. Jeannette always believed that the strength of a movement came from the grass roots, with many people working toward the same goal in their own ways. Remarkably, the strong-minded women of the Washington suffrage movement managed to cooperate without too much public dissension although afterwards, according to the Seattle *Town Crier* (February 4, 1911), Carrie Hill and Nellie Fick refused to go to a farewell party for Emma DeVoe, and May Hutton was cold-shouldered at a political meeting in Tacoma.

During the campaign, however, peace was maintained, and the suffragists soft-pedaled the prohibition issue. Society leader Nellie Fick gave an interview saying she opposed prohibition, and temperance leader Carrie Hill kept quiet. And despite the conflicts, DeVoe's central headquarters saw to it that every county and every precinct had someone responsible for it, who worked to ascertain the stand of every registered voter, so the suffragists would know where to concentrate their efforts. Jeannette was to follow this tactic of organizing by precinct in future campaigns.

The women used every means of dramatizing the issue— booths at fairs, theatrical productions, speaking engagements. Dr. Cora Smith Eaton hiked up snowy Mount Rainier and planted a pennant reading "Votes for Women" at the summit, nearly three miles high. There were parades, some women marching in yellow, the NAWSA color, some in green, the state color, and some in orange, to compliment the Honorable Orange Jacobs, a Washington pioneer advocate of woman's suffrage. The suffragists enlisted the support of men's organizations: farmers' groups, unions, most of the newspapers, and most of the clergy. There were no large meetings or quarrelsome debates. Instead, they went to meetings of other organizations and received permission to speak briefly; these speeches were a large part of Jeannette's work. They gave teas, luncheons, dinners, and receptions. To show that suffragists had not rejected the home, they issued a cookbook and ran an essay contest on household hints.

Adella M. Parker of the collegiate group, the tactician of the movement, outlined the principles of the campaign in a 1912 article:

> Keep the issue single. Be for nothing but suffrage and against nothing but anti-suffrage. Pin your faith to the printed word. It carries conviction. Rely on facts rather than argument. Plead affirmative arguments. Put your opponent on the defensive. Convert the indifferent—there are thousands of them; let the incorrigible alone—there are only a few. Avoid big meetings—they rouse your enemies. Avoid antagonizing "big business," but get the labor vote, quietly. Be confident of winning. Try to have every voter in the state asked by some woman to vote for the amendment; this will carry it. Always be good-natured.

Jeannette absorbed these principles, which would guide her throughout her suffrage work.

After working with Minnie J. Reynolds, Jeannette was sent out on her own, to Ballard, a Norwegian lumber mill district of northwest Seattle. She visited schoolteachers and newspaper editors and decided to hold a public meeting. She worked so hard she thought twenty or thirty people might attend. When only fifteen showed up, she felt she had failed. But her impromptu street meetings went better. A local newspaper reported: "An audience of 300 people stood for half an hour listening to a little woman with a sweet voice and appealing gestures. . . . The lady carefully explained that this amendment . . . confers suffrage on the women of Washington. . . . [She] was sought out by some of the bystanders and beseeched to address the crowd a second time, which she finally consented to do."

Jeannette had a pleasant resonant voice that carried well without seeming loud or strained—an important attribute in the days before electronic amplification. Whether the audience was six or six thousand, she seemed to be speaking directly to each person. She spoke simply and to the point, avoiding the oratorical flourishes and impassioned phrases still in fashion in 1910.

She had a smooth and easy speaking formula. First she would say something personal or provocative, to get the audience's attention. "Your representative is a fine man, honest and independent. The only thing wrong with him is, he's against woman suffrage, and that's your fault. You haven't told him how you feel."

Then, to relax the listeners, she would offer a little joke and a little flattery. "Our men of the West are afraid of nothing. There was a timid little boy, sitting on his father's lap, and his father was trying to tell him there was nothing to be afraid of. 'Well,' said the little boy, 'what if you'd see a great big lion?' 'Oh, lions are way out in the woods. They don't come around and wouldn't bother you if they did.' 'But wouldn't you be scared of a great big black bear?' 'No,' said the father, 'the bear wouldn't hurt you, and I wouldn't let it.' 'Wouldn't you be afraid of a wolf or a big dog or something?' 'No,' said the father. The little boy was silent awhile, and then said, 'Paw, is Maw the only thing you're afraid of?' " (Laughter) "But you men of the West are not afraid of your women, and you're not afraid to give them the vote."

Then she would make her pitch in simple earnest language with concrete evidence. "It's a woman's place to make a home, but she can't make it if she has no say in community conditions. It's beautiful and right that a woman should nurse her sick children through typhoid fever, but it's also beautiful and right that she should vote for sanitary measures to prevent that typhoid from spreading." This formula could be adapted to any situation, and Jeannette used it for sixty-two years.

Her gestures were few and quiet, usually arms extended to the audience, rather widely apart, as if to embrace, hands open, palms up. She did not, however, confine herself to the advice given by a speech teacher to Dr. Anna Howard Shaw, the silver-tongued orator of the suffrage movement. Jeannette enjoyed telling the story of how the speech teacher advised his students to gesture from the shoulder, except for Dr. Shaw, who, as a woman, was to gesture only from the elbows.

Jeannette's speaking technique probably reflected that of her old instructor, Professor Daggy, a man who as a Chautauqua speaker had learned how to please a crowd. In any case, she was so successful that she was moved from town to town; in autumn 1910 she traveled to nearly every county west of the Cascade Mountains and helped to carry all of them. In fact the women won every county in the state, the total vote being 52,299 to 29,676. Yet many men abstained; some 56,000 men who voted for a congressional representative failed to vote on the amendment. Perhaps the small vote showed that the women, with their single-issue campaign, had not aroused their enemies. In any case, it would be typical of most suffrage votes. Apparently, many men could not bring themselves to vote either for or against woman's suffrage.

At the end of the campaign, Minnie J. Reynolds described Jeannette's service in an article in the *Woman's Journal,* the organ of the NAWSA: "Jeannette worked for several months without pay. No service was too commonplace, difficult, or disagreeable. All this was enhanced by her singularly sweet personality. I prophesy that she will be heard of in future campaigns." The prediction was accurate, with a little help from the oracle herself. The Washington campaign became a stepping-stone for Jeannette when Reynolds recommended her to New York suffrage leaders. Harriet Laidlaw, wife of a wealthy banker, agreed to hire Jeannette from her personal funds for six months at fifty dollars a month, and after several months in Montana—where she urged the Montana legislature to pass a suffrage amendment—Jeannette boarded a train for New York in spring 1911 to take up the job.

When Jeannette returned to New York, she joined a vibrant movement. Young, well-educated, militant women who understood organizing and publicity techniques led the fight. Working women had joined because they wanted the protection they hoped the ballot offered; the well-to-do because they wanted to improve society. Many women were angry at being second-class citizens.

The militancy of the English suffragettes had crossed the ocean. The English women had demonstrated, paraded, chained themselves to Parliament fences, gone to jail, gone on hunger strikes, endured forcible feeding, and when released had done it all over again. Harriot Stanton Blatch, daughter of early American suffragist Elizabeth Cady Stanton, had been living in England. She returned to America in 1902 impatient with the quiescence of American women. In 1907 she organized the Equality League (later the Women's Political Union) and by 1908 was organizing demonstrations, open-air meetings, and bazaars. In 1910 the fiery Alice Paul returned from a stay in England with the same message and even more dramatic methods.

The death of 146 women in the Triangle Shirtwaist factory fire on March 25, 1911—tragic proof of the necessity for protective legislation—further galvanized the suffrage movement. An investigation revealed the factory had been a firetrap, of which the doors and windows had been kept locked (to prevent theft). A wave of anger swept New York, for the Triangle workers had previously struck for better wages and conditions, and prominent socialites and suffragists had rallied to their cause. The workers had lost the strike, but people remembered it when the women died in the fire.

So on May 6, when the suffragists held New York's second grand suffrage parade, three thousand garment workers, college women, and socialites, accompanied by a few brave men, marched together under banners proclaiming "Women Need Votes to End Sweat Shops." Bystanders jeered. "Laugh," said one of the marching young men. "How many of your wives have got jobs, and your mothers, and your sisters? What wages do they get? . . . [We're] marching for better hours and fairer wages for [our] own folks . . . and you stand there and jeer." Held shortly after Jeannette's arrival in New York, the parade offered her a heady introduction to the movement there.

Jeannette's employer, Harriet Laidlaw, soon became Jeannette's good friend. According to one astute observer, Laidlaw was "a pretty woman . . . with a gift of graceful womanly talk." Like Jeannette, she was something of a maverick, who did not always follow the lead of the top suffrage officials. Nevertheless, Laidlaw offered Jeannette's services to the New York Woman Suffrage Party, and Jeannette began work in Manhattan, organizing suffrage clubs and speaking extemporaneously on street corners. She and a colleague would ask people to wait until a crowd had collected. Jeannette would speak and her associate would pass out slips of paper asking for names and addresses and opinions on woman's suffrage. They then visited those who responded favorably, hoping to enlist them as precinct workers.

Leaders at headquarters grumbled that Jeannette did not get enough names; they said she spent too much time talking, explaining the suffrage movement. Jeannette was irritated; she was following her training in Seattle and the words of *The Woman Voter*, which said that the leader "makes her appeal solely to the intellect and the moral sentiments of her neighbors. . . . Results must come slowly to her . . . for the voters aren't accustomed to appeals based on ideas of justice." Believing in education through action, she showed the officers how quickly she could get signatures. She merely asked people to sign her petitions if they had voted for a certain candidate for mayor. She got many signatures, meaningless signatures, and hoped her superiors would realize they had to be satisfied with more gradual results.

In the middle of August 1911, Laidlaw sent Jeannette to California to work on the suffrage campaign there. She worked first in San Francisco and then in rural districts and mining camps. She helped organize bands, parades, and meetings and continued with her specialty, informal speaking on the streets. "I have not slept in the same bed two nights in succession since I came to California, so you know I have been busy," she wrote Laidlaw. "Have spoken 14 times." She had been there thirteen days. "It has been like a lovely summer outing." The California suffragists concentrated their campaign heavily in the rural areas, where they needed to win a large majority; liquor would defeat them in the cities. Jeannette even took a stagecoach over the Sierras to the picturesque old mining district around Weaverville, an interesting trip because she knew the old mining camps of Montana. In Weaverville she found an all-girl band and pressed it into service. When victory came in California in November, it was narrow but important. Woman's suffrage carried by a majority of only 3,500 votes out of 247,000, a margin of only one vote for each precinct. California was now the fifth state in the suffrage column.

Jeannette wrote an article for the *Woman's Journal*, in December 1911, explaining the victory. According to Jeannette, the class structure in the West was less rigid than that in the East. A well-dressed, cultured man with whom she had discussed tax reform turned out to be the same one she met later in work clothes. The owner of a flour mill, he worked with his men. And men respected women, she argued, especially in the rural districts where "they work and achieve things." In Jeannette's somewhat romanticized view, wealthy California women lived democratically, doing their own housework and working on community and church affairs beside their less affluent sisters. She also attributed much of the victory to Socialist and Progressive political organizations.

As publication of the article showed, Jeannette was becoming known in the higher echelons of the movement. Her next assignment raised her profile higher: she was tapped to lead the legislative lobby in Albany, New York, for the 1912 session, at a salary of $125 a month. In Albany she worked with a number of volunteers, including Harriot Stanton Blatch, president of the militant Women's Political Union. Jeannette learned much from Blatch, who had grown up in the movement. A strong, innovative,

unstoppable woman, Blatch had the best mind of her generation, according to historian Mary Ritter Beard.

Indifference was the rule in the legislature, said Blatch, who
had worked there the previous year. Suffrage resolutions had died
in committee; even to get one reported out to the floor would be
a triumph. To combat this indifference, Jeannette assumed chief
responsibility for lobbying, delegating other work. And, in response
to legislators' comments that "the women of my district don't want
it" or "some of the women have spoken to me about it, but not a
single man," she organized a statewide letter-writing campaign.

She met a charming freshman senator, Franklin Delano Roosevelt,
who said he was sympathetic but unconvinced. Woman's suffrage
was necessary, she told him, to secure protective legislation for
women and children. That might work in the West, he said, but it
would not work in New England, for instance in the sardine can-
neries at Eastport, Maine, across the strait from his summer home
on Campobello. The women and children had to work when the
boats loaded with fish came in, and if another boat arrived they
might work all night, even if they had worked all day, "Otherwise, the fish might spoil."

Jeannette was to tell this story many times. She always held
against Roosevelt the fact that he could not see the difference between children and fish. (Later, of course, she was to blame him
for American involvement in World War II.) Roosevelt later claimed
he had always been for woman's suffrage, but other workers had
similar stories about him. Harriot Stanton Blatch remembered
that Roosevelt avoided voting on the 1912 suffrage resolution.
His excuse: he had to "help his missus" make the journey to their
summer home at Campobello with the babies and their carriages.
Only later, after Blatch found out how efficient Eleanor Roosevelt
was, did she realize the weakness of this excuse. Even at the time,
though, she put Roosevelt down on her list as "unreliable." But
in 1912 even Eleanor Roosevelt opposed woman's suffrage.

Jeannette managed to get a suffrage amendment reported to the
floor—a victory in itself—but there it was narrowly rejected. Her lobbying had a sustained effect, however, for the measure was to pass the
next session. "Miss Rankin's work has been most gratifying," said *The
Woman Voter*, while three New York legislators wrote of her ability, "her
tact, her gentle feminine persuasion, and her ever ready logic," in an
unusual letter to James Laidlaw, the husband of her employer.

The gratifying achievement in New York contrasted with frustration in Ohio, where she went in May 1912. She conducted street meetings, spoke at factory gates in Canton, Cleveland, and Akron, and hired a buggy to travel into the rural districts. She encountered only apathy; she thought midwestern women were too much held down by the church, the Apostle Paul having told them to "learn in silence with all subjection." She lacked money and printed matter. She lost her voice in Akron from too much speaking and had to rest it by speaking only once a day.

Then there was a strange quarrel with her supervisor, Harriet Taylor Upton, treasurer of the NAWSA and a fat, jolly, motherly woman, given to jokes in ordinary times and tears in moments of stress. Probably Upton kept a tight rein, and Jeannette never worked well under direction; where she shone was in positions like the New York legislature–lobbying job where she was in charge. Jeannette later wrote that she was sorry there had been misunderstandings but that Upton should have realized that when someone is used to planning and directing her own work, it is impossible to work too closely with anyone else. "I have had no complaints where I have worked elsewhere," she said.

She went back to Montana for a six month's "rest," which she spent organizing the state and preparing for the 1913 session of the legislature. She was unable to attend the session, however, for she accepted a year's paid appointment as field secretary with NAWSA. She would be traveling wherever they needed her, making her own plans and running her own campaigns.

She went first to North Dakota, where she addressed large, enthusiastic crowds and received positive press coverage. The Fargo, North Dakota, *Forum and Daily Republican*, for example, commented approvingly: "these ladies . . . [are] very peaceable in contrast to the English suffragists." At that very moment, however, Alice Paul, a tiny, dark-haired Quaker who had learned from and suffered with the English suffragists, was organizing a dramatic parade in Washington, D.C., to demonstrate for a national suffrage amendment. Jeannette liked Alice Paul; they were nearly the same age, both social workers, both graduates of the New York School of Philanthropy; they had even both majored in biology in college. They became lifelong friends.

Held on March 3, 1913, the day before President Woodrow Wilson's inauguration, the parade succeeded in drawing attention to the cause. Wilson, coming into the city, expected the streets to be lined with welcoming citizens; instead, he was told, they were several blocks away watching the suffrage parade. The five thousand marchers were in costume, marching state by state. Organized by Jeannette, the Montana delegation had dressed as Indians, led by a girl representing Sacajawea, the Shoshone woman who interpreted for the explorers Meriwether Lewis and William Clark. (Montana suffragists always used Sacajawea as their symbol, calling her, with considerable exaggeration, Montana's first suffragist, based on the generally accepted myth that Sacajawea voted along with other members of the Corps of Discovery at critical points on the journey and was thus America's first woman voter.) Jeannette's pretty little sister, Edna, about twenty, marched in white buckskin. Jeannette was proud of the presentation, although the Montana banners did not arrive, so no one could tell where they were from.

Disorderliness among the spectators along the line of march and refusal of the police to keep order turned the parade into a riot. The women had to fight their way against rioters in the street; it took an hour to make the first ten blocks; then progress became impossible. Men in the Massachusetts National Guard regiment laughed when asked to help keep order; police were rioting with the spectators. Finally, a rapidly organized squad of Maryland Agricultural College students took over. Some students locked arms and formed a crowd-breaking vanguard; others made a protective file on each side of the marchers. Several times they had to use their fists. Because of the riot, the suffragists got more publicity than did the inauguration; the brutal behavior of the crowd aroused a reaction of sympathy. But fifty years later Jeannette could not remember anything about it, perhaps because she had encountered heckling and rioting so many times.

Still working as NAWSA field secretary, she then took a short trip to Michigan and then to Florida for several weeks, at the invitation of the Jacksonville Equal Franchise League. They cordially received Jeannette, whom they described to the local press as "one of the best schooled and enthusiastic suffragettes to be found in America." Two Florida legislators agreed to introduce the resolution; Jeannette took charge of promoting it.

The Senate and House convened as a committee of the whole and invited the women to be guests. From all over the state women

crowded into Tallahassee and stood on chairs in the Capitol halls
to "hear the first call for the rights of women ever uttered in the
Capital of Florida." Jeannette addressed the legislature, but it
came to nothing. One legislator said she was invading the South
as a paid lobbyist of Yankee women. Florida women did not want
to vote. Men wanted "women of the South to remain in that realm
of reverence which had been made for them by the men of the
South." Votes for women would result in broken homes. There
was also fear among whites about enfranchising black women,
though the suffragists believed this a spurious excuse. They
pointed out that many more whites than blacks would be enfranchised. It made no difference; the issue was emotional. At the
end of the legislative session, Jeannette good-naturedly retired
from Florida telling the women, "It is a winning fight and is bound
to prevail."

From Florida she traveled to Montana in June 1913 to prepare for that state's part in another of Alice Paul's mammoth
demonstrations in Washington. Enthusiasm greeted her everywhere since the Montana legislature had just passed the equal
suffrage resolution. She collected signatures by the hundreds on
petitions that were to be presented to the United States Congress and, accompanied by Mary Land, a friend from Whitehall,
began a difficult cross-country drive to Washington, D.C.

Few people, men or women, dared a transcontinental automobile trip in those days. Cars had to be cranked, gears shifted,
the choke adjusted, tires changed, side curtains put up in the
rain. Carburetors became gummed with dirt. Roads were twist-
ing, narrow, and mostly unpaved. Garages or service stations were
few and far between. Little wonder, then, that Jeannette's transcontinental automobile trip impressed everyone.

On July 9, 1913, shortly before the women left, The Anaconda
Standard ran a two-column interview with a picture of Jeannette.
She was wearing a light blouse, with elbow-length sleeves and a
comfortable V-neck, a dark belt, a moderately full, long skirt, and
an enormous wristwatch. She told the Standard the suffragists had
a two-pronged plan of attack: education first, then organization,
precinct by precinct. Asked about the behavior of the English suffragettes, she said it was hard to get unbiased news, implying their
behavior was probably not as bad as it had been painted. But, she
said, "I do not want to be understood as advocating violence. I am

thankful that in this country we do not have to even think of it, for the men are so chivalrous and sensible and so imbued by the sense of justice, that all we have to do to win is appeal to their common sense." The interview was typical of Jeannette's best efforts. She made it clear she was peaceful and expected to win by peaceful means; she flattered her listeners; and somewhere in those few words of commonsense there was a little smile.

Stopping frequently to collect signatures for petitions, the two women were three weeks en route. They met other suffragists in Maryland, and drove into Washington, D.C., in a seventy-two-car procession headed by Alice Paul on July 31, 1913. One by one each state delegation requested its congressional representatives to meet them and receive the petitions. This was the suffragists' first direct assault on Congress, in line with Alice Paul's strategy of working for a national amendment. Paul and her allies despaired of the state-by-state approach, in which each state legislature had to be convinced to pass an amendment to that state's constitution, which then had to pass by a popular vote in a statewide election. The old state-by-state plan was too slow and bound to fail in many states, they felt. Instead, they favored passage of a federal amendment. This method required both houses of Congress to pass the amendment by a two-thirds majority and be ratified by three-fourths of the state legislatures within a proscribed period.

Some of the leaders stayed in Washington to lobby Congress; Jeannette, who seemed to get the most difficult jobs, was assigned the southern congressmen. She found them polite but uninterested. Said John Sharp Williams of Mississippi, "Suffrage is all right for the women of the North; the South can't have it on account of the colored women." Excuses, excuses, reflected Jeannette. In the East, they said it was all right for western women to vote. She well knew that few black men voted in the South. They had been disenfranchised by intimidation, literacy tests, poll taxes, and the "grandfather" clause, which permitted men to vote whose grandfathers had voted before the Civil War (in other words not the descendants of former slaves). So she said, "Can't you use the same thing against the women that you use against the men?" The question upset Senator Williams, who jumped from his chair and shouted, "You can't hit your baby's nurse over the head with a club."

After visiting congressmen during the day Jeannette spoke on the streets of Washington despite the capital's heat and humidity.

There followed quick trips to other states, several to Montana to rally the movement there, and one to New Hampshire, where she took her mother to visit relatives.

Through all this traveling Jeannette was always impeccably dressed. A symbol of womankind, she had to make a good impression on the man in the street or the congressman. She wore long, narrow skirts, in the fashion of the moment, and a hat and gloves. She was addicted to overly ornate hats, with large brims that shaded her face. It was a movement joke that suffrage would simply have to succeed, so that Jeannette could get a better paying job and stop making her own hats. The new fashion of detachable, launderable collars and cuffs helped her look well-groomed despite her busy schedule, but they had to be washed, ironed, and sewed back every night. And she had a mass of hair to care for.

Obviously there was little time for diversion, which Jeannette never seemed to need anyway. She did some reading. Sixty years later she would remember with pleasure the gentle satire of Canadian humorist and economist Stephen Leacock, whose books *Literary Lapses* (1910) and *Nonsense Novels* (1911) she enjoyed. She bought Olive Schreiner's *Woman and Labor* (1911) and stamped on its flyleaf "Votes for Women." Many of the suffragists were reading Schreiner, who wrote that society was poorer for its refusal to make use of women's talents. The upper classes made women into idlers and parasites; the lower classes ground them down. She advocated opening all work to women, giving them equal responsibilities, equal opportunities, and equal pay. Even marriage and sex relations would be improved, she claimed, since they would no longer be based on financial considerations.

The Englishwoman Schreiner pointed out the hypocrisy of the upper-class Englishman, standing in front of his comfortable fire, who argued against suffrage on the grounds that women should be spared from worldly toil for the divine act of childbirth. If his housekeeper, about to give birth to her ninth child, should forget to bring up his scuttle of coal, she wrote, he would soon turn her and her family out into the streets.

But Schreiner's position on women was not the only view. Arguing for the opposite perspective was Lyman Abbott, pastor of the fashionable New York Plymouth Congregational Church, who asserted in his popular 1908 tract, *The Home Builder*: "She [the homebuilder] laughs at the cynical reformer who tells her that she has bartered away her independence for her board and clothes. Economic independence has no charms for her. . . . Her one dominating desire is . . . to be dependent on the man she loves. . . . She has no ambition to become a public woman."

The anti-suffrage movement was strong, and in addition to vocal men like Lyman Abbott, it contained many women. Anti-suffrage women needed to be educated, Jeannette felt, their "consciousness raised," in a phrase to be used half a century later, before the men could be prodded into action. It demanded hard, continuous work on the part of many women, and Jeannette certainly did her share. In the five years she was in the movement she made at least a dozen trips across the continent by train, sleeping in upper berths or staying with colleagues to save money. She drove primitive cars great distances over primitive roads. She planned and marched in parades, organized political districts, gathered signatures on petitions, made hundreds of formal and informal speeches. She lobbied the New York and Florida legislatures and the United States Congress, and worked in New York, California, Ohio, North Dakota, Tennessee, Nebraska, New Hampshire, Michigan, Missouri, Delaware, Oklahoma, Florida, Wisconsin, Pennsylvania, Washington State, and Washington, D.C. Between these jobs she dashed back to Montana six times to help the movement there. For a little rest she would make clothes and discuss politics with Wellington. Now she was determined that the women of Montana should have the vote. Even during her furious activity across the United States, woman's suffrage in her native state remained a primary concern.

CHAPTER FIVE

Suffrage Success in Montana

"WOMEN IN OUR ORGANIZATION
ARE FROM ALL WALKS OF LIFE. . . .
WE UNITE ON ONE POINT:
WE WANT TO VOTE."

ONE FREEZING FEBRUARY day Jeannette Rankin stood in the flower-decked hall of the Montana House of Representatives and asked for the right to vote. Instead she received violets, but she had begun her political career. The year was 1911. Fresh from her suffrage training in Washington State, her employment with the national movement had not yet begun; she was unknown in Montana. Yet three years later Montana women won the vote, and two years after that Jeannette was elected to the United States Congress.

After the 1910 Washington victory, Jeannette was determined that her native state should also have woman's suffrage, though the cause was so little known in Montana that after her speech to the legislature she received letters from the far corners, saying "Why didn't you let us know?" or "Why didn't anyone tell us about that?" In the 1890s, a brief flurry of suffrage activity, due mostly to the Populists, had gained both Colorado and Idaho women the vote. In Helena, Montana, women organized a small suffrage club in 1890. A statewide group, the Montana Woman's Suffrage Organization, formed in 1895, and that same year John Huseby, a Populist representative from Lewis and Clark County, introduced an amendment to give women the ballot. The amendment failed and went down again in 1897 and 1899. A tiny handful of stalwart workers had kept the state movement from dying, mostly members of the WCTU plus a few professional women: teachers, a doctor, a lawyer, and a newspaperwoman.

By the end of the century, Helena had the only active club, and even it withdrew its affiliation from the NAWSA when its members became angry with National's president, Carrie Chapman Catt. Catt had chided them for inactivity, and, later, when they had put their best feet forward to entertain her, she had condescendingly remarked on the way people in little western towns put on airs.

In 1902 Catt and two of her best organizers spent the greater part of the summer in Montana working for suffrage. Some progress must have been made, despite the fact that the twenty-two-year-old Jeannette had not heard about it, for a convention was held in Butte that fall. In 1903 Governor Joseph K. Toole and other prominent men, as well as the state trades and labor council, endorsed woman's suffrage. Nevertheless, the 1903 and 1905 legislatures decisively defeated the suffrage resolution and refused even to consider it in 1907 and 1909.

When Jeannette arrived home to Missoula from Washington at Christmas 1910, this seeming apathy masked a favorable climate. The recent victory in Washington had set people to thinking. Additionally, the Progressive wings of both parties were still strong. People were tired of corrupt politics, of having senators elected by legislatures bribed with money thrown through hotel transoms. (This and worse had actually happened; the heavy hand of the Anaconda Company had spawned notorious corruption in Montana politics.)

Reformers hoped that women, ostensibly more moral and less self-interested than men, could exercise a cleansing and civilizing influence on government. Finally it had become clear from looking at Wyoming, Colorado, and Idaho, where women had voted for years, that equal suffrage could work. Even the Great Falls (Montana) *Tribune,* formerly an adamant suffrage opponent, admitted that none of the dire predictions of the anti-suffragists had come true in states where women voted.

When Jeannette read in the December 11, 1910, *Missoulian* that a Montana legislator planned to introduce a suffrage resolution during the next session, she saw opportunity. She asked

friends to call a suffrage meeting and invite her to address it;
when they did not, she did it herself. About forty men and women
attended the organizing meeting of the Political Equality Club
of Missoula, held at the Missoula High School gym. They elected
Jeannette secretary and approved her suggestion that she go to
Helena for the coming legislative session. Her behavior was un-
characteristically brash. Calling the meeting herself, after an apparent rebuff, was bold enough; planning to lobby the legislature
was astounding. The experiences of the Washington campaign
had fed her ego and stiffened her spine.

She traveled to Helena, where she met with prominent women—
among them Hattie Nolan, wife of Representative C. B. Nolan,
and Dr. Maria Dean—to form the Equal Franchise Society. She
also met with Representative Dr. D. J. Donohue of the eastern
Montana town of Glendive, whose announcement that he would
introduce a suffrage resolution had kindled her enthusiasm. She
found he considered it a joke, but she had encountered such
male risibility before. "Well," she said, "you've gotten the publicity. Now you'll have to introduce the resolution."

After the session commenced, she proceeded to lobby the legislature but found much opposition and became so discouraged
she returned to Missoula. Yet suddenly the committee passed the
bill into the house and asked Jeannette to speak in its favor on
February 1, 1911. She quickly agreed. Then she began to practice her speech over and over, trying to recall all the precepts she
had learned in oral expression. Her brother, Wellington, now
practicing law in Helena, listened to her rehearsals, corrected
her delivery, and kept reminding her of the speech's importance.
The more he talked, the more nervous she became.

She was to speak in a trying time. The legislature was tense
over the election of a United States senator. Citizens had passed
a referendum selecting the Democrat Thomas Walsh, but in 1910
the legislature, not the voters, actually elected senators. The contest between Progressives of both parties, who supported Walsh,
and the Anaconda Copper Mining Company, commonly called
the Company, which wanted to reelect Republican Thomas Carter,
would take two months and eighty ballots to be resolved. (Ultimately it ended with the election of compromise candidate Henry
L. Myers.) Probably the men thought of Jeannette's speech as a
diversion—as entertaining as the Chinese New Year celebration

they had attended two evenings before. They assessed themselves fifty cents apiece for flowers to decorate the hall and banned smoking. They sat in the gallery while their seats were taken by the suffragists in their long full gowns and elaborately trimmed hats. Jeannette was elegant in green velvet.

In introducing Jeannette representatives C. B. Nolan of Helena and Dan O'Hern of Missoula spoke of her work in other parts of the country, her studies in New York, her social work in San Francisco, and the Washington State campaign. Sensitive to the emphasis put on her absences from the state, Jeannette found the introduction disconcerting. Also some of the older suffragists, those who had carried the burden for so many years, had made her feel like an interloper. She therefore began her speech, "I was born in Montana." In response the men broke into loud applause, boisterousness so uncalled for that Jeannette nearly forgot her speech.

Recovering, she asked the legislators to think of the six million women who worked to support themselves and their children. She spoke of enlightened countries where women did vote: Norway, Finland, and New Zealand. Here in the northern Rockies all the women but those of Montana voted, and now the women of Washington had joined them. Women were struggling against "taxation without representation." And paraphrasing Jane Addams—the founder of Hull House in Chicago—Jeannette argued that if a woman's place was indeed in the home, she could not make it a home when she had no control of the influences coming into it. She spoke calmly for twenty minutes without further interruption.

There was great applause. A legislator rose and presented her with a bouquet of violets. Again great applause. But now came the usual jokes at the expense of the suffragists. Burton K. Wheeler, a freshman legislator leading the fight against the Company's candidate for Senate, presented an amendment. Later a senator himself and an ally of Jeannette's, Wheeler was a man who liked a jolly time, all-night poker parties with the boys. He once said he was unalterably opposed to woman's suffrage, but he had to vote for it, or his wife would quit him. He wrote in his memoir: "I voted for it [suffrage] but I could not resist some prearranged byplay . . . I proposed amending the Amendment so as to limit the right to vote to women with six children . . . [The] suffragettes . . . must have thought we were taking their crusade lightly."

The oratory then went from the ridiculous to the sublime. Colonel C. B. Nolan, long a proponent of women suffrage, in whose offices the young Wellington worked, rose in its favor. His rich Irish brogue stilled the laughter: an Irish accent was a political asset in Montana. He spoke of his old Irish mother, how hard she had worked to support the family. "A woman like that ought to have the vote," he said.

The house gave the resolution a good majority, but two-thirds was needed to pass the constitutional amendment. Even then it would require two-thirds of the senate, followed by acceptance in a voters' referendum, so the issue would have to be brought up again in 1913. Yet Jeannette had made a striking impression and was instantly and favorably known all over the state. The February 2, 1911, Helena *Independent* wrote, "to Jeannette Rankin belonged the glory . . . to her logic, argument, and pleadings . . . the House succumbed." She "spoke simply and . . . her argument was sound as a dollar." She "neither begged . . . threatened, [nor] cajoled."

Hired in spring 1911 to work in New York, Jeannette did not spend much time in Montana for more than a year, but she kept in frequent touch with Wellington. Just beginning an active, expansive career in business and politics, Wellington kept informed about everything—and seemingly everyone—in Montana. Of great interest to both siblings were the maneuverings of the state's largest employer, the Anaconda Copper Mining Company. The Company dominated Montana politics: it had flexed its political muscles in 1903, when it closed down its operation (putting fifteen thousand men out of work) until the governor called a special session of the legislature to enact the legislation it demanded. Many Montanans were angry and stayed angry for half a century; just to suggest that a man "wore a copper collar" would make votes against him. On the other hand, many men of genuine conservative opinions favored the Company, and many others could be reached with Company money.

Both Wellington and Jeannette believed Anaconda would cause problems for the suffrage campaign. The Company controlled most of Montana's major newspapers, and, like many big businesses, it opposed woman's suffrage, believing that women were likely to favor humanitarian laws that would interfere with operations or result in higher taxes. And even if the Company did not work directly against suffrage, it had proven that it would go to great lengths to oppose progressive politicians from both parties who tried to curb its political influence; it was these reformers who were the suffrage movement's most likely allies.

A second problem would be the prohibition issue, for Montanans —from the lumbermen in the northwest, through the miners in the middle, to the cowhands in the east—had the reputation of being joyful drinkers. Every little crossroads had its saloon, the social center for miles around. Towns and cities prided themselves on the number and size of their bars. Butte had a saloon with a bar a block long. Still, times were changing. The dry winds of reform blowing over the nation had reached Montana. The mayor of Butte had announced the closing of the red-light district in January 1911. True to Butte's heritage, the closure only lasted a few weeks: the city was proud of the district, Venus' Alley, reputed to be the largest north of New Orleans.

A third problem was the incredible diversity of population. Of Montana's 376,000 residents, more than 100,000 were of foreign birth or parentage; 2,000 citizenship papers a year were taken out. Irish, Welsh, Cornish, Scandinavian, and German immigrants had come by the shipload to mine or farm or log. Scottish cattle and sheep ranchers settled on the eastern plains. Later the southern Europeans arrived, along with large numbers of Finns. Of these groups, the Irish were the most numerous, most vocal, and most political.

Montana was a politicized, organized state. Among the groups a politician had to deal with were the Cristofero Colombo Club, the Ancient Order of Hibernia, Sons of St. George, Narodjini Com and Trobjaica, Sons of Hermann, St. Jean Baptiste, Baron de Hirsch, Sons of Norway, Bing Kong Tong, and the Robert Burns Society, as well as Masonic lodges and other native orders. There were Roman and Greek Orthodox and Catholic churches; Swedish, Norwegian, and German Lutheran, both conservative and reformed; Presbyterian, Methodist, Baptist, Christian, Brethren, Unitarian, Buddhist, Jewish, Quaker, Mormon, Congregational, Confucian, Moslem, and Baha'i. This diversity had its positive aspects, for such a variety of ideas made for tolerance: freedom of opinion was easily accepted. Running for governor in 1920, Burton K. Wheeler said about his religion: "My mother was a Methodist, my father was a Quaker, I attended the Baptist Sunday School as a child, I am married to a Methodist and like most of you men most of my religion is in my wife's name."

Still a fourth problem was the huge size of the state, the third largest in the country, with one of the smallest populations. There were towering mountains, few and bad roads, some of them covered with snow six months or more of the year. Here again, though, there was a positive side: Montanans were used to coping. They were sociable and mobile.

Thinking of these factors Jeannette returned from the heat and frustrations of Ohio in summer 1912. Local suffragists, including Ida Auerbach, Dr. Maria Dean, and Frieda Fligelman, had kept the movement alive. Now Jeannette helped them set up a loose organization with no constitution, no dues, no affiliation with NAWSA. Such an organization would act more and argue less; it gave Jeannette, as chairman, the kind of freedom in which she worked best. She went from county to county, appointing chairmen and urging women to set up permanent local organizations. Since the immediate goal was the election of a favorable legislature, the women canvased the candidates directly and spoke at political meetings. They secured the endorsement of all four parties, Democratic, Republican, Progressive, and Socialist. In some cases they campaigned against candidates who had opposed them in the past, such as James McNally, who had been adamant and vocal against suffrage in 1911. They did not defeat him, but they scared him enough that he voted with them when the time came.

In the 1912 elections the Democrats received a good majority in the legislature, and most were suffrage supporters. Jeannette organized a letter-writing campaign to the lawmakers elect; as the 1913 legislature opened, she called a state meeting of suffragists in Helena. Foreseeing victory the women made plans for the 1914 referendum. While they were meeting in Helena, the suffragists received invitations to Governor Sam V. Stewart's inaugural ball. Helena women, who had a reputation for dressing well (it was said there were three hundred millionaires in that small city), attended in beautiful evening gowns, but Jeannette's guests from the far reaches of the state had not brought formals, if indeed they owned any, so Jeannette herself just wore a nice daytime dress. The women from the hinterlands appreciated the gesture. Indeed, one of them remembered it sixty years later.

The vote on the suffrage bill—to submit to the voters an amendment to the state constitution granting woman suffrage— came early in the session. It passed by an overwhelming majority:

twenty-six to two in the senate and seventy-four to two in the house. Suffragists held celebrations all over the state, and not just for themselves. Arizona, Alaska, California, Kansas, and Oregon had, in the last three years, given women the vote, so there was great euphoria. The next task was to see the suffrage amendment through the popular referendum to be held in November 1914.

After the amendment passed the legislature, Jeannette headed east to begin her work as NAWSA's field secretary, but she took a quick trip back to Montana in the summer (preparing for her famous drive to Washington, D.C.), during which she took the opportunity to generate publicity and organize. Then in January 1914, although she had been offered another year's employment with the national association, she returned to Montana to work without pay on the referendum.

As usual, there were financial problems. Jeannette raised half the money for the nine-thousand-dollar suffrage referendum campaign out of state. In state the women raised money with teas, baked goods, and self-denial weeks. They gave lectures on how to be beautiful and wrote and presented a musical comedy that played in Helena, Butte, and Missoula. They lost nearly one thousand dollars when the State Savings Bank in Butte failed two months before the election, but Jeannette's former New York employers the Laidlaws replaced the money with a loan. Jeannette did not publicize the Laidlaw's loan; she did not want to draw attention to out-of-state money, and besides it helped, she said, "that everybody felt sorry for us because we lost our money."

The liquor problem was solved by avoiding it as much as possible. Jeannette had learned in the Washington campaign to "keep the issue single." She sent a letter to every registered voter in the state saying, "Women in our organization are from all walks of life, every political party, and every religion and faith. We unite on one point: we want to vote."

In a newspaper interview run in the Anaconda *Standard* on July 9, 1913, she said, "We want the people informed first of all, as we believe that education will overcome prejudice and that we can safely appeal to the sense of justice in men to stand uppermost and overcome any commercial interests that might tend in the other direction." The commercial interests, of course, were the liquor interests, which feared women would vote for prohibition.

Jeannette kept saying what was not entirely true, that suffragists were "neither for nor against social reform."

The liquor interests, however, had the same problem as the suffragists: it was bad tactics to come out publicly against suffrage, and women anti-suffragists did not want to be identified with saloons. The National Anti-Suffrage Association sent a representative to Butte to confer with and obtain funds from the Montana Protective Association, a group of liquor promoters, and asked them specifically not to oppose votes for women in their magazine. Jeannette found out about it and wrote an article called "Gumshoe Methods Not Popular in Montana."

The incident made votes for the suffragists, but Jeannette's article was the pot calling the kettle black; she was careful to keep the suffrage movement a clear distance from the temperance movement. The WCTU was not even allowed to march with the suffragists in the great state fair parade under its own banners. Since many of the older women had come into the suffrage movement through the WCTU, feelings were hurt. Jeannette, for her part, felt the temperance women were not much help; they were too concerned with their own issue.

Rhetoric hostile to foreigners was too common and inappropriate, Jeannette recognized later. Campaigners tended to echo inappropriate arguments of the educated upper-middle-class women who made up the bulk of the national movement: educated women of old American stock would vote more intelligently and had a better right than the recent flood of immigrants. Even though a quarter of Montanans were of foreign birth or parentage, speakers made remarks like: "As an American mother, I feel that I deserve as much voice in the government under which I and my children must live as does my Chinese laundry man who has been in this country only a few years, or an Italian laborer who has just taken out his naturalization papers." Jeannette herself sometimes echoed these sentiments, once inexplicably saying there were fortunately few immigrants in Montana.

Since the problems of the foreigners, liquor, and the Company converged in Butte, the largest and most important city in the state, suffrage headquarters was set up in a hotel there. Publicity was placed in the hands of the lively Mary O'Neill, a Butte newspaperwoman. She knew politics, was active in school elections (in which women long had voted), and she became Jeannette's close adviser. Since the Company owned most of the state's major newspapers, it was difficult to publicize the suffrage campaign; the Anaconda Company had had a policy for fifty years of ignoring any issue it opposed. So Miss O'Neill resorted to dramatization. She labeled the campaign the Suffragette Express, and put up posters like these two:

> STOP LOOK LISTEN, Provided you are a live one. If dead already, stay where you are and be run over by the Suffragette Express that will overtake the fast male at the Missoula Theatre.
>
> Miss Jeannette Rankin of the greatest city on earth will act as an engineer and introduce Mr. James L. Laidlaw of New York, second greatest city, and Mrs. James L. Laidlaw, who will discourse eloquently on the latest agricultural stunt of making two votes grow where one grew before . . . Have your life insured and bring your firearms for there are going to be many bombs exploded and many balloons punctured.

The Laidlaws, Jeannette's friends and ex-employers, had come to campaign in Montana in their own private railroad car. It was February 1914 and far below zero, but the shivering Laidlaws spoke at meetings all along the way. Also out from New York was "General" Rosalie Jones with her rough-and-ready wit; she had made national headlines with her colorful parades in the East. Another friend of Jeannette's, New York school principal and pacifist Kathryn Blake, and NAWSA past president Dr. Anna Howard Shaw came, too. There was some criticism of these carpetbaggers, and cowboys and miners could be rough on eastern tenderfeet. One story has it that cowpunchers at the 1914 Miles City Fourth of July parade roped Rosalie Jones as she marched by.

An effective outside campaigner was the New York laundry worker, Margaret Hinchley. Large, lively, and red-haired, she was popular with the loggers and miners. "Let's hear the big girl again," they would shout. Her theme was protection for working women; women worked seventeen to eighteen hours a day in laundries, she said, for $3.00 to $3.50 a week (the miners got more than that a day). Average weekly wages for women in the United States were $6.00.

"We have in New York," she said, "14,000 women over 65 who must work or starve . . . you may see them in jail, scrubbing hard rough concrete floors that make their knees bleed—women who have committed no crime but being old and poor." Workingmen could understand this kind of talk. Jeannette's sister Edna toured the rough logging district in northwest Montana with Hinchley. When a drunken logger broke into their hotel room, Margaret Hinchley picked him up and threw him out.

Jeannette traveled six thousand miles during the 1914 campaign, using trains, stages, and borrowed Fords. On one trip of thirteen hundred miles in one month she made twenty-six speeches, oversaw the election of twenty precinct leaders, and set up county central committees. The precinct and county committees were the keys to the campaign. Headquarters could coordinate and send out literature, but activity at the grass roots, as Jeannette was always to say, was what counted.

One of the best tactics of the campaign was for the women to ask for a few minutes at the many community events that Montanans always seemed to be holding: meetings of clubs, churches, unions, and farmers. The suffragists also organized claques to attend every possible meeting, regardless of whether suffrage was on the agenda. These women would clap whenever woman's suffrage was mentioned, so it behooved campaigning politicians to mention it. When national workers tried to follow their old tactics and asked for introductions to the wives of prominent men, Jeannette would reply that she did not care who the banker's wife was; what was important was the precinct organizations. Jeannette had learned the technique in the Washington State campaign.

To overcome the distances in the large and sparsely settled state, Jeannette encouraged people in rural areas to campaign on their own. It worked well. Jeannette did not know, until she visited there, that one county printed its own *Suffragist Weekly*. Nor did Jeannette know until later that one of her best supporters in the extreme eastern part of the state was a prostitute who contributed money and wrote letters to the *New Republic*. As a former social worker, Jeannette was saddened but not shocked by prostitution. When men would say to her, "But if you have woman suffrage, the bad women will vote," she would retort, "Well, the bad men do now."

In another county she found to her surprise that the chairman of the local suffrage organization was a Catholic with eight children and a saloonkeeper husband. Another suffrage worker, whose husband had died and left her the owner of a profitable saloon, was often asked why she was a suffragist when woman's suffrage would destroy her means of making a living—the assumption being that if suffrage passed, prohibition would not be far behind. Jeannette remembered her reply: "Oh, I can earn my living some other way."

One of the best workers operated entirely independently: Maggie Smith Hathaway, state suffrage chairman for the WCTU and later a state representative from Ravalli County from 1916 to 1922. Hathaway knew that campaigning as a temperance worker was not wise, but the WCTU would not finance her unless she spoke for suffrage and prohibition. She, therefore, went to suffrage headquarters, but there they were afraid of her white ribbon. So Hathaway dipped into her own slender purse, made her own itinerary, provided her own publicity, wrote her own speeches, and traveled 5,379 miles in five months. She even managed to have one of her speeches printed in full in the Miles City *Star*, though the editor had never printed anything in favor of woman's suffrage before and would not even mention the name of Jeannette Rankin. The editor relented in Hathaway's case because he and her deceased husband had spent hours together discussing English literature.

These organizing tactics did not mask the substantive issues at stake. Suffrage campaigners made impassioned arguments in favor of female enfranchisement. Women should have the vote, they said, not only out of simple justice, but also for public welfare, health measures, protection of children, and honest politics. After World War I broke out in July, speakers often mentioned that women would be for peace. Said Judge E. K. Cheadle at a giant rally in Helena during the state fair: "If equal suffrage does nothing but convince the people that government is not founded upon physical force, upon cannon and Gattling guns, but upon opinions, upon love and faith, it will be worth any cost to get it."

Jeannette's speech at the June 1914 meeting of the State Federation of Women's Clubs in Lewistown was typical. Her speech was important because many of the women active in Montana's club movement had a history of opposing woman's suffrage. As Belle Fligelman Winestine, who later became Jeannette's very good friend and publicist, remembered the speech:

When Miss Rankin came forward to speak the air became electric. She immediately dispelled the notion that suffragists were all middle-aged and masculine. Young, attractive, energetic, and glowing with friendliness and reason, Jeannette Rankin commanded attention as soon as she spoke. She wore a gold-colored velvet suit, and the Lewistown editor said she looked like a young panther ready to spring. . . . Women should not have to give their reasons for voting, she said. . . . No one asked men to make any such defense.

Nevertheless she did give reasons: "Governmental actions directly affected their lives, but they had nothing to say about any of them. . . . Montana's infant and maternity mortality rates were among the highest in the nation . . . the need for food and safety inspectors."

Afterwards Mary O'Neill wrote Jeannette: "give the same talk you gave at the state federation meeting. . . . You will know what I mean, but do give them all the dope you can about the influence of the women in behalf of CHILDREN AND APPEAL TO THE HIGHER STANDARD OF MOTHERHOOD and truer homelife . . . but even more so. That's the gush that gets the public. . . . That speech of yours . . . will do more to make suffragists than all the purely intellectual guff we might give them in a whole hundred years."

Severe interruption to the campaign occurred in June 1914. In Butte war broke out between pro- and anti-Company factions of the Butte Miners' Union, a powerful influence in state politics. Dissident miners said their officers wore the Company's copper collar and had refused to do anything about enforcing mine safety and an equitable hiring system. There were riots, dynamitings, and shootings in Butte, followed by martial law. Complicating the problem were radicals of the Industrial Workers of the World and labor spies brought in by the Anaconda Company. The affair broke the union and ended organized labor opposition to the Company, but serious discontent continued. The upheaval prevented campaigning for suffrage in Butte. Butte labor politics would again haunt Jeannette when she served in Congress three years later.

When the campaign could not be carried on in Butte, it was taken with renewed intensity to the rest of the state. On Election Day Jeannette publicly expressed optimism, but privately she was anxious. No politicians had publicly opposed equal suffrage, but there was a strong undercurrent of disapproval. Jeannette drove a borrowed Ford from polling place to polling place in Butte, making sure poll watchers were on the job. Results came in late, and Jeannette feared fraud; she was afraid they would be "counted out" in a few counties whose officials would wait until they saw how many "No" votes they needed to deliver. It was an old Montana tactic. She telegraphed her good friend, the politically knowledgeable Ruth Hanna McCormick, daughter of the Ohio political boss Mark Hanna and chairman of the NAWSA's congressional committee. McCormick recommended that Jeannette send delegations to watch ballot boxes in Anaconda and Boulder until they were opened and counted. Jeannette did so.

The victory was narrow: 41,301 to 37,588—52 percent for woman's suffrage. Maggie Hathaway's Ravalli County magnificently gave the suffragists 70 percent, and Jeannette carried Missoula with 64 percent. Small agricultural and lumbering counties in the northwest gave solid support. A cluster of cattle counties around Miles City approved, possibly a tribute to Hathaway and the Miles City *Star.* Unhappy Butte, still under martial law, where there was strong labor support for suffrage, was a toss-up. But the older suffragists long established in Helena and Bozeman had not been able to carry their counties.

Nearly twelve thousand voters did not express themselves on the suffrage issue; such had been the experience in other states. It is interesting to note that prohibition sentiment was rising, for in the wet state of Montana, the voters, all of them men, elected a legislature that two months later approved a state referendum on prohibition. The same would happen in the United States, and prohibition would be added to the Constitution before woman's suffrage. A reform tide was running strong.

In the same year, 1914, Nevada women also received the vote. Since Jeannette had begun working in Seattle four years before, six states and one territory had approved woman's suffrage. These victories were the work of thousands of devoted women and many equally devoted men. Still, Jeannette herself could take some credit. In Montana she was instantly famous. Said Montana Democratic congressman Tom Stout: "[The suffragists] have such a splendid leader. Jeannette Rankin is one of the most successful campaigners that I ever knew. I have seen her go into a Democratic convention and secure an endorsement. . . . Then she went into the Republican convention where the opposition was stronger and won there. She achieved all of this by the charm of her manner and the force of her argument." Quite a feat for a "timid girl, who worked hard for what she got."

CHAPTER SIX

Jeannette Rankin for Congress

"I WAS NEVER A REPUBLICAN.
I RAN ON THE REPUBLICAN TICKET."

JEANNETTE'S BRILLIANT SUCCESS in the Montana suffrage campaign turned her thoughts toward politics. She believed she could
be elected to Congress. Well and favorably known across the state,
she had a strong organization behind her—the one she had built
to pass woman's suffrage. And the grateful, newly enfranchised
women would vote for her. An accident of history also favored
her election: the homestead boom had increased Montana's
population to the point where the state was due two congressmen, but Montana had not yet been redistricted. Jeannette reasoned that since each congressman would be elected at large,
each voter voting for two people, she easily might run second,
which would be good enough.

She had to find something to do, for she no longer had a job.
Early in 1915 she had severed her connections with NAWSA. She
was tired, disappointed with Carrie Chapman Catt's election to
the NAWSA presidency, dissatisfied with her own role in the movement, and uncomfortable with a serious split in the movement.
To Jeannette's dismay, Alice Paul's Congressional Union, soon to
be renamed the Woman's Party, had broken from the NAWSA in
February 1914. A year earlier, Alice Paul had reinvigorated the
NAWSA's long-moribund congressional committee, the mission

of which was to promote a national suffrage amendment. In so doing, she angered some of NAWSA's more conservative members, including its president Carrie Chapman Catt.

Quarrels over money and tactics ultimately led to the split. Catt objected to Paul's spending the money she raised without first running it through the NAWSA treasury, where Catt could scrutinize its uses. She also objected to Paul's militant methods and the tactic (more suitable to a parliamentary government like that of England, where Alice Paul had lived for so long) of working against all Democratic congressional candidates, regardless of their position on suffrage, because Democratic president Woodrow Wilson would not speak in favor of an amendment. On the other hand, many of the younger suffragists objected to Carrie Chapman Catt's dictatorial ways and the attitude of Catt's companion, Mary Garrett Hay, who conveyed the impression that "Mrs. Catt is Mrs. Catt and I am her prophet." They disagreed with Catt's state-by-state strategy, feeling that all energies should be bent toward securing a national amendment.

Alice Paul and the younger suffragists were Jeannette's good friends, although she thought their overly dramatic methods were apt to alienate the public. Too, Jeannette objected to Catt's bossiness, and there was some longstanding feud between Jeannette and Mary Garrett Hay. Harriet Laidlaw, who though something of a maverick herself was able to get along with both factions, wrote Jeannette: "Funny about your letter to Mary [Garrett Hay]. . . . There can be no friction between you and Mrs. Catt. Of course there is none between you and the national. Any trouble with Mrs. Catt is through Mary. All you can do is just to put her aside as a jealous 'brimstone heart'."

As for her role in the movement, Jeannette felt her experience, hard work, and ability entitled her to more recognition and influence. Part of the problem was the old East-West antagonism. The easterners ran NAWSA, and the western women had the vote. Westerners wondered why the easterners should tell them what to do. Anne Martin of Nevada and Abigail Scott Duniway of Oregon had expressed the same dissatisfaction. There was also, in that class-conscious era, especially in the East, a strong division between volunteer management of an organization and paid staff. Volunteers set policy, and staff did as it was told. This made it difficult for Jeannette to penetrate the upper councils of NAWSA; besides, she was not good at doing what she was told. Twenty years later, Jeannette's sister Edna McKinnon encountered the same difficulties in the birth control movement.

Jeannette had complained to Antoinette Funk, executive vice chairman of the NAWSA congressional committee, about her work assignments, and Funk replied in April 1915: "I have heard from Mrs. McCormick [committee chairman] and we will do our very best to arrange something for you that will be satisfactory. You know we can't lose you and we will find some stationary work for you to do. I know the work is hard and seems to be unsatisfactory, but you are a very important spoke in the wheel, my dear, and we need all our spokes." It sounded like a runaround. Jeannette felt that this time she had earned better. She had headed important and successful campaigns, spoken thousands of times. She had traveled across the continent more than a dozen times in four years, sleeping in upper berths or the homes of newly met suffragists, washing and ironing at night after the evening meeting so as to look neat and respectable by day. One can imagine her, utterly fatigued, being asked to share a bed with some child, and saying, with the comradely grin children always responded to, "which side of the bed would you like me to sleep on?"

She had worked intensively with strangers and done it well, but inside she was still timid. It had cost much inner effort and was hard on her well-developed temper. Usually through all the fatigues and disappointments, failures of fellow workers to come up to expectations, and public jeering, she had been able to control herself, but occasionally she could not. She had had a violent public tantrum, screaming and throwing things, at state suffrage headquarters in Butte, likely in July 1914, until Mary O'Neill steered her to her room and locked her in.

Later O'Neill had written:

> Lively maiden:
>
> Now a word of advice. . . .
> Above all things keep yourself sweet, young, pretty,—by that I mean just natural. You have a great work to do—do not try to do it in thirty days—even God knows better than to try it. . . . In the meantime remember that the beautiful personality you possess is yours by right of countless efforts through the past lives; then preserve what you have and ADD to it, not take from it

being careless of your health and extreme fatigue. Neither of them will buy you anything in your work. Never mind if you do not convert the multitude—others will follow after you who can complete the job. Try and not be selfish in the work, leave a twig or two of laurel for someone else who must come after!!! Discouragement and irritability will rob you of your priceless winsomeness and beauty, so forget you ever have a chance for either.

Does this seem like a dreadful 'jacking up'? Well, I mean every word even though it is all said with the sweetest love in my heart for you. I appreciate what you are and feel that I must help protect you against yourself in the intense and even reckless passion to turn the world over like a flapjack. Just try and work in harmony with God's plan; I have a sneaking notion that He knows a wee bit about it.

Here in Butte we are all ready to kowtow before you—that is everyone but me—for once in a while I want to spank you good and hard.

Now, will you be good?

> Lovingly,
> Mary O'Neill

A reflection of her exhaustion, Jeannette's temper may also have been precipitated in part by illness. Mary O'Neill wrote Carrie Chapman Catt a few months later: "the long strenuous suffrage work done by this brilliant young woman quite undermined her health." For Jeannette had trigeminal neuralgia, or, as it is sometimes called and as she called it, tic douloureux. Characterized by searing, burning, lightning-like jabs in the cheek (in Jeannette's case, the right one), the excruciatingly painful disease attacks without warning and may leave as rapidly. It may last a minute or two or fifteen minutes or longer. It may happen many times a day or a few times a month. In those days it was treated with opium or its derivatives, milder analgesics having no effect.

Although the disease is more common in the elderly, and seldom attacks before age thirty-five, Jeannette had had at least one bad attack in 1913, at age thirty-three, while campaigning in Michigan. Apparently she had gained relief from "little black pills," for she wrote in 1917, while she was in Congress, to a doctor in Saginaw, Michigan, thanking him for

> your kindness to me when I was sick in the Fordney Hotel. . . . I have been thinking for a long time that I would write you and

tell you that you have made my life very much happier by giving me the "little black pills." I hesitated about writing because I was afraid you would advise me to stop using them. I did not want to receive such advice because I have been taking them so long now that I do not wish to get along without them.

The phrase "made my life much happier" suggests that the attack in Saginaw was not her first. She did not ask the doctor for a new prescription, and if he ever replied, his letter has been lost, but two months later she received a letter from a Michigan drug store: "Answering your query, you may of course get what amount you wish of these pills at any time, at the rate of 300 pills for $2.00.... Your recent order ... received today, and package goes forward tonight."

Such a malady must have been a terrible handicap to a woman who was constantly in the public eye. Sometimes treated by severing the trigeminal nerve, this operation could leave one side of the face sagging and the voice slurred, an inappropriate remedy for a public speaker. Some years later Jeannette adopted, apparently with some success, the preventive measure of taking six aspirins each night and morning. At age eighty-nine she did have the nerve severed, with the unfortunate result of sagging face and difficult speech, but by then she had put sixty years of public speaking behind her.

Considering the heroic intensity of Jeannette's campaigning, her losses of temper seem almost inevitable, even without the added disability of tic douloureux. More surprising—given the intensity of the work—is that others in the movement did not duplicate Jeannette's fits of temper. Unlike Jeannette, however, her compatriots showed remarkably good self-control in very trying circumstances. These passionate, intense women made a revolution without throwing a stone or firing a gun. They turned masculine jeers into vote-getting jokes, endured calumny, forgave stupidity, fought apathy, defied tradition, and kept their sanity.

In this they were helped by an extensive network of female support. Letters went out constantly from feminist to feminist, praising, exhorting, encouraging. But Jeannette, unfortunately a loner, seems not to have participated in this network. Letters to and from her are mostly concerned with facts and plans. Nor did she have an especially close friend as did many others. The close friendship of Elizabeth Cady Stanton and Susan B. Anthony is legendary. Alice Paul, Carrie Chapman Catt, and Jane Addams all had their special friends. Of Jeannette's coworkers probably only Mary O'Neill and Minnie J. Reynolds were really close to her, but each was associated with her only a few years and was twenty years older. In addition, most of the suffragists found consolation in religion, but Jeannette was not religious. Her family supported her, but mostly she had to find her strength within herself.

So in 1915 she made a series of lonely decisions—to quit NAWSA, to go to New Zealand, to run for Congress. She was thirty-five years old, middle-aged. She had discovered gray streaks in her brown hair, and it caused her pause. In spring 1915 she realized she was, indeed, tired of trying to "convert the multitude." After a heavy several months' schedule of suffrage campaigning in the East she returned to Montana, planning on taking a vacation with her family in the cool sunny summer.

Of course she did not vacation. She lectured on economics at Montana State University, chaired the state convention of the Good Government League—an organization that had grown out of the old suffrage clubs—arranged for a series of citizenship lectures, wrote a course on civics, made a quick trip to New York for a peace conference, and went to Seattle for some long delayed surgery. Recovering she suddenly decided to vacation in earnest. She took the train to Vancouver, British Columbia, and then a Pacific-Orient Express ship to New Zealand and had two weeks at sea to do nothing but think.

New Zealand at this time was a most appropriate place to study social conditions. Women had voted there since 1893; there were old-age pensions, child welfare laws, mothers' pensions, workmen's compensation, and labor arbitration laws. The newly formed United States Children's Bureau had just published a pamphlet extolling New Zealand's program for the health of women and children. A famous private organization, the Plunkett Society, had set up health clinics all over the country. It was exactly the kind of situation that would interest Jeannette.

Jeannette arrived in New Zealand during their summer (winter in the United States), glad to miss the sub-zero winter in Montana and the damp winds and slush of New York. She lodged in "Girls' Friendlies," cooperative homes for women, in Wellington and Auckland. She looked into maternal and child health programs, unions, arbitration and conciliation laws. She went to the docks to observe a strike and talked with the leader, Peter Fraser, who later became prime minister of New Zealand.

She needed money and worked as a professional seamstress, sometimes going out to homes, sometimes in shops. She wrote Harriet Laidlaw: "I had very little money, and when I found what a delightful, restful country it is, I wanted to stay, so I went out sewing by the day. It was such a splendid way to learn of the living conditions of the people." Years later she told an interviewer that she had forgotten how to sew and just faked it as she went along, excusing herself by saying, "that's how we do it in the United States." Any seamstress will know little had been forgotten. Actually she capitalized on her Americanism, refusing to take the standard wage of six shillings a day plus carfare. Advertising that she was an American dressmaker familiar with all the latest styles who would work for twelve shillings, she got all the work she wanted. She encouraged other seamstresses to raise their prices, too, and suggested they should organize.

While her hands were busy, her mind had time to work. She needed to decide what to do when she returned home in the spring. All along, she had wanted to improve social conditions through beneficial legislation; running for Congress seemed a logical, if audacious step toward that goal. Her suffrage work had taught Jeannette the importance of organization, and she planned to turn for campaign help to Montana's Good Government League, which she had helped found.

Victorious suffragists in Washington State had created the Good Government League to use the network they had created to win woman's suffrage to promote reform legislation. Other states had followed suit. There was even a loose national organization with headquarters in Washington, D.C. Jeannette had recognized its uses earlier and had probably already considered running for Congress, for while she was getting vague assurances that NAWSA might find her a better job, she had received this letter with its veiled remarks from an executive in the Good Government League headquarters:

> I have been thinking a great deal about the matter which looms big to you. The cause would surely profit by such a move on your part. Of course I am referring to your political plan. So far as I can see, there could be no objection to the kind of preliminary

campaign about which you talked—one in which the work of
the League might be placed before the people of Montana. That
ought to be the most effective kind of a campaign measured in
personal political results, and at the same time a campaign in
the orthodox sense.

Jeannette's work in Montana the previous summer, then, had
been a foresighted effort to increase her profile in Montana and
to rally her allies for the upcoming election. She returned to Montana in spring 1916 rested and ready. She invited a score of women
leaders from all over the state to the family home in Missoula and
asked for their support. Consternation greeted her. Some women
thought she should set her sights a little lower and run for the
state legislature. The family's old Missoula friend, Joseph M. Dixon,
newspaper owner, progressive Republican, and ex-senator, begged
Wellington not to let his sister run. "She will make a laughing stock
of herself," Dixon predicted. But Wellington told Jeannette, "You
run and I'll elect you." Later he wrote: "I am shocked at the prejudice that exists against a woman going to Congress . . . the biggest
campaign of education that is going to be required is to the effect
that a woman can do the work there and should probably be sent
there, rather than the question of you, individually, going. . . . The
prejudice is substantial."

Carrie Chapman Catt wrote Jeannette a condescending letter, asking about her program and political ambitions. Catt opposed women sticking their heads up for politicians to chop off
until national suffrage was won; whatever one woman did, all
would be blamed. And if someone were to run, Jeannette felt,
Catt wanted someone with more distinction, with a law degree,
someone more "intellectual," more commanding. The easterners
put Jeannette down as coming from a state full of cowboys and
Indians and called her the "young Jeannette" when she was well
over thirty.

Even Anna Howard Shaw, former president of NAWSA, discouraged her. Jeannette had been disappointed when Catt took
over the presidency from Shaw, and now Shaw tried to dissuade
her, telling her she should not aim higher than the state legislature. So embarrassed about this after Jeannette actually won election to Congress, Shaw did not get around to congratulating
Jeannette for four months. "I told the eastern women," said

Jeannette, "that maybe I wasn't the best person to be the first congressman, but I could be elected."

In July 1916 the Good Government League formally nominated Jeannette as a candidate of "all the women of Montana and a majority of the men." Among the seconders was Olive Rankin's first Montana friend, Emma Dickinson. Three days later Jeannette announced for the Republican nomination. It made sense for her to run as a Republican, although it was the minority party. After all, her father had been a Republican, and Wellington—who would serve as Jeannette's campaign manager—was active in the (then declining) progressive wing of the Republican Party. She later would say, however, "I was never a Republican. I ran on the Republican ticket."

Optimistic as to her chances, she wrote Harriet Laidlaw that she would face "seven mediocre men who have only a local following." The "regular" Republicans, that is those conservatives who might oppose her, were weak in Montana, while the progressives and suffragists were solid for her. Anyway, the regular Republicans were "scared to death of the woman vote" and might support her as an appeasement policy. Women were indeed registering to vote all over the state, even, the astonished Helena *Independent* reported, "two little Chinese girls," who the county attorney said had as much right as anyone. As for the men, they were impressed with Jeannette's experience as a lobbyist in Congress and in legislatures of several states, as well as by the frequent mention of her name in eastern newspapers. She was a celebrity.

Jeannette and her aides campaigned as they had for suffrage, going into all parts of the state, organizing telephone brigades, hiring bands, speaking on street corners. The Helena *Independent* (a Democratic paper) grumpily remarked on her flamboyant style; male candidates were too dignified for soapboxes. On August 29, 1916, she won the Republican nomination with 22,549 votes, 7,080 votes more than her nearest opponent, George W. Farr of Miles City. Together Rankin and Farr would fight for the two, at-large House seats against Democrats John M. Evans, Missoula, the incumbent, and Harry B. Mitchell, editor of the influential Great Falls *Tribune*, a man who had "not an enemy in the state."

Old-line Republicans were displeased by her candidacy, though they might have looked at the primary figures and seen that Jeannette Rankin enhanced the party; the Republicans, usually the minority, polled 80,000 votes for Congress, and the Democrats only 65,000. (These figures should be halved, of course, to find the number of voters, since each person voted for two candidates.) It looked as if Democrats had crossed party lines just to give Jeannette Rankin a vote. Nevertheless, the politicians tried to keep her out of sight, and state Republican leaders gave her a difficult speaking schedule in the more thinly populated parts of the state. She had to threaten to expose their tactics to the public before they would give her a more practical schedule.

If the party did not solidly support Jeannette, neither did she go out of her way to support the Republican Party. Believing that the Democratic incumbent Evans would win easily, she pushed her own candidacy more than the rest of the ticket. Her campaigners said, "Vote for your local candidate and vote for Jeannette Rankin." Some of the Democrats did as well by her. Elinor Walsh, wife of Democratic senator Thomas J. Walsh, and a longtime Helena suffragist, wrote regretfully to a fellow Democrat that the Democrats could not recommend Jeannette, because she was a Republican, but of course she would support her if she had run on the Democratic ticket. It amounted to saying to Democrats, "Vote for Jeannette Rankin but don't tell anybody about it."

A lively and indefatigable worker and an excellent writer, Belle Fligelman, a former Helena *Independent* reporter, handled Jeannette's publicity. Mary O'Neill could not do it; she was too well known as a Democrat. Smaller papers, especially weeklies, used most of Fligelman's material, but Company papers like the Butte and Anaconda *Standard* and Livingston *Enterprise* scarcely mentioned Jeannette. The Miles City *Star*, which two years earlier had said the name of Jeannette Rankin would never be mentioned, did report her speeches, because the other Republican candidate was from Miles City. The Great Falls *Tribune* enthusiastically supported its editor. The *Missoulian*, owned by old family friend Joseph M. Dixon, gave her some space. The vituperative editor of the Helena *Independent*, who in print called Wellington a "baboon," said there would be no sniping at Jeannette Rankin and there was none, but news of her campaign usually appeared on the society page.

Bad newspaper coverage made travel essential. Jeannette used cars, trains, and once or twice a horse-drawn buggy, usually depending for transportation and hospitality on old suffragist friends. Once in a Miles City hotel, waiting for a promised car that never came, she fell into conversation with a lanky red-haired writer named Sinclair Lewis. He offered his car. They were to meet later in Washington, D.C., after both had become famous, and they became lifelong friends. At Baker, in the southeastern corner of Montana, where ranches are miles apart and towns even farther, a sixteen-year-old boy—an enthusiastic fan—drove her to a community picnic. At the picnic he fought a cowpuncher who jeered at the idea of women in office. Later, in the early morning, he drove her to Miles City through a thunderstorm to catch a 3:00 a.m. train. The car lights went out, and they drove by flashes of lightning. They talked of the European war.

Jeannette's pacifism was well known in Montana; peace had been mentioned frequently as a reason to support woman's suffrage. Jeannette's pacifism had crystallized in 1910 through a conversation with her mentor in the suffrage movement, Minnie J. Reynolds. They had passed a store window full of little chicks, and the beauty and vulnerability of the fluffy yellow creatures somehow had started the two women talking about violence and war. Reynolds had said that pacifism should be part of woman's suffrage; it was truly a woman's issue. "The women produce the boys and the men take them off and kill them in war," she said.

When war came to Europe in 1914 people were shocked. Jeannette had been sitting on a friend's front porch in Lewistown when she heard. She was furious with herself for being so ignorant as not to have seen it coming, she remembered, and furious at the rest of the world. "I felt the end of the world was coming if we were stupid enough to go to war. I said, 'Well, if we don't win suffrage, I'll just let God take care of it himself. I'll just not do any more.' I wasn't going to go on with everything against us."

It was, of course, an idle threat; Jeannette always marched on. But she was, indeed, upset. In a careless moment during the suffrage campaign in Butte, she said: "If they are going to have war, they ought to take the old men and leave the young to propagate the race." Not a nice thing for an unmarried woman to say, said the newspapers. Describing the suffrage campaign, Jeannette said: "we said over and over again that war was stupid and futile and couldn't be used successfully in adjusting human relationships. It was women's work that was destroyed by war. Their work was raising human beings, and war destroyed human beings to protect profits and property."

In 1915 Jeannette had taken part in a conference called by Jane Addams in New York to organize the Woman's Peace Party. Jeannette had presented a petition to Secretary of State William Jennings Bryan signed by 350,000 school children asking him to intercede to end the war in Europe. So Jeannette's view on war was well known in Montana, but with President Wilson campaigning for reelection with the slogan "he kept us out of war," war was not a campaign issue. Happy with the high prices the European conflict brought for copper, timber, wheat, wool, and beef, Montanans had no other use for the fighting in Europe. Montana's Irish did not want to fight on the side of Britain; nor did its Germans and southern Europeans. Many of the Scandinavians, especially Finns, were pacifists. Jeannette's platform advocated "preparedness for peace: a system of coastal defense and no foreign entanglements." It was a position advocated by most politicians at the time.

Instead of foreign policy, Jeannette emphasized social issues. She told Montanans that her first motive in seeking election was to further the equal suffrage movement; she hoped to serve responsibly and convince men that women could vote wisely and serve well in office. Secondly, she wished to serve the interests of children; she pointed out that the previous Congress had appropriated $300,000 to study hog feed, and only $30,000 to study the needs of children. "There are hundreds of men to care for the nation's tariff and foreign policy and irrigation projects. But there isn't a single woman to look after the nation's greatest asset: its children." She also advocated prohibition, tariff revision, and revision of the rules of the House of Representatives so that constituents could find out how each representative voted, not only on the floor but in committees.

Wellington reminded Jeannette that she must study community issues. He wrote:

> In Sheridan, Richland, and Dawson counties prohibition will be an excellent plan; in Billings you will be confronted with the tariff on wool, and you will have to bear in mind that the Republican Party has been based upon tariff issues chiefly, and in those sections where they are dependent upon a tariff on wool for prosperity they will not vote for anyone that does not favor protection.

Jeannette adopted most of the platform of the Montana Society of Equity, a flourishing progressive farmers' group. It asked for a program of state grain inspection (to prevent cheating on grading at terminals), construction of state-owned storage facilities, a state farm-loan credit system, and mine taxation revision, because taxes on the state's predominant industry were so low. Of course, the Company adamantly opposed increasing the tax on mining property, but Jeannette and Anaconda were not yet locked in battle. Mostly it ignored her. "They let me win the first time," she was to say later, "because they didn't think I amounted to anything."

She did win, second, as she and Wellington had predicted. When the ballots were counted in November 1916, the Democratic incumbent, Evans, had 84,499 votes; Jeannette 76,932, Democrat Mitchell 70,578, and Republican Farr 66,974. State newspapers were reluctant to concede her the victory, and outside the state there was astonishment and disbelief. A Tennessean wrote the *New York Times* on November 18, 1916, that Rankin's election was plainly illegal, for the Constitution used the word "he" in describing the qualifications of a congressman. A week later, the *Times* published a Bostonian's response: any student of language knew that "he" was often used as a general term to include both sexes. Some said third-place winner Mitchell should contest the election, but he declined. Miss Rankin had won the election fairly, he said, and he wished her every success.

How did she do it? First, she ran an excellently managed campaign. Compared to the Rankin organization, the Helena *Independent* said, the campaign of the losing Republican candidate for governor, "run by men who are supposed to have political astuteness, was a joke." Here, Wellington deserved much credit. Too, Jeannette ran a nearly nonpartisan campaign. She could not afford to alienate the Democratic majority, especially as she could not depend on support from her own party's machine. Of course, the main reason Jeannette won was—as she and Wellington probably predicted two years earlier—the combination of two factors: the election of two congressmen at-large and the new enfranchisement of women. Grateful to Jeannette for the privilege, women voted in large numbers, and many cast their ballot for her. In the previous presidential year, 1912, close to 80,000 Montanans voted; over 177,000 Montanans voted in 1916.

Following the election, Jeannette was besieged by publicity, speaking offers, and requests to endorse products. A toothpaste company would pay $5,000 for a picture of her teeth, an automobile company would give her a car. Offers of marriage were reported. She found she could not tolerate all the publicity. On the advice of Republican politicians, possibly her friend Dixon who had been afraid she might make a laughing stock of herself, she refused to meet reporters, answer telegrams, or even leave the house when cameramen were present. She issued one public statement, saying, "I am deeply conscious of the responsibility resting upon me. I earnestly hope that I may be of some substantial service, however slight, to the men and women of Montana, my native state, and of the nation." She later remembered, "To be suddenly thrown into so much limelight was a great shock. It was very hard for me to understand, to realize that it made a difference what I did and didn't do from then on."

In early January 1917 she signed a contract with the Chicago *Sunday Herald* to produce fifty articles in the next year (Belle Fligelman would write most of them) and one with a New York speakers' bureau for public appearances at $250 a speech. She would give some twenty speeches across the country before Congress opened with a special session in April. Added to her congressional salary of $7,500, it was, as Wellington said, "a lot of money for a girl from the country."

CHAPTER SEVEN

First Congresswoman: Pacifist

"I VOTE 'NO.'"

"THE FIRST VOTE of the first woman member of Congress was a vote against war," Jeannette was to say many times in the future. "It was not only the most significant thing I ever did, it was a significant thing in itself." She had not expected, when she ran for Congress, to be voting on American involvement in the European war. Her constituents knew she was a pacifist, and they had reelected Wilson on the slogan "He Kept Us Out of War." Wilson's majority in Montana was large, and little war sentiment had been expressed during summer and fall 1916.

The situation changed rapidly, however, in January 1917. Gambling on a quick victory before America could act, Germany announced resumption of unrestricted submarine warfare. When the Germans torpedoed several American merchant ships without warning, American public opinion was inflamed. Even President Wilson was alarmed at the way hysterical public opinion outran him when he announced the end of diplomatic relations with Germany.

In this climate of opinion, Jeannette and Wellington arrived in New York on February 21 to stay with their friends James and Harriet Laidlaw. With Wellington at her side, in the Laidlaw drawing room, Jeannette gave her first newspaper interview, evading questions about

House politics and universal military training. She said women would support their country. She would support upcoming tariff legislation if she thought it would benefit the workers. She was in favor of national woman's suffrage, a farm loan law, extension of child welfare benefits, and open congressional hearings.

She and Harriet went shopping for clothes. Jeannette paid two hundred dollars for an afternoon dress to wear at the opening of Congress. Only a year before she had been sewing in New Zealand for a few dollars a day. She also bought three evening dresses, which she would remember fondly more than half a century later. Clothes were elegant in those days, she would say. The new congressman from New York City, Fiorello LaGuardia, asked them to lunch. He just had had almost as astounding a victory as Jeannette's. Bucking Tammany Hall, he was the first Republican to be elected from his district for years. His liberal views matched Jeannette's, and their lunch was the beginning of a friendship that would warm her life for nearly thirty years.

Other social events crowded her life. The Laidlaws gave a reception for Jeannette and Wellington; hundreds attended. But the main event was Jeannette's speech in Carnegie Hall on March 17, 1917. Carrie Chapman Catt introduced her to the audience, perhaps regretting her previous hints that Jeannette should stay out of politics (but who would suppose the woman would be elected?). Although both Jeannette and Catt had direct manners, and neither was given to idle chitchat, one can imagine they smoothed over the awkward situation with talk of mutual friends in Seattle, where both had begun their suffrage careers.

Jeannette spoke on "Democracy in Government," illustrating her theme with references to Montana. She reminded her audience of the nation's egalitarian traditions, begun when the nation was smaller and life was simpler. Montana, she said, retained some of that simplicity, especially in homesteading communities filled with new pioneers. Unfortunately, she explained, the state's great mineral wealth, like other forms of wealth in the United States, was concentrated in the hands of a few.

We needed more democracy, not only in government, but also in industry, business, and society, Jeannette said, so that the masses could profit from that great wealth. People needed more than the right to vote. They also needed the machinery to make it effective. She wanted a corrupt practices act, so that great wealth would not unduly influence the electorate, and she wanted a direct popular vote for president. "True democracy demands," she said, "that each man have a vote and one man one vote." (She did not think it necessary to use the word "woman," agreeing with the *Times* correspondent who had defended her election that the word "man" in such contexts included "women." She even preferred to call herself "congressman.")

She went on to ask for a direct nominating primary, which would make the candidate more important than the party. She endorsed the recall, the referendum, and the initiative, measures common in the West but not in the East. She explained that such measures gave the electorate not only more voice, but also more responsibility: they were educational. She wanted proportional representation, so that minority ideas might be represented.

She did not mention what was in everybody's mind, the war, which rushed ever closer. Harriet Laidlaw and Wellington were both terribly afraid Jeannette's pacifism would ruin her political future. Wellington used every pressure, for her own good, he thought, to convince her to support the United States' entry into the war. He talked to her, and he recruited her friends to talk to her, until Jeannette was pounded from all sides. "I've been a little ashamed of it since," he admitted half a century later.

A dinner invitation to Oyster Bay came from former president Theodore Roosevelt. Roosevelt knew of the Rankins through their friend former congressman Joseph M. Dixon of Missoula. Dixon had been Roosevelt's national Bull Moose (third party) campaign manager in 1912. Wellington was very excited. The Laidlaws' chauffeur lost his way to Oyster Bay, and they were forty-five minutes late. "It was the most important engagement I had ever had," said Wellington. "That guy [the chauffeur] came as near being killed as any man could. I never suffered so much as then."

Roosevelt and Wellington did most of the talking. "There's no need of this war at all," Roosevelt said, "and we're going to war. . . . It's a crime and a shame and if that fellow in the White House had a lick of sense or an ounce of courage he would have stopped all this. . . . But this fellow talked about peace and keeping out of war, and his old slogan—the Kaiser was convinced we wouldn't go into it. If he had thought we would, he never would have started it." Roosevelt did not advise Jeannette on how she should vote when the declaration of war came before the House.

Congress was not to meet in regular session until December, so Jeannette left for a month's speaking tour, twenty engagements in the East and South. Suddenly, President Wilson called a special session for April 2. Because of her commitments, and possibly to avoid further lobbying, she did not arrive in Washington, D.C., until April 1. She spoke to reporters in the large apartment on California Street that she had rented for herself, her mother, and two secretaries. She would not say how she would vote on the war, only that she would "study the situation. You know, I am in a pretty predicament. I had no idea Congress was going to open so soon. . . . I have so much to learn that I don't know what to say and what not to say. So I have just decided not to say anything at all, for the present at least."

On the day Congress opened Jeannette was honored by suffragists at a breakfast at the Shoreham Hotel. The two national organizations—the NAWSA and the Congressional Union—were divided not only over tactics, money, and strong personal conflicts between Carrie Chapman Catt and Alice Paul, but also over the war. Sitting between the war supporter Catt and the pacifist Paul, Jeannette could see her difficult position in visual and dramatic form. Many women were wearing pacifist white arm bands, yet at a mass meeting Catt and former NASWA president Anna Howard Shaw had pledged the services of the entire suffrage movement to the war effort. The pacifist wing of the movement was incensed that Catt had not even waited for a declaration of war. Jeannette and others believed it part of a deal she had made with President Wilson in September 1916, when he endorsed woman's suffrage at the NAWSA convention, saying, "I have come to fight not for you but with you, and in the end I think we shall not quarrel over the method."

A southerner who had always opposed woman's suffrage, Wilson grudgingly announced at that meeting that he favored its adoption state by state: the NAWSA's method. The forum Catt provided Wilson by inviting him to speak at the convention, and the timing of the convention itself, suggested a back room deal, for Catt had called the convention in September—two months before the national election—instead of at its usual time, December, a month after the election. She offered him women's votes and women's support of the war, and, in return, he came out for woman's suffrage.

Jeannette addresses a crowd from the balcony of the National American Woman Suffrage Association headquarters in Washington, D.C., shortly before becoming the first female representative in the United States Congress. Behind her stands NAWSA president Carrie Chapman Catt.

Though Jeannette's sympathies lay with Alice Paul and the pacifists of the Congressional Union (her assistant Belle Fligelman was a member of the Union), she knew she must steer a wary course between the two factions. Catt had reassured the NAWSA board that Jeannette was "well-poised and apparently very level-headed and sensible." "Probably," she said, "the rival Congressional Union would claim the new Congressman," but she correctly foresaw that Jeannette would not make an open break with NAWSA.

Catt and Shaw well knew that Jeannette was angry with NAWSA, for Jeannette had only recently, after the special session was announced, received a long, belated, apologetic letter from Shaw congratulating her on her election. Four months after the event, Shaw was trying to make amends for earlier discouraging Jeannette from running. The timing of the letter, after the announcement of the special session, which everyone knew was called to consider war measures, suggests that Shaw was really concerned with Jeannette's war vote. At the top of this letter is written, in Jeannette's handwriting, "No reply."

At the breakfast everyone smiled and was friendly, and women of both factions rose to commend Jeannette with praise so fulsome it undermined her composure. Her lips trembled as she said, "There will be many times when I will make mistakes. And I need your encouragement and support. I know I will get it. I promise . . . I promise . . ." She could not continue. Twenty-five flag-draped cars, some decorated with the yellow and white of NAWSA and some the purple, gold, and white of the Congressional Union escorted her to the Capitol. Going to her office, Jeannette found it filled with flowers. She chose the Congressional Union's yellow and purple to carry with her onto the floor of the House.

Her Montana colleague, the Democrat John M. Evans, who also happened to be from Missoula, escorted her onto the House floor. That acute observer of the Washington scene and connoisseur of women's clothes and manners, Ellen Maury Slayden, the wife of a Texas representative, recorded in her journal:

> Not more than a year ago men would say . . . "Next thing you'll be wanting women in Congress," as if that was the reductio ad absurdum, and here she was coming in, escorted by an elderly colleague, looking like a mature bride rather than a strong-minded female, and the men were clapping and cheering in the friendliest way. She wore a well-made dark blue silk and chiffon suit, with open neck, and wide white crepe collar and cuffs; her skirt was a modest walking length, and she walked well and unselfconsciously. . . . She carried a bouquet of yellow and purple flowers. . . . She didn't look to right or left until she reached her seat, far back on the Republican side, but before she could sit down she was surrounded by men shaking hands with her. I rejoiced to see that she met each one with a big-mouthed frank smile and shook hands cordially and unaffectedly. . . . She was a sensible young woman going about her business. When her name was called, the House cheered and rose, so that she had to rise and bow twice, which she did with entire self-possession. She was not pretty, but had an intellectual face and a nice manner.

That night the House and Senate met in joint session to hear President Wilson ask for a declaration of war, "for the right of those who submit to authority to have a voice in their own governments, for the rights and liberties of small nations, for a universal dominion of right by a concert of free peoples . . . and [to make the world] safe for democracy." Three days later the House met to consider the resolution already passed by the Senate with

only six dissenting. Five minutes speaking time was given alter-
nately to opposing sides. Proponents spoke of the brutality of
the Germans and the importance of upholding American interests by not "knuckling under." They spoke of loyalty to our fair
country, to our flag, red, white, and blue, and mourned lives lost
to German submarines. Opponents said the measure was being
jammed through, that the people did not want war, that they did
not want conscription, and that they did not want the war loans
and the high cost of living that would follow.

Claude Kitchin of North Carolina, the Democratic majority
leader, was impassioned. Opposed to the war, he was about to
break with his president and his party, and he knew his political
career had ended. "In view of the many assumptions of loyalty
and patriotism on the part of some who favor the resolution," he
said, "and insinuation by them of cowardice and disloyalty on the
part of those who oppose it, offshoots doubtless of a passionate
moment, let me at once remind the House that it takes neither
moral nor physical courage to declare a war for others to fight."
On and on went the speeches, past midnight and into the morning of Good Friday. One member suggested the vote be post-
poned until Monday, so as not to vote for war on the anniversary
of the murder of the prince of peace. He was ignored.

Jeannette retired briefly to her office for some rest. She had
been under intense pressure all week. Wellington had told her
she should vote a "man's vote" in order not to jeopardize a bright
career. Harriet Laidlaw had made a trip from New York to urge
her to support the declaration. Suffragists had pointed out that
if she voted against the declaration, she would hurt the cause.
On the other hand, Alice Paul had called her out from the floor
to ask her to oppose the resolution. "I knew," Jeannette said later
in a formal statement,

> that we were asked to vote for a commercial war, that none of the
> idealistic hopes would be carried out, and I was aware of the false-
> ness of much of the propaganda. It was easy to stand against the
> propaganda of the militarists but very difficult to go against friends
> and dear ones who felt that I was making a needless sacrifice by
> voting against the war, since my vote would not be a decisive one.
> In trying to be fair, I said I would listen to only those who wanted
> war and would not vote until the last opportunity and if I could
> see any reason for going to war I would try to change.

Therefore, having promised to wait, and knowing from lobby-ing experience with Congress that there would be two roll calls, she did not answer the first. "Uncle Joe" Cannon, the Republican leader, thought she did not understand the situation. "Little woman," he said, "you cannot afford not to vote. You represent the womanhood of the country in the American Congress. I shall not advise you how to vote, but you should vote one way or an-other—as your conscience dictates." When the second roll was called and Jeannette heard "Miss Rankin," she rose and with a shaking voice said, "I want to stand by my country, but I cannot vote for war. I vote No."

The clerk could not hear for the hubbub on the floor and in the galleries. It was contrary to the unwritten rules of the House to make a speech during a vote. There was a scattering of ap-plause. Some members shouted, "Vote. Vote. Vote." The chief clerk asked if she intended to vote "No." She nodded, pressed her hands to her eyes, and sat down. On went the vote: 373 for, 50 against, 9 not voting. The House adjourned at 3:14 a.m. Wellington, walking Jeannette home in the dark dawn of Good Friday, told her she had crucified herself. "You know you're not going to be reelected. You know there will be a lot of feeling." She replied: "I'm not interested in that. All I'm interested in [is] what they'll say fifty years from now."

The papers made much of Jeannette's vote. Although fifty men had also opposed the resolution, hers was the vote that attracted attention. She had wept, they said, just like a woman. Others said she did not. It became a public issue: did or did not Miss Rankin weep? Fiorello LaGuardia, whose desk was near hers, said he did not know. "I could not see because of the tears in my own eyes." He had voted for the declaration and four months later signed up in the Signal Corps. He had promised his constituents that if he sent them to fight he would go himself. The April 7, 1918, Atlanta *Constitution* said if there were tears, it was on an issue dear to a mother's heart. Tears did not prove her weak, it said, but womanly, and some day "tears will move all the women of the world to be consulted before the War Lords tear their sons from their bosoms."

Jeannette said she did not cry. She had cried for a week and had no more tears left. The *Congressional Record* says she did not cry. Only a few months later, at a House hearing on woman's suffrage, a witness, explaining why women should not be allowed to vote and deploring their weakness, said, "Never was their a more eloquent confession of woman's inability to support the strains of a war council than that so pathetically made by Miss Rankin in that moment of national crisis when in her agony she cried, 'I want to stand by my country, but I cannot vote for war.' "

Jeannette, a member of the committee and sitting right there, did not reply, but she had a champion in the committee chairman, John Raker of California: "Let me say right now and then, this is the first I have had the opportunity of saying it—that statement that Miss Rankin cried is absolutely false . . . I want it said publicly. I sat within four feet of Miss Rankin. She was impressed, as men were. What she did when she went out I do not know. But I think the public has not treated her that way. I think they have treated her scandalously. She did not cry. (Applause). This is the first time I have had an opportunity to say that . . . and I want to say it on behalf of Miss Rankin and the women."

Whatever the manner of her vote, she was attacked nationally for the vote itself. The April 7, 1917, *New York Times* said she had justified distrust of her judgment and opinions. A Presbyterian minister said that if she would not stand by her country in time of trial she should resign. Hardest to bear was the thought that her vote had hurt the suffrage movement. In New York some suffragists canceled a coming reception and a number of speaking engagements they had arranged for her. But publicly most of them excused her. Harriet Laidlaw told the *Times* she was sorry about the vote, "but she did her duty as she saw it after the most terrible mental struggles any woman ever had." Carrie Chapman Catt said that no matter which way Jeannette had voted she would be criticized, but she put a clear distance between herself and Jeannette. "Miss Rankin was not voting for the suffragists of the nation—she represents Montana." Privately she wrote, "Our Congress Lady is a sure enough joker. Whatever she has done or will do . . . she loses us a million votes."

While many Montanans were also critical, there was some public commendation back home. The Helena *Independent* wrote on April 26, "Montana's Congresswoman is Now Very Popular. . . . Her mind is honest and open and she has evident courage to back her convictions." Grace Erickson, the suffragist wife of a prominent Democratic politician (future Montana governor J. E. Erickson), also publicly voiced her support: "In that tense gray dawn, there arose in the cold Congressional Halls a strange sound, a new born sound, like the sob of a mother's heart. By virtue of the heroic stand of Jeannette Rankin, I herein voice our appreciation, our deepest gratitude, and our loyalty to her." Jeannette wrote a Montanan who complained of her vote, "In the campaign last fall, I judged the sentiment in Montana was overwhelmingly against war. Of course, the situation had changed when the vote was taken and yet the letters and telegrams that came to me were sixteen to one against the war resolution."

Afterwards, since the voice of democracy had spoken, she supported the war effort, spoke for Liberty Bonds, and voted for most of the administration measures, including the selective draft. (There were draft riots in Butte.) She did, however, vote against the War Espionage Act of 1917, an act that became a vehicle for baiting aliens and suppressing dissent. When the question of the declaration of war against Austria-Hungary came up, she said:

> I still believe war is a stupid and futile way of attempting to settle international difficulties. I believe war can be avoided and will be avoided when the people, the men and women in America, as well as in Germany, have the controlling voice in their government. Today special privileged commercial interests are controlling the world. . . . This is a vote on a mere technicality in the prosecution of a war already declared. I shall vote for this as I voted for money and men.

She never regretted her vote. She believed the issue of war and peace to be peculiarly a woman's issue. Women spent themselves, physically, mentally, emotionally bearing children and raising them. Women's social concerns focused on building an environment, not only in which children could grow in the present, but also in which they could live happily and constructively in the future. War destroyed all. The issues were never settled. Wars continued, many people suffered, a few got rich, and the quarrels remained. War also diminished the ability of people to govern themselves. Even democracy in America suffered in the war to make the world safe for democracy, witness the War Espionage Acts, for instance, and the witch hunting and red baiting that followed. Twenty years later, four years before America's entry into the Second World War, she was to say, prophetically, "I would vote 'No' again."

CHAPTER EIGHT

First Congresswoman: Suffragist

⟨flourish⟩

"THE WOMEN OF THE COUNTRY
HAVE SOMETHING OF VALUE
TO GIVE THE NATION."

IN SPITE OF HER antiwar vote, Jeannette was making a favorable reputation. Her every move was publicly discussed because she was that eighth wonder of the world, a woman member of Congress. Entering the House on the first day, she was besieged with visitors, newspaper reporters, and curiosity seekers asking for statements and autographs. Visitors crowded her one-room office, where she worked at a mahogany rolltop desk in the back, three secretaries in front. In her guest book, right under the signature of David Starr Jordan, former Stanford University president, peace worker, and popular lecturer, appeared that of Benny Leonard, champion light-weight prize fighter. Mothers wrote they had named their new babies for her. She answered each letter asking for a photograph. A May 31, 1917, _Nation_ article described her attraction for children, telling of an embassy party where she was immediately surrounded by children, sitting on her lap, leaning against her.

No week went by without an article about Jeannette in some national magazine. Said the _Literary Digest_ in an August 11, 1917, article:

Her mail reaches approximately three hundred letters a day. . . .
In her first speech Miss Rankin showed little nervousness and handled her subject capably. She is no stranger to the stump. . . .

The Lady from Montana is not of the militant-suffragist type; in fact she is gentle, modest, and a bit retiring. . . . Her voice is pleasing. . . . One wouldn't describe her as beautiful, neither can she be called plain. She has a trim, neat figure, a winning smile, twinkling blue-gray eyes, and a well-set head.

Miss Rankin dresses smartly, and altogether is prepossessing and is a better-looking woman than the average House member is a man. The House today has about accustomed itself to the presence of a woman on the floor. There was wonderment of whether Miss Rankin would use the cloakrooms, whether she would want to talk frequently, seek special privileges, or harangue the members on suffrage. She hasn't used the cloakrooms, where male members tell stories and smoke cigars; she hasn't pestered anybody about suffrage and she has asked no special privileges.

No fault can be found with the demeanor of Miss Rankin on the floor. She is amiable, friendly, and an excellent conversationalist when members are talking in an undertone during a dull debate. She occupies a seat near the center aisle, well toward the rear of the hall. Sometimes a Congressman will invite her to lunch in the House restaurant. Miss Rankin will insist upon receiving her check and paying the bill.

People speculated on her single state. They wanted romance. Her office, they noted, was across the hall from that of the only bachelor representative, Fiorello LaGuardia. (Although LaGuardia and Jeannette were to become very close, at that time he had a beautiful blonde fiancée in New York.) People wanted to know if her voluminous correspondence contained offers of marriage. Jeannette mostly ignored such questions, but she did pick a seat near a very elderly white-haired congressman, so people could not accuse her of flirting.

She bought a car, a source of much satisfaction. For the next fifty years her car would be her most important possession though in less affluent times it would be a beat-up, second-hand jalopy. She arrived at her office by nine o'clock and attended all the House debates. Her executive assistant, Belle Fligelman—a tiny young woman "looking like a little boy" with short hair, flat shoes, and a Buster Brown collar—ran on and off the floor with messages. Fligelman later made a national reputation as a writer. Jeannette had a knack for choosing extraordinarily competent and loyal assistants.

A dependable source of help to the women clerks, typists, and other government employees, Jeannette became a champion of the overworked women of the Bureau of Printing and Engraving. In order to speed printing Liberty Loan bonds, the bureau had canceled all leaves and made overtime work compulsory. Some of the women worked twelve to fifteen hours a day in violation of the federal eight-hour law; several fainted from exhaustion. When they asked Jeannette for help, she joined a group of tourists and unobtrusively observed the bureau and then hired a private detective. After discussing the complaints with a delegation of fifty women, she went to the bureau director and asked him to restore the eight-hour schedule within a week, threatening a congressional investigation.

"You can't do that," he said. "Things don't work that fast in government." The girls preferred the overtime, he said, for the extra money, and, in any case, he could not get more workers in such busy times. Jeannette stood firm, and the threat of congressional investigation induced the Treasury Department to proceed with an investigation of its own. Two hundred employees, mostly women, came forward to testify that overtime was compulsory and that they had been deprived of rest periods, sick leaves, and vacations. Though the bureau's excuse was wartime necessity, one employee produced a time card showing she had worked overtime for the last three years.

The Treasury Department ordered an eight-hour day and restored vacations, but it was not an unmixed success. About two hundred of the bureau's four thousand employees protested the shorter hours, saying they needed the extra money on account of wartime's high cost of living. The maximum possible full-time wage was seven hundred dollars a year. A few months later some employees had to go back to twelve-hour shifts.

Most bureau employees were grateful, though. Encouraged by Jeannette, they organized a union. They also presented her with a silk banner and wrote in their national journal, The *Plate-Printer*: "the great army of labor did not realize that in sending Miss Rankin to Washington, Montana was sending an angel in disguise, the woman we love best in all the world."

Other interventions on the part of the staff were more humorous. When female staffers came to Jeannette to report a man in the ladies' room, Jeannette investigated, only to find Dr. Mary Walker, who always wore trousers, stretched out asleep on a couch.

A tiny, shriveled figure in a Prince Albert coat, crocheted cape, and high hat, Walker was an aged eccentric who had served as a physician in the Civil War. She was so fragile that she was once blown off the Capitol steps. When Jeannette asked her how long she had worn men's clothes, Walker replied, "I've never worn men's clothes; I've always worn my own."

The onslaught of war meant less time and interest in social legislation than Jeannette would have liked. As she watched war measures pass through Congress, she tried to protect women and children where she could. She introduced a bill requiring the same wages for men and women in government work and a bill for pensioning families of soldiers. She also introduced a bill requiring the president to require employers in private industry to pay women equal wages to men for similar work.

Another of her bills would have given women citizenship independently of their husbands. Still another was the forerunner of the Tennessee Valley Authority, the creation of a federal board to build and operate hydroelectric plants to produce power for the manufacture of fertilizer and munitions, the surplus power to be sold to the public. She was soundly criticized for offering a resolution favoring Irish independence, an idea that appealed to Jeannette's sense of democracy, was appropriate to Wilson's cherished self-determination of peoples, and was popular among her large Irish constituency. None of the measures she advocated were adopted; they were too far ahead of their times, although they were all to become law within her lifetime.

She was successful in an amendment she introduced to a bill on food supply; she asked that women be employed as far as practicable in gathering information on production, storage, and use of food. A similar amendment, also introduced by Jeannette and passed without a dissenting vote, required that in the 1920 census "wherever practicable women should be employed." She compromised with the southern members, who objected to female preference, by assenting to the inclusion of "disabled soldiers and sailors."

Closest to Jeannette's heart was the Rankin-Robinson bill for maternity and child hygiene. The origins of this measure went back to Florence Kelley, who in 1905 had advocated a national commission for children and suggested it concern itself with infant mortality, birth registration, child labor, desertion, illegitimacy, and

degeneracy. Kelley's leadership had led to the formation of the
Children's Bureau in 1912, which, among other activities, conducted
research on child and maternal health. One of its studies found
that a quarter-million American children died every year and that
the United States had the highest maternal death rate of any
civilized country. Another of its publications described the tremendous success of New Zealand's public health program, which
Jeannette had studied first hand.

Encouraged by the Children's Bureau, Jeannette proposed a
program to improve maternal and infant health. Since people in
cities ostensibly had access to medical care through urban hospi-
tals and settlement houses, Jeannette decided to emphasize rural
health care as a first step; she knew a small program was all she
would be able to get away with. Congress had only halfheartedly
funded the Children's Bureau, and a measure sufficiently financed
to cover the whole country could not hope to pass. Thus, she proposed a bill to provide federal funds for rural health education:
$480,000 in matching funds the first year, gradually increasing to
$2 million for the fifth year and thereafter. Even this limited pro-
posal faced bitter opposition. Opponents called it socialistic,
Bolshevistic, state medicine and fretted about the possible inter-
ference with private practice. They also worried it might teach contraception or discuss venereal disease and other subjects unsuitable
for women's ears. Certainly, opponents believed, the old maids in
the Children's Bureau were unfit to administer the program.

The thinking of opponents of the Rankin-Robinson bill can
be seen from a colloquy that took place in a hearing on woman's
suffrage. One Dr. Howe said women should stay home and take
care of their babies instead of worrying about the vote. He pointed
out that of every one hundred children born sixteen were dead
by the end of the year, twenty-two at the end of the fifth year:
therefore, women should stay home and not vote. Why, he said,
there were even babies born blind because the mothers did not
have sense enough to use silver nitrate. Jeannette replied:

> How do you expect women to know this disease when you do
> not feel it proper to call it by its correct name? Do they not in
> some states have legislation which prevents women knowing these
> diseases, and only recently after the women's work for political
> power were women admitted into medical schools. You yourself,

from your actions, believe it is not possible for women to know the names of these diseases. (Pause.)

Dr. Howe: I did not like to use the word "gonorrhea."

Miss Rankin: Do you think anything should shock a woman as much as blind children? Do you not think they ought to be hardened enough to stand the name of a disease when they must stand the fact that children are blind?

The Rankin-Robinson bill stalled in the House Labor Committee, but Jeannette returned to lobby for similar legislation the following session, and would see it pass in 1921 as the Shepard-Towner bill. The passage of national woman's suffrage in 1920 made Congress more responsive to calls for funding for women and children's health.

Thus, in 1917–18 a federal suffrage amendment was Jeannette's primary goal. As the only woman member of Congress, she felt particular responsibility for pushing through an amendment. And the climate was becoming favorable. In 1916, for the first time, both major party conventions had discussed the question at length. The *New York Times* expressed surprise at the time spent on this "minor" issue. Montana's senator Thomas J. Walsh had told the Democrats that they would have to come out for the amendment or give up the votes of the suffrage states. Neither party would go so far, but both had given ground.

After the 1916 election the New York *Herald*, disgruntled over the narrow loss of its candidate Charles Evans Hughes, a loss attributed to the women of the West voting for peace and Wilson ("He Kept Us Out of War"), said it was a national scandal that some women could vote but not others. The only way to cure this inequity was by a federal amendment. Then, in November 1917, New York enacted woman's suffrage. Northern Democrats had seen the inevitable, and Tammany Hall had withdrawn its previous opposition. In addition to New York eleven western states had full woman's suffrage, and seven in the Midwest allowed women to vote for president. New York alone had forty-five electoral votes; looking toward future presidential victories in "suffrage states," both parties began to think seriously about supporting suffrage. The arithmetic of the Electoral College was forcing politicians into a position they had long opposed.

Immediately after being sworn in Jeannette had drafted a resolution calling for a constitutional amendment for woman's suffrage.

It did not come up for consideration in the House until the following January, and, in the meantime, the militant tactics of the National Woman's Party (formerly called the Congressional Union) became an embarrassment to Jeannette. As Wilson's new administration took office, the National Woman's Party began picketing the White House. Alice Paul said she had sent deputations of all kinds to President Wilson; now she would send a permanent deputation. Women stood silent and motionless at the east and west gates. Soon crowds of unruly young men began to taunt them and throw stones. Riots began. Police made no attempt to quell the mob.

In June the pickets were arrested and found guilty of obstructing traffic. Refusing to pay their fines, the women spent three days in jail. Next month sixteen women were sent across the Potomac River to Occoquan Workhouse for sixty days for obstructing traffic. Pardoning them after three days, Wilson said they should not be indulged in their desire for martyrdom. In August a mob wrecked National Woman's Party headquarters. Two days later police attacked the demonstrating suffragists. Arrests continued; the women continued to refuse to pay fines and were sent to the workhouse. Alice Paul was sent in October.

Conditions at Occoquan, filled mostly with prostitutes and other petty criminals, were sordid. Some suffragists objected to being housed with Negroes; they were made to paint the colored women's toilets. Such stories leaked out and angered the public, as racist as it was sexist. Many women refused to eat and were forcibly fed gruel through tubes forced down their throats or noses. Alice Paul was held incommunicado, although the president is said to have agreed that if she would call off the picketing he would come out for the federal amendment and push it through the House (he well knew he could not get it through the Senate on account of thirty-four southern senators). Paul wanted all or nothing; she remained in jail and picketing continued.

Jails became so crowded that many women slept on the floor. Many of the jailed women were Jeannette's personal friends. She took her secretary and a friendly senator to visit Occoquan. She asked one friend who had several times been to Occoquan how to get there. "I don't know," was the cheerful response. "I've always gone in a Black Maria"—the vehicle used to transport prisoners.

Publication of the abuses at Occoquan secured some sympathy for the women, but, on the other hand, the riots angered many members of the public, who saw them as unpatriotic in wartime and blamed them on the suffragists. Jeannette told the press: "The public . . . does not confuse the pickets with the whole suffrage organization and they do not blame the mass of women . . . for the mistaken policies of a few." Suddenly, at the end of November, all prisoners were released. An appellate court decided all the arrests were illegal; Congress had to make a special appropriation to pay costs of the suit.

The picketing and concomitant rioting and bad publicity had only just ended when the House Suffrage Committee began its hearings on January 3, 1918. Jeannette had a technical block to overcome; suffrage was locked up in the Judiciary Committee, which refused to report it out. So, in spite of a gentleman's agreement between the two parties to deal only with war measures for the duration of the special session, she persuaded the House to set up a special suffrage committee; she told it that the committee was only part of the business of organizing the House. With the help of a public statement from Wilson, who called it "a very wise act of public policy, and . . . an act of fairness," the special committee was approved but did not actually meet until the following session. Jeannette was gallantly suggested for chairman, but she declined. The chairman should be a member of the majority party, the Democrats. An exception would not only be out of order, but also look as if the House took the matter lightly. John Raker of California, a good friend from a suffrage state, was named chairman.

The Senate had its own Suffrage Committee, to which Jeannette testified twice, representing each faction of the movement. As a member of the House committee, she did not speak to it, but proved an adroit questioner. She pushed one Eichelberger, introduced as a good American "in spite of his German name," into saying that Socialists carried the suffrage vote in New York, that lots of Socialists were Germans, that lots of Germans were Jews, but Jews were mostly against suffrage, but they voted for Hilquit, who was for suffrage. He ended up in knots. When he said women were trying to change constitutions that were adopted by the people, Jeannette replied, "May I ask you who are the people?"

She also got in a jab at former Texas senator Joseph W. Bailey, who appeared before the House committee to testify against suffrage. Referring to the fact that women could not serve in the armed forces, Bailey said, "If I were to state as an abstract proposition that no persons are entitled to exercise all the privileges of citizenship unless they are capable of performing all the duties of citizenship, everybody would agree that I had stated a sound maxim of political justice." Jeannette responded, "I would not. We have men in the United States Senate who cannot serve in the Army, and yet they make splendid Senators."

The committee reported the measure out to the floor, the first time the House had ever had an opportunity to consider woman's suffrage. Representative Joseph Walsh of Massachusetts asked Chairman Raker to allow Jeannette to lead the debate. It was a personal tribute. Her relationship with this man who could have been a dangerous enemy offers an interesting insight into her political ability, for Walsh was a vehement opponent of woman's suffrage. Jeannette even made a point of sitting behind him, so that the sight of her would not get on his nerves. ("Don't rouse your enemies," she had learned from Adela Parker in Seattle.) But as weeks went by, she came to admire his independence and integrity. She liked the way he refused to change his votes at the behest of colleagues.

Speaking in his district, she had praised him to his constituents, spoke of his fairness and integrity. She regretted his opposition to woman's suffrage, she said, but they would have to change that. Later he sought her out and thanked her, and they had a pleasant chat. Thus, when she asked him not to speak against suffrage, he agreed. Furthermore, when the vote was taken, so close that the clerk had to call the roll again, Walsh—although he had voted against the resolution—told those wavering congressmen who had voted for it, "If you change your vote I'll change mine."

For the historic occasion of the first debate on woman's suffrage in the House of Representatives, Jeannette had prepared carefully. From New York she had ordered a special dress, "a pretty brown silk, to cost $75," while Belle Fligelman had worked on her speech for months, and Jeannette had rehearsed it repeatedly. Addressing the House, Jeannette spoke of how women had aided the war effort, much as they hated war and of how women were more apt to think of human needs than were men. She spoke directly to the South, reminding them that "there are more white women of voting age in the South today than there are

Negro men and women together. She related woman's suffrage to democracy and asked, since war had been declared by federal action, why not woman's suffrage?

> We as a nation were born in a land of unparalleled resources . . . opportunities for development . . . people imbued with the buoyancy of youth . . . the will and energy to make their dreams of freedom come true.
>
> . . . But something is still lacking . . . babies are dying from cold and hunger; soldiers have died for lack of a woolen shirt. Might it not be that the men who have spent their lives thinking in terms of commercial profit find it hard to adjust themselves to thinking in terms of human needs? . . . Is it not possible that the women of the country have something of value to give the Nation at this time?
>
> . . . We declared war not State by State but by Federal action . . . Shall our women, our home defense, be our only fighters in the struggle for democracy who shall be denied federal action? It is time for our old political doctrines to give way to new visions.
>
> . . . How shall we explain . . . the meaning of democracy if the same Congress that voted for war to make the world safe for democracy refuses to give this small measure of democracy to the women of our country? (Prolonged applause)

The debate lasted five hours. Opponents mentioned states' rights; proponents said these same men had voted for federal prohibition. Opponents spoke of the unladylike behavior of the pickets; proponents said reform always brought a few extremists and that women had waited patiently for seventy years. Opponents said women were already represented by their husbands, and the measure would cause dissension at home; proponents said eight million women did not have husbands, and that although usually husbands and wives thought alike, on those occasions when they differed, women were entitled to their opinions, which likely would reflect morality and children's welfare. Opponents said St. Paul preached that if women wanted to know anything they should ask their husbands, and he permitted not a woman to teach or have dominion over men; proponents said no wonder people were so ignorant in those days, and also where would go our school system, our churches without women teachers? Opponents said women would not fight, and proponents said why should they, having the loftiest, most essential duty of citizenship, that of childbearing. Opponents said women were divine and should not be sullied by the mud of politics; a proponent said he was reminded of that great southern poet who wrote:

> Woman, woman, thou art divine.
> Oh, that I had one I could call mine,
> To soothe me in my worstest woes,
> And cook my dinner and wash my clothes.

In the midst of the argument, Congressman Richard Wilson Austin of Tennessee asked for two minutes "to pay a simple, sincere, and deserved tribute to the fair member of this House who so well and faithfully represents the State of Montana and who is in fact the real leader and invincible champion of the just cause of the noble woman." He continued:

> The highest, best, and strongest evidence that woman's suffrage is a success has been established in this House by the enviable record made by our colleague from Montana, who has won the respect, confidence, and admiration of the members and officials of this House. The greatest ovation given a member on opening a debate was accorded to the Member from Montana this morning. It was not so much an endorsement of the subject she championed as it was a just tribute to an able, popular and successful woman.

Probably neither the tribute nor the arguments swung any votes. The Deep South voted "No" in a bloc; the resolution won by 274–136, only a fraction more than the needed two-thirds. Two congressmen came from sick beds, one from a hospital in Baltimore, to vote for the resolution. One congressman had just broken his arm and had it in a sling. Another rushed from his wife's deathbed in New York to vote "Yes," and rushed back to make arrangements for her funeral before Jeannette could thank him. Fiorello LaGuardia, on leave from the House to serve in the armed forces in Italy, cabled his "Yes."

When the vote was announced there was prolonged cheering and congratulations on the floor. In the gallery women burst into tears and outside in the hall, where suffragists were crowded, they lifted their voices in unison,

Praise God, from whom all blessings flow,
Praise Him all creatures here below,
Praise Him above, ye Heavenly Host,
Praise Father, Son, and Holy Ghost.

There was tremendous euphoria in the suffrage movement, for this bare two-thirds was their first national victory. For seventy years, thousands of women had organized campaigns, faced jeers and taunts, kept card files, and written and spoken and agitated. Of course, the victory was by no means Jeannette's alone, but she had had more than her share in it. Besides all those years working for suffrage, she now sat in Congress as living evidence that a woman could participate in politics responsibly, sensibly (in spite of her antiwar vote), and gracefully.

Yet the victory in the House was only a beginning. The measure had to go to the Senate, where thirty-four senators representing the South easily blocked the amendment, which needed two-thirds (or sixty-six votes out of one hundred) to pass. Suffrage forces tried four times in that Senate, failing each time by two votes. They took to the field in the 1918 campaign to try to defeat opponents they considered vulnerable. Opinions were changing. In the new House the vote was 305–90. In the Senate the measure narrowly passed, 66–33. Only four votes had been changed. The amendment then had to go to the state legislatures, thirty-six of which had to ratify it. The states were dilatory; not until August 18, 1920, did Tennessee become the thirty-sixth state to ratify the amendment. If Jeannette's antiwar vote or Alice Paul's picketing the White House had damaged the cause, there was little evidence. Probably a majority of men had favored woman's suffrage for years, but the difficulty of amending the constitution had been too much to overcome.

When woman's suffrage became law, Jeannette had been out of office for a year and a half. Though she had been much praised, she had not been reelected. The story of her defeat was an old one in Montana: by championing the cause of Butte labor in its struggles with the Anaconda Copper Mining Company, she had earned the Company's determined opposition. In the face of war hysteria, a red scare, violence, and martial law, the Company was easily the victor.

CHAPTER NINE

Defeated Politician

JEANNETTE RANKIN MISSED the 1918 Republican nomination for senate by less than a 5 percent margin before running a losing race on a third-party ticket. Her problems went back to 1917, when she had taken the part of Butte's miners, on strike in response to a tragic fire in the Granite Mountain shaft of the Speculator mine. The nation's worst hard-rock mining disaster, the June 8 fire took the lives of over 167 men. Miners blamed the deaths on the Company's lack of concern for safety and were enraged to discover that, contrary to state law, concrete bulkheads blocked some of the mine exits. Safety enforcement had been an issue for years, and the tragedy galvanized the men, who walked off the job within a few days of the disaster. Strike leaders wrote Jeannette for help. She agreed to try to intervene in the dispute and, in so doing, found herself on the wrong side of the powerful Anaconda Copper Mining Company.

Since Butte produced 20 percent of the nation's copper, which was used to produce armaments, and half of all quality zinc used by the army, the strike had possible national security consequences. From the Company's perspective, high wartime prices also meant huge profits, which the strike imperiled. When copper miners led by the radical Industrial Workers of the World

(IWW) struck for higher wages in Bisbee, Arizona, that same summer, vigilantes rounded up twelve hundred strikers and dumped them in the desert, most without food and water. Public officials condoned the action or looked the other way. In opposing the IWW and keeping up wartime production of a strategically important metal, anything went.

The IWW, or the "Wobblies" as its members were called, became an important factor in the Butte strike as well, and an equally important issue in Jeannette's 1918 reelection campaign. A flamboyant radical organization, the IWW flashed across the Progressive Era and died in the flames of World War I. Believing that employers manipulated the democratic process, they renounced the ballot in favor of "direct action," by which they meant primarily the strike. They had conducted successful strikes before the war at rubber plants in Ohio, textile mills in Massachusetts, and logging camps in the Northwest. Full of song and laughter, they were "One Big Union" and, unlike the more traditional American Federation of Labor, would organize anybody, even women, blacks, and immigrants.

The IWW ran soup kitchens and printed propaganda in many languages. In an era when soapbox speakers were denied the right to speak if they held unpopular views, its members conducted "free speech wars," standing on street corners reading the Declaration of Independence or the Bill of Rights, in order to assert their right to public assembly. As fast as one was arrested, another would mount the soap box, until the jails were full. Hated by the conservative craft unions and feared by government and industry, IWW members courted imprisonment and martyrdom.

The press was almost universally against them—especially Montana's Company-controlled press. Lurid stories of sabotage and violence made farmers expect to see their wheat fields in flames, employers to find their machinery dynamited. Yet the movement was very small, at its height no more than eighteen thousand paid up members (including a large number of labor spies). Workers found the IWW too radical in aims and too impractical in methods. Nevertheless, its toughness and activism made it a force to be reckoned with, especially in Butte where the problems were so acute and labor so divided.

Broken by dissension and violence in 1914, the venerable, once-powerful Butte Miners' Union had splintered into three smaller unions—the Western Federation of Miners, the Butte Mine Workers' Union, and the IWW; the Company dealt with none. Union activity could lose a man his job—and the rustling card system helped the Company make sure he was not rehired. When a miner looked for a job in Butte, or even in other parts of Montana, he received a card issued from a central office. When a miner was hired, he surrendered his rustling card. If he quit or was fired he could not get another job without a new rustling card. The central office kept track of everybody.

The system had been the main issue in the union breakup. It enabled the Company to deny employment to union activists and had made it difficult to build a union powerful enough to do anything about wages or mine safety. But now, with 167 of their fellows burned to death, the miners were angry enough to defy the Company. Two old union activists organized a new union, the Metal Mine Workers Union (MMWU), and pulled five thousand men out of the mines. Others quit of their own accord. Turmoil spread. Carpenters, electricians, streetcar operators, and telephone operators also struck. By June fifteen thousand men had joined the strike.

Jeannette was in Washington when she received a wire on June 20 from the new union asking her to influence the secretary of labor to send an investigator to Butte. Her old friend and advisor Mary O'Neill also wrote and asked her to do something personal about the strike; a personal settlement, she said, would be a political masterstroke. The Butte miners, according to O'Neill, were counting on help from Washington. Rankin approached Bernard Baruch, head of the war metals division, and President Wilson on the miners' behalf; each man told her to go see the other. She went to the attorney general and the secretary of labor; they would not act. The miners also telegraphed, asking Jeannette to come herself. Then, at midnight (ten o'clock Montana time) on July 31, she received another wire: the miners feared violence.

The violence was already under way, for on August 1, the nearly naked body of Frank Little, an IWW organizer recently come from the copper fields of Arizona, was found hanging from a trestle, a placard affixed, "Others Take Notice. First and Last Warning." He had been taken from his boarding house bed and dragged behind a car. No one knew who did it, but miners considered the lynching the work of the notorious Company goon squad. Company

newspapers and respectable opinion said Little was good riddance.
Much of Butte, however, was incensed. On August 5, in the largest
funeral ever held in Butte, three thousand people escorted Little's
casket on a four mile march past thousands of onlookers.

As a result, the IWW—previously only one of several factions
in the Butte labor movement—came to the fore in the strike.
Though there were only seventy-five to one hundred Wobblies
and ten thousand miners, IWW militancy magnified its importance. As a proponent of mine safety laws, Jeannette necessarily
became entangled with the IWW. She was familiar with the
Wobblies; their roots went back to Montana and the Western Federation of Miners, and they had conducted their first free speech
war in Missoula in 1909. Dedicated to reform by means of the
ballot, Jeannette did not condone their methods, but she did
support their immediate aim, the improvement of working conditions in the mines. After receiving a telegram about Frank
Little's lynching, she decided to bring the matter to the attention of Congress.

First she wired John D. Ryan, who was president of both the
Anaconda Company and the American Red Cross, that she would
like a conference with him before she spoke to Congress. He did
not answer her wires, so on August 7 she introduced a joint resolution, empowering the president to seize and operate metalliferous
mines whose products were essential to the war effort. There was
precedent, for the government had already taken over the railroads. In presenting the resolution, she spoke of the rustling card
system and how it prevented men from complaining about safety
practices or discussing any grievances. Interrupted by a representative asking if she knew the murdered man was a member of the
IWW, she said, "Yes. It is not a question of whom they hanged. It is
a question of lawlessness." There was applause. She went on:

> Mr. John D. Ryan of New York, the president of the Anaconda
> Copper Mining Company, is the man responsible for this situa-
> tion. You are probably all familiar with Mr. Ryan's name in con-
> nection with his recent affiliation with the activities of the
> American Red Cross. If Mr. Ryan says the rustling card system
> must be abolished, it will be. I have tried in vain to draw this fact
> to his attention, however.
>
> My telegrams have received no response. The question I

wished to ask Mr. Ryan was whether at this time, considering the great needs of the country in war, he would agree to abolish the rustling-card system, to meet grievance committees, and to recognize a union.

Jeannette was expressing Montana's feelings about the state's absentee landlords, her humanitarian revulsion to mine accidents, her democratic opposition to men being forced to secure permission to look for work, and her fervent belief that men should not be allowed to make profits from war.

She then took the train for Butte, to which federal troops had already been ordered. Though Wellington had advised her not to come at all ("O'Neill is visionary," he said), he met her in Miles City, three hundred miles east, and escorted her west. The union planned to honor her with a parade when she arrived on August 14, but city officials would not allow it. Nor was she allowed to speak to a cheering crowd of five thousand at the station. Police hustled her into a cab ("abducted me," she said indignantly). She shouted to the crowd, "Good Americans must obey the law. There will be no demonstration tonight."

Six days earlier, an article in the Washington *Times* had quoted Jeannette on the political risks of defying the Company:

> I think I know perfectly well what the Anaconda Company will try to do to me. They'll try to do to me just what they have done to everyone who ever tried to oppose them. . . . They own the State. They own the Government. They own the press. . . . First I'll be roasted from one end of the State to the other. Every newspaper will print my shortcomings, real or fancied, in the largest type. All the mud and all the bricks in the State will come hurtling in my direction. . . . They probably won't assassinate me; they use more subtle methods now. . . . If the Company prevents my ever returning to Congress, I'll at least have the satisfaction of having done what I could for my constituency while I was here. I didn't want to fight the copper crowd. I wanted above and beyond everything else, to get some relief for those poor miners out there. I didn't put my resolution before the House until I had exhausted every other means.

On her arrival in Butte, a reporter from the Anaconda *Standard*, a Company-controlled newspaper, asked her about her remarks in the August 8, 1917, Washington *Times*. Jeannette replied:

I never said the copper interests of Butte were fighting me any more, of course, than they would anyone else who happened to be in opposition to them. And as to the statement that every newspaper would throw mud and bricks at me; that is absurd on the face of it. True, I have had my share of criticism, but the papers throughout the state, taking them as a whole, have been very fair and generous to me and I should regret very much the impression going abroad that I felt otherwise. Other statements, in that same Washington *Times* story, such as my alleged reference to assassination and deportation, are fiction pure and simple.

But the *Times* story does sound a bit like Jeannette in a temper.

Perhaps it was true that the "papers on the whole have been fair and generous," but the Anaconda *Standard* had already struck behind her back. In an August 8 article, headlined "Miss Rankin Doing Strange Things," the *Standard* alleged that Jeannette had advance notice of Frank Little's lynching and quoted miners accusing her of consistently doing "the wrong thing at the wrong time" in regard to the strike.

Jeannette had hoped to serve as a mediator, but since the Company would meet neither with her nor with the union, Jeannette carried her campaign to the public. On August 18, a fine Saturday under deep blue skies, she spoke at Columbia Gardens, a recreational park several miles outside the city, away from the slag and smelter fumes, where there were trees, flowers, picnic spots, and a ball park. Free streetcars ran from the city to the park. She spoke to fifteen thousand people, said Wellington Rankin; sixty-five hundred, one-third of whom were women, said the Anaconda *Standard*. Beside her on the platform were union leaders Tom Campbell from the MMWU, James Larkin from the IWW, and a local district judge, J. J. Lynch. Cheered repeatedly she gave a calm, impartial speech, attempting to find a compromise.

She scolded the mine owners for unsafe conditions and unfair hiring practices. She scolded the IWW for its policy of sabotage; they were striking in the wheat fields of Oregon, and she pleaded with them not to destroy the country's wheat. She urged the men to return to their jobs. She condemned the lynchers of Frank Little; such an act was lawlessness no matter who Little was or what he had done. "It is unpatriotic for labor to strike without just cause, especially in time of war. But it is equally unpatriotic for capital to take advantage of men whose patriotism causes them to continue to work under conditions which mean the daily un-necessary risk of lives . . . I pledge you my word that I shall always do my utmost to bring about better conditions."

She asked for a compromise because the country was at war, a war that, as a good American, she now supported even though she had voted against it. She asked the men to go back to work at their old wages (they wanted $6.00 a day, up from $4.50); she asked the Company to abolish the rustling card and institute safety measures. In any case, they must try to find some peaceful solution.

She was cheered for fifteen minutes, the greatest ovation any-body in Montana ever had, said Wellington; two or three minutes, said the Anaconda *Standard.* But neither the Company nor the IWW would yield on anything. Moderate unionists supported her and would have accepted the compromise. At this point, if the Com-pany had yielded, the strike would have been over; the IWW with its small membership could not have kept it going. But the Company loftily ignored the whole thing; it would not talk to the unions, it would not talk to Jeannette. Miners' tempers were inflamed and the strike continued, with the IWW becoming prominent.

Leaders ordered the men to remain quiet and orderly. "If things get too heated up just go fishing." There was none of the dynamiting and murders that had occurred in 1914. The gov-ernment raided IWW headquarters and seized pounds of printed material regarding grievances that for weeks the strikers had been trying to bring to its attention. Nothing subversive was found. But one by one, as money ran out, men drifted back to work. By December the mines were running at full capacity, with the rus-tling card, the old wages, and the old working conditions. The Company was getting the new high prices for copper.

For Jeannette the affair was a fiasco. She had accomplished noth-ing for the men and had damaged her political future, incurring the enmity of the powerful Company and the suspicion of some of the general public, which connected her name with the feared IWW. Nevertheless, in 1918 she decided to run for the Senate. She did not think she could win reelection to the House, despite labor support from Butte, because Montana was no longer electing two congressmen at large. After her dramatic victory in 1916, state officials divided the state into two districts—one comprised of counties in the mountainous mining west, the other of the home-steading counties to the east. Wellington and others believed that the legislature purposely aligned the districts to make it harder for Jeannette to be reelected to the House; Republican Jeannette lived in the western, Democratic First District. In the senatorial election she could run in the whole state, including its Republican eastern half, which had strongly supported her first bid.

The incumbent senator, the popular Democrat Thomas J. Walsh, might not run again. He, too, was in deep trouble with the Company and conservatives; he had built his reputation by opposing the Company. And he was in deep depression over the death of his wife; they had been intellectual partners, studied mining law together, and worked for woman's suffrage. Since 1918 looked like a Republican year, he might not think it worthwhile to run. If the Democrats did not have a strong candidate, Jeannette and Wellington believed she would have a good chance in spite of her vote against the war and the enmity of the Anaconda Company.

As for the Republican nomination, some political analysts expected Jeannette to get it by default. "What will deter nearly any Republican from entering the primaries against her is the humiliation which would attach to being defeated there by a woman. And if a man should come out for the nomination, then possibly some other man would also announce his candidacy, and the vote in the primaries would be divided between two men and one woman, thus giving Miss Rankin this added advantage," Montana's lieutenant governor W. W. McDowell theorized in a letter to his friend Senator Walsh. McDowell continued: Dr. Oscar Lanstrum, well-known conservative Republican, Helena physician, and newspaper owner, was the logical candidate, but he was "too foxy" to run; he would be "too mortified" if Jeannette beat him. Besides, Miss Rankin's "notoriety and prominence" as the first woman member of Congress, her pictures in nearly all the newspapers and magazines in the United States, her contributions to papers and magazines over her own signature, her $500 payments for lectures (actually $250), no doubt made her feel "much more important than two years ago, and she probably thinks she would be very suitable Senatorial timber."

Jeannette took a long time to make up her mind. She told Wellington she would not want family and friends to make sacrifices unless there was some chance of success. But by early July they were confident, and she announced her candidacy. Dr. Lanstrum also announced, as did two political unknowns, Harry H. Parsons of Missoula and Edmund Nichols of Billings. Thomas J. Walsh had also decided to run, despite his troubles with the Company and the smear campaign the newspapers, most of them Company-owned, were running because of his association with "Bolshevik Burt" Wheeler.

Wheeler, Walsh, and Jeannette had all begun their political careers in the 1911 legislature: Jeannette speaking on woman's suffrage and Wheeler and Walsh campaigning against the Company. Walsh had lost his bid for Senate in 1910–11, when legislators still elected senators, but he won a senate seat in 1912, the first year Montanans were allowed to elect senators by popular ballot. Later Wheeler, with Walsh support, had been appointed United States District Attorney. In that post Wheeler had outraged conservatives because he refused to lose his head during the war hysteria that followed the United States entry into World War I. He would not prosecute people just because they had German names, were aliens, Socialists, members of the IWW, or said things conservatives believed to be treasonable. "As a matter of law there is treason," he said, "but there is no such thing as treasonable utterance." Company papers demanded that Walsh, as Montana's senior senator, withdraw his patronage from Wheeler.

Jeannette and Wellington were friendly with Walsh and Wheeler, and ideologically sympathetic, but politics was politics. Jeannette prepared for the Republican nomination, running on the slogan "Win the War First," an idea borrowed from Women's Peace Party founder Jane Addams. She would support President Wilson in "whatever measures he may recommend to more efficiently prosecute the war." She wanted legislation to prevent war profiteering, better prices for farmers, administration power to fix food prices, national prohibition, national equal suffrage, and prohibition of the use of grain to manufacture liquor and beer. She sent out materials on baby care and spoke of her record for the protection of women and children. She distributed a letter of appreciation from the women in the Bureau of Printing and Engraving, and Gertrude McNally of the bureau came to Montana to campaign for her. She secured the support of the state Nonpartisan League. It must have been an adroit piece of political maneuvering, for nationally the league supported Walsh. One suspects Wellington's hand.

The Nonpartisan League was a new farmers' organization, dominant in North Dakota and spilling over into Montana. It worked within both parties, as did the Company, and its members voted as a bloc. With seventeen thousand members in Montana, it hoped to affect a coalition with labor; such a coalition, if successful, could offer a credible threat to the Company's stranglehold on Montana politics. The Nonpartisan League had developed from the old Society of Equity, whose platform Jeannette had adopted in 1916. The league protested the low price of wheat, the high cost of living, Company control of Montana politics, and the Company's avoidance of its share of taxes. (In 1916 the mines, by far the richest segment of the state's economy, paid 8.79 percent of taxes, compared with farming's 32 percent, livestock's 11 percent, railroads' 18 percent, all others' 30 percent. In 1922 the metal mines would pay less than $14,000 in taxes on $20 million of production.)

The league also wanted publicly owned grain terminals, a rural credit system, and public development of water power. Jeannette had already come out for public power; the matter was just becoming an issue. The Anaconda Company was against it, for the Company and the Montana Power Company were known as the "Montana Twins," both companies having the same president. Walsh complained to the national Nonpartisan League about state support of Jeannette, but the state league continued to endorse Jeannette, probably because of her stand on power. Walsh, already in trouble with the Company, did not dare to come out for public utilities.

Had the league flourished, it would have been a more serious threat to the Company than the IWW, for it worked within the democratic framework. So the Company press attacked, smearing the league as radical, socialistic, Bolshevik, disloyal, unpatriotic, and advocating free love. Many towns prohibited the league, which did have ties with the Socialists, from holding meetings, while other towns actually deported its members. Even the university denied it a meeting place. Having first maligned the league, the papers attacked Jeannette because of her association with it. She was denied permission to speak for a Liberty Loan in Deer Lodge because of her "IWW and Nonpartisan League leanings." She defended herself, saying, "The man we can point to as unpatriotic is the man who comes out of the war with a bigger bank account than when he entered it."

Louis Levine, a Montana economics professor, effectively described the press campaign against Jeannette in a November 2,
1918, article in *The Nation*:

> Miss Rankin voted against the declaration of war. That is used
> effectively against her. But the real cause of the bitter opposi-
> tion to her on the part of those whose views are voiced by the
> Butte *Miner*, the Anaconda *Standard*, the Helena *Independent* and
> similar newspapers, is her economic radicalism. Nominally a
> Republican, Miss Rankin has championed the cause of the work-
> ers of Montana and attacked the mining companies of the State.
> . . . The Butte *Miner* falsely brands her as a "rabid Socialist of the
> IWW type."

Despite the rough treatment Jeannette received from the papers, both Democrats and Republicans feared she would win the
Republican nomination. The national Republican chairman sent
an emissary to Montana to adjudicate the differences among the
three male candidates, in the hope of getting two of them to
withdraw and not split the vote, but the effort failed. Very well,
then, the chairman declared, if Jeannette did get the nomination she would be asked to sign a "declaration of Republican principles." If, and only if, she did so, the Republican National
Committee would make a determined effort to elect her and
would send prominent national speakers into Montana to "certify her Republicanism" and stump for her. It is amusing to suppose Jeannette would sign a declaration of someone else's
principles, but the Republicans were right in their fear that she
might be nominated. She actually lost by only 1,714 votes out of
46,027. Lanstrum received 18,805, Jeannette 17,091, and the
other two candidates split 9,321. It was a good showing.

Immediately rumors started circulating that the nomination
had been stolen from her in the ballot counting, certainly a possi-
bility. She began to consider running on a third-party ticket. Walsh
was alarmed; she would not be elected, but she might siphon off
liberal votes that would otherwise go to him. Wellington, Jeannette,
and Wheeler, however, thought differently. Wellington was "feeling rather sore and terribly bitter against the Doctor [Lanstrum],"
Walsh's political confidant and former law partner, C. B. Nolan,
reported to Walsh. "His [Wellington's] idea is that she should

run so as to insure his [Lanstrum's] defeat." Nolan, however, disagreed. "Her running would be disastrous to you," he wrote Walsh.
"Every influence should be brought to bear upon Wellington not
to have her run."

Some Democrats suggested the administration give Jeannette
a good government job, preferably overseas, to enable her to re-
tire from politics gracefully. Then rumors started that she was offered money to run, or, alternatively, not to run. Walsh's campaign
manager, A. E. Spriggs, an old party hack of thirty years experience, believed Republicans were bribing her. He wrote Walsh, that
it was impossible to prevent her from running "because the Republican organization has outbid us at every turn. . . . It was folly
for us to raise their bid, because we were not in a position to do it,
and it would only result in their offer being increased and thus
fattening the treasury of the people we are to fight."

This letter has been adduced to support the theory that
Jeannette was bribed to run and split the liberal vote, but the
idea is ridiculous. She had taken high risks for high principles;
she would not be likely to succumb to petty bribery. When, forty
years later, a writer who did not understand that there were different shades of politicians was to say that Wellington had "negotiated" with the Democrats, she angrily threatened to sue. She
had to run, she said, to quash rumors that she was bribed not to.

So Jeannette announced her candidacy on the National Party
ticket, a coalition of Socialists, Progressives, Prohibitionists, and
the state Nonpartisan League. Walsh was worried. Nationally, it
was a bad year for Democrats, and Walsh was in trouble at home
over his support of "Bolshevik Burt" Wheeler, who nevertheless
kept telling Walsh he had nothing to worry about. Wheeler said
many Republicans would vote for Walsh, some to defeat Lanstrum
and some to defeat Rankin. Even while the newspapers were
screaming for Wheeler's scalp, Walsh asked him to use his influence with radical elements to secure their support. Wheeler was
given the impossible job of delivering radical votes without alien-
ating conservatives.

Walsh himself began to court conservatives. He even asked
some of his liberal friends not to campaign for him. He culti-
vated the conservative Democrat governor Samuel Stewart, with
whom he had formerly been on the outs. He wrote a congratula-
tory letter to C. F. Kelley on his promotion to the presidency of

Anaconda. Colonel Nolan wrote that some conservatives, among them Bruce Kremer, Company attorney, Democratic national committeeman, and head of the Council of Defense, were coming over to him, but the Company would not deliver its "Instructions" until about the first of October.

With Company support in doubt, Walsh decided that Wheeler's actions as United States district attorney were too great a political liability. In September he offered Wheeler a job as attorney for the Federal Trade Commission. Wheeler refused it. Finally, as the newspapers increased their attacks, blaming Walsh for the actions of "Bolshevik Burt," the pressure became too much, and Walsh asked Wheeler to resign. Wheeler did so, while reminding Walsh, "I made my enemies in the first place by supporting you." Walsh arranged for Wheeler to be offered a federal judgeship in Panama and a colonelcy in the army. Disappointed that his old friend had been "gullible" enough to fall into the conservative trap set by "political pirates," Wheeler once again angrily refused the offers. If he was to be deported, he said, he would prefer to go to Siberia where the climate was more congenial. Despite Wheeler's anger—he refused to publicly endorse Walsh's campaign—and his influence among liberals, Walsh's campaign prospects only brightened after Wheeler's resignation.

Campaigning was vigorous. Jeannette had her usual carefully organized speaking schedule and postcard mailings. But the Helena postmaster reported that Walsh's organization sent out five times as much literature as the others. Walsh sent to every woman a copy of a personal letter from Carrie Chapman Catt and Anna Howard Shaw praising him for his support of woman's suffrage. It was true; except for Jeannette Rankin, Senator Walsh was the best friend the suffragists had in Congress. Yet why should Walsh get credit in order to take votes from Jeannette? It looked as if the two hawks in NAWSA wanted to punish Jeannette for her antiwar vote.

Jeannette countered with a letter of approval from the WCTU, though their relationship previously had been cool. Walsh received the support of the Anti-Saloon League. Lanstrum panicked and unsuccessfully tried to stir up the Masonic Lodge against the Catholic Walsh and then tried to make an improbable deal with the Nonpartisan League. Walsh heard reports that Lanstrum was losing heart and would be happy just to "beat Miss R. If Miss

R. had any party to back her she would be dangerous." Jeannette was expected to get the labor and Irish vote in Butte, and sympathy had been created for her by the "brutal conduct of some of the local satellites of the copper company . . . when she was denied access to a public building for purposes of speaking for the Liberty Loan."

Just before the election the popular former president Theodore Roosevelt visited Montana. He did not endorse anyone, but he castigated the Industrial Workers of the World and the Nonpartisan League in the same breath. There was no real connection between the two; he misrepresented the league and hurt Jeannette. Toward the end of the campaign the influenza epidemic began. Meeting places were closed, especially hard on Jeannette because she had to make public appearances to counteract Company newspapers. Nevertheless, she spoke twenty-two times in the last twelve days of the campaign. Election Day, November 5, was cold and miserable, with snow in the west and rain in the east. People were afraid to go out on account of the flu. Mothers stayed home with their babies. Only two-thirds as many people voted as had in 1916.

Walsh won with 46,160 votes; Lanstrum received 40,229, Jeannette 26,013. She carried three sparsely settled Nonpartisan League counties in eastern Montana and received a heavy labor vote in unhappy Butte, where federal troops were still patrolling. Wheeler, Wellington, and Jeannette had been right, and Wheeler crowed, "I said Walsh would win if she ran and I was right." Wheeler was to prove his political acumen many times in the future.

Nationally, except for the solid South, the country went Republican, dooming Wilson's efforts for world peace. Walsh said the country was punishing the Democrats for the selfishness of southern congressmen, who had, for instance, fixed the price of wheat but not of cotton. So he went back to the Senate as a minority member. Unfortunately in order to win Walsh had had to make peace with his old enemy, the Company. Colonel Nolan wrote: "The election returns show most conclusively that the Company did all that it possibly could do to bring about your election, and without the financial assistance that was given by Con Kelley [Company president] our situation would be critical in meeting the expense account that was contracted." The Company understood politics meant compromise. Lanstrum would have served them better in the Senate, but they were afraid of Jeannette. So they financed their old enemy Walsh, and he had to pay for their support by abandoning Wheeler.

The protagonists of this drama were all good friends of longstanding and similar ideas. Wellington Rankin had begun his law practice in the Walsh and Nolan offices; they had worked together for woman's suffrage and other progressive and anti-Company causes. The Republican Wellington had told the Democrat Nolan that he would do anything to defeat the Republican Lanstrum. The Democrat Walsh had criticized the Democrat Wheeler: "Complaint is made that when you go to Helena you confer with Wellington Rankin, Sam Ford [a progressive Republican], and their associates, rather than with Democratic leaders there."

They were all to have great futures. Thomas J. Walsh went on to national prominence, especially as investigator of the Teapot Dome oil scandals of the Warren G. Harding administration. In 1933, out of respect for Walsh's reputation as a constitutional lawyer, President Franklin D. Roosevelt appointed him attorney general; Walsh died on his way to Washington to assume office. Wellington Rankin was elected state attorney general in 1920. Though his future ventures into elective politics were unsuccessful, he became a Republican national committeeman and had considerable influence in the party through the 1950s. He would become one of the state's most prominent lawyers and businessmen.

Burton K. Wheeler said he was disgusted and through with politics, but he ran for governor in 1920 and was soundly trounced. But to defeat him the Company had to accept the liberal Republican Joseph M. Dixon, an old Rankin friend, and Dixon was able to put through a small but significant tax reform that increased the levy on mines, a breakthrough in the long fight against the Company. By 1922 the Company could no longer beat Wheeler, and Bolshevik Burt was elected to the United States Senate, serving there with his old friend Walsh. He became a strong force in the Democratic Party nationally, one of the first to push Franklin D. Roosevelt's candidacy for the presidency, and later a leader of anti-Roosevelt forces in the Senate.

The Montana State University economics professor Louis Levine—who reported on Jeannette's campaign in *The Nation*—published an essay called *The Taxation of Mines in Montana* in 1919, which revealed what many people already knew: the minute amount the Anaconda Company paid the state in taxes. The Company forced the university to fire him. This egregious exercise of corporate power motivated Dixon to enter the 1920 gubernatorial campaign and pursue tax reform. Levine went on to a distinguished career as a Brookings Institution economist. Jeannette Rankin, like Wheeler and Levine, found herself temporarily defeated, but as a lobbyist in the 1920s and 1930s, she spent more time in Congress than some congressmen. Twenty-two years later she would win a second term, and she and Wheeler would work together to try to keep America out of yet another war. But now, at the age of thirty-eight, she had to find a new career.

CHAPTER TEN

Miss Rankin,
Former Congresswoman

"THOSE WERE WONDERFUL YEARS."

JEANNETTE CONTINUED, after she left Congress, to work for twin goals: peace and the protection of women and children. She attended a women's conference in Zurich, Switzerland, in 1919 and came home to work for protective legislation. Her traveling schedule was almost as hectic as it had been when she was working for suffrage, and she rarely slept in the same bed twice in succession. A noticeable aspect of these years is that she began to make many personal friends, some of worldwide renown and some obscure farmers' wives. Four years earlier, unhappy with herself and her position in life, she had escaped to New Zealand. On her return, she had entered the political arena and found herself in the public eye for four extraordinarily difficult years. She had risen to the occasion, and her comportment had earned her praise from allies and opponents alike. That turbulent period seemed to have made her more at peace with herself and others. It gave her self-confidence.

In April 1919 she went to Europe with Jane Addams, Florence Kelley, and other peace workers to the Second International Congress of Women for Permanent Peace (which soon became the Women's International League for Peace and Freedom). The congress had its origin in a 1915 meeting in The Hague, at which Jane Addams and others conceived of a meeting of women at the end of the war to discuss the prevention of future wars. The Second International Congress was to have been held in conjunction with the official peace talks in Paris near the Versailles Conference called by the Allies. Unfortunately, France refused to admit women from the Central Powers, and the women's meeting had to move to Zurich. Even then, the French government tried to refuse French women permission to attend.

In Paris, waiting for arrangements to be made, Jeannette, Jane Addams, Lillian Wald, and Dr. Alice Hamilton hired a car and toured some of the French battlefields. At Vimy Ridge their car broke down, and they had to wait for repairs. It was a dreary, cold, rainy day in late fall. Although they knew what to expect, the women were distressed at what they saw: rolls of rusted barbed wire, trees burnt and broken, the mud plowed by trenching and shells, scarcely a blade of grass. Casualties had been heavy at Vimy. Chinese laborers were hastily digging up bodies of Canadian soldiers for proper burial. Back in Paris the women saw emaciated, sick, frightened French children under the care of an American relief organization. Jeannette could hardly face these sights; later, when Jane Addams went on to Germany and Austria, where conditions were even worse, she stayed behind.

In Zurich the women enjoyed international comradeship in their search for peace, but they were appalled at the opposite nature of the male conference at Versailles with its vindictiveness and "spoils to the victors" mentality. Noting that representatives of the defeated nations had not even been invited to Versailles, the women resolved:

> This international Congress of Women expresses its deep regret. . . . The terms of peace deny the principles of self-determination, recognize the right of the victors to the spoils of war, and create all over Europe discords and animosities which can only lead to future wars. . . . A hundred million people of this generation in the heart of Europe are condemned to poverty, disease, and despair which must result in the spread of anarchy within each nation. With a deep sense of responsibility this Congress strongly urges the Allied and Associated Governments to accept such amendments of the terms as shall bring peace into harmony with those principles first enumerated by President Wilson.

It was tactful of them to speak of "principles first enumerated by President Wilson," since actually the "Fourteen Points" were essentially those promulgated by the 1915 women's conference in The Hague. A year later the economist John Maynard Keynes said that the women's congress had been largely right in its view of the peace terms. Later events in Europe—economic collapse and the rise of militaristic political movements—would vindicate the women's judgment. Jeannette herself said the Treaty of Versailles was "vicious." She wrote the only Republican member of the United States delegation: "There will be war as long as we have secret international relations and governments . . . [that] protect special economic privileges."

Difficult to deal with was the issue of Bolshevism. The revolution in Russia was a year old; Americans feared revolutionary leaders Lenin and Leon Trotsky more than they had the Kaiser. Jeannette told the *New York Times* that she expected to "place the problem of stopping the spread of Bolshevism before the [women's] Congress and expect[ed] to receive many suggestions from delegates who come from the countries where it is prevalent." She did not mean, however, stopping the spread of Bolshevism by armed intervention. In fact she later supported the women's congress resolution to immediately end all western intervention in Communist Russia and Hungary, "whether by armed force, by supply of munitions or money, or by blockade." The women argued: "Warfare was being waged without open declaration . . . upon people who are experimenting in a new social and economic order which has not yet had a fair trial, but which may prove to have a great contribution to make to the future of the world."

This was a reasonable expression of Jeannette's pragmatic approach to life: let us examine others' methods and try to learn. She was not a Communist. She had no quarrel with free enterprise. She merely opposed monopoly capitalism. Huge industrial and financial interests fomented war, blocked efforts to protect human beings, and frustrated democracy. She just had witnessed a good example in the American war hysteria. If other nations wanted to try Communism, she believed that, instead of making war on them, the United States should leave them alone in the hopes of learning from their successes or failures.

On her trip to Europe, Jeannette met some of the most brilliant and active women in Europe and America, and as an ex-congresswoman

she was made much of. She especially enjoyed getting to know
Mary Church Terrell, president of the National Association of
Colored Women, with whom she traveled and shared hotel rooms.
Terrell spoke fluent French and German and was frequently called
on to interpret. The daughter of a wealthy Memphis real estate
dealer, she had been educated by private tutors, special schools,
and at Oberlin College in Ohio, a Quaker school founded by abo-
litionists with a long history of accepting black students. Jeannette
admired her excellent education.

The women at the international congress formed themselves
into a permanent body, the Women's International League for
Peace and Freedom. At the league's behest, Jeannette went to
Washington, D.C., in January 1920 to lobby Congress for the early
release of prisoners of war and political offenders. These included
Wobblies and other labor organizers, socialists, and pacifists arrested under the Sedition Act for discussing the flag or the government using "disloyal, profane, scurrilous or abusive language."
Try as she might, she could accomplish little. Men had run the
war and were running the peace like a war.

A position in the National Consumers' League followed in
November 1920. So named because it tried to use pressure from
consumers to improve conditions of workers, the National Consumers' League encouraged consumers to buy only goods bearing the league's white label. The label vouched for the working
conditions under which the item had been made—Consumers'
League inspectors guaranteed that white label goods were made
in sanitary factories that did not employ child labor. Most of the
goods were clothing or other items sold in department stores.
Jeannette's boss, Florence Kelley, had spent her life in this work.

One of the most interesting women of her generation, Kelley
had the art of inspiring others. It was said that, when she entered a
room, "everyone was brave." The strong and brilliant daughter of
a Pennsylvania congressman, Kelley had studied at Cornell University in Ithaca, New York, and in Zurich, Switzerland, where she
had become a socialist and married a young Polish physician. They
had come to New York, where her husband could not establish a
practice; debts and estrangement followed. Determined to support her three children herself, she had moved to Illinois, where
she could get a divorce on grounds of nonsupport. She found a
home at Hull House, Jane Addams's settlement house in the slums

of Chicago. Her investigation of the lives of the residents of slums surrounding Hull House helped pass the first factory law in Illinois, which limited the number of hours women could work to eight and banned employment of children under fourteen. In 1893 Illinois governor John P. Altgeld appointed her chief inspector of factories, giving her the job of enforcing the protective legislation that she had helped pass. In 1899 she moved to New York to head up the recently formed National Consumers' League. She served as the league's general secretary until her death in 1932.

Hired by the National Consumers' League as field secretary, Jeannette spent most of her time working for state factory laws and other protective legislation. But she spent her first months on the job lobbying Congress for the passage of the Shepard-Towner bill for maternity and infant care, a modest version of her Rankin-Robinson bill. Careful not to infringe upon the purview of physicians, the bill proposed a system, overseen by the Children's Bureau, of public health nurses, who would offer education rather than direct services. While Jeannette lobbied members of Congress privately, the eloquent Kelley testified passionately on behalf of the measure:

> when we are told that this country is so poor and this Congress so harassed by things of greater importance than the deaths of a quarter of a million children a year, we say to ourselves, "surely, we are not to take this seriously." . . . Will Congress let Christmas come and go and New Year's come and go, and the legislatures come, and seven of them adjourn after 30 days, and half of them after 60 days, without . . . [taking] action for saving the lives of children? . . . What answer can be given to the women who are marveling and asking, "Why does Congress wish women and children to die?"

Despite the fierce attacks against it as socialistic, unwomanly, and subversive, the bill had the support of women's organizations. Assuming that these organizations accurately represented the views of recently enfranchised women voters, Congress bowed under the pressure, and the bill became law on November 23, 1921. For seven years, the Sheppard-Towner Act provided federal funds to improve maternal and child health, the first federal funds ever provided for social welfare.

Glowing from that legislative success, Jeannette went to the Midwest to work for minimum hour legislation for women. Although in 1895 the Illinois Supreme Court had declared unconstitutional an Illinois law calling for an eight-hour day for women and forbidding the employment of children under fourteen in factories or in hazardous conditions, legal tides were turning. The Illinois court had reasoned that the law violated the right of an individual to freely enter into a contract by restricting the terms of that contract, but in 1908 Louis Brandeis had persuaded the Supreme Court not to strike down an Oregon law limiting women workers to a ten-hour day by arguing that the state had a special interest in protecting the health of mothers. In 1916 President Wilson had named Brandeis to the Supreme Court, and the Consumers' League stepped up its campaign to pass state wage-and-hour laws for women and children.

For Jeannette this meant a heavy travel schedule throughout the Mississippi valley, where she spoke to social organizations, unions, schools, churches, and universities. She explained how to introduce legislation, plan hearings, and conduct lobbying. She organized the Mississippi Valley Conference for Labor and Welfare Legislation for Women and Children held in Chicago on January 5–6, 1923, which delegates from eleven midwestern states attended.

Part of the time she traveled alone, but sometimes Jane Addams, Florence Kelley, and Julia Lathrop, the director of the Children's Bureau, accompanied her. They would take a "drummers' room," one with several beds, in a hotel in the capital of the state in which they were lobbying. These three women were among the most interesting in the country. Jane Addams had wisdom and humor; she could balance complicated situations and ignore personal attacks. Though an ardent reformer she was no socialist; she thought legislation could cure the inequities of society. A socialist and the most class conscious of the group, Florence Kelley would settle for temporary reforms until socialism was achieved. Julia Lathrop was a pragmatist and diplomat, merry and witty. They were all well-balanced women, hopeful for the future and dauntless in defeat. We can imagine them at night after their legislative business was disposed of, in their common hotel room, speaking of the increasing freedom of women, of short skirts, coeducational colleges, moving pictures, lipstick, and rouge.

Especially, they must have discussed the birth control movement. Margaret Sanger set up a permanent birth control clinic in New York in 1923, and Marie Stopes established one in London in 1922. As Jeannette and her compatriots lobbied for protective legislation, Dr. Stopes, on trial for sending contraceptive information through the mails, was receiving a great deal of publicity. Although still controversial, contraception was beginning to win wide public acceptance among the upper classes. Like abortion in a later day, the rich widely practiced it, but knowledge of it was kept from the poor. The early twenties marked the start of the gradual spread of contraception, which would prove more emancipating to women than suffrage. Although never directly involved in the birth control movement herself, Jeannette followed its progress closely. Her sister Edna would take on birth control as her life's work. In the 1930s and 1940s Edna helped to establish clinics across the United States; in the 1960s she took her work to Asia, the Middle East, and Africa.

In between trips Jeannette's headquarters was at Hull House, where reformers often stayed when in Chicago. Some of the best conversation in the world took place there. Writers and theorists, social workers and politicians, exiled radicals, progressive business men, and poets dined there. It was a stimulating place to live. "Those were wonderful times," Jeannette said. It pleased and flattered her that Jane Addams often asked Jeannette to sit by her at table and to accompany her when she greeted visiting dignitaries. "But it was really because," Jeannette would say with her habitual self-disparagement, "I was so easy to introduce. She would just say, 'This is Miss Rankin, the former Congressman.' "

Of all the people she had ever known, Jeannette said many times, she most admired Jane Addams. "She was a perfect blend of thought and action. She had a grasp of economics, finance, law, administration, international affairs, everything. She should have been president." Jeannette herself borrowed much from Jane Addams. The speech she made many times for woman's suffrage, "It's beautiful and right that a woman should nurse her sick children through typhoid fever, but it's also beautiful and right that she should vote for sanitary measures to prevent that typhoid from spreading," closely paraphrased Addams's argument in a January 1910 *Ladies Home Journal* article, "Why Women Should Vote."

She also admired Addams's method of educating through doing, for instance Addams's practical campaign to improve garbage collection in her ward in Chicago. Addams pestered the mayor until he finally made her garbage inspector for the ward. According to legend, she took a shovel and inspected, finding one narrow street with the pavement eighteen inches below the surface of the filth. Some of the foreign-born women who lived in the ward were shocked to see her doing a man's job; she explained that it was as womanly to clean up the district and prevent illness as it was to go about the tenements and nurse the sick. That was Jeannette's kind of educational activity.

While life at Hull House was stimulating, in fact Jeannette was accomplishing little. It was a bad time for reformers. The Harding administration wanted to get back to "normalcy." President Calvin Coolidge said the "business of America is business." People were making money; the standard of living of the influential sector of society was rapidly rising. Reformers were not wanted. At best, they hurt profits; at worst, they were Bolsheviks. In spite of Jeannette's four years of hard traveling, as Kelley remarked, "at a rate equaled only at the height of the old suffrage campaigns," she could see little progress. And then the Supreme Court, in *Adkins vs. Children's Hospital* (1923), overturned earlier decisions to rule that minimum wage laws for women were denial of liberty without due process of law. Not until 1937 would the Court uphold the constitutionality of wages-and-hours laws.

Discouraged, Jeannette asked for a temporary leave of absence in 1924; it soon became permanent. She wanted to spend the summer in cool Montana and help her brother campaign for the Senate. Elected state attorney general in 1920, Wellington had lost the Republican senatorial nomination in 1922. In 1924 he decided to try again, and Jeannette went back to Montana to stump for him. After a hard fought campaign, Wellington lost the nomination to Frank Bird Linderman in the Republican primary. Some sting was taken out of the defeat when Governor Joseph Dixon, the Rankins' old Missoula friend and sometime political rival, appointed Wellington associate justice of the state supreme court.

After Wellington's campaign, Jeannette—tired of not having a place to really call her own—decided to look for property in Georgia. The rural south seemed like an odd place for Jeannette to settle, and her decision to build a home there aroused comment. When people asked Jeannette why she made her home in the backwoods of north Georgia, she would tell them she chose the location for its proximity to New York. She meant the remark to be provocative, but it was not unreasonable. Her Georgia home was only a day by train from friends and colleagues in New York and Washington; from Montana, changing in Chicago, the trip could take four days. Also, thought Jeannette, living would be cheap in the South. She had little income. And she liked the people, thought of them as quiet, simple, unmaterialistic, even unmilitaristic, possibly confusing their insularity with pacifistic leanings. She admitted later that she had thought the winters would be warmer; she had not expected the ice storms and cold damp winds prevalent at the southern tip of the Appalachians.

However right or wrong her perceptions of Georgia were in the beginning, she was to live happily there for nearly half a century. There was much time away, working, traveling, summering in Montana. She voted in Montana, registered her car there, and owned a small farm there, which she rented out but considered her legal residence. But actually she was a guest in Montana, either at relatives' homes in Missoula, or the Placer Hotel that her brother owned in Helena, or at his ranch in Avalanche Gulch, forty miles east of Helena. Georgia was home.

She bought sixty-four acres of scrub land covered with shortleaf pine and kudzu vine, near the village of Bogart, eight miles from the university town of Athens. She hired carpenters and built a one-room house with a bay window and screened porch. A fireplace at one end of the room was connected with water pipes to a car radiator at the other. As the fire heated the water it circulated through the radiator. The contraption probably did not work as well as she had hoped; a pump or fan would have helped, but there was no electricity. The heating mechanism, like the house itself, was Jeannette's own design.

An old cotton house was connected to the main house with a covered runway; it served as kitchen and bathroom. Jeannette cooked on a black iron stove and poured the waste dish water into a gasoline funnel sunk into a countertop; the water ran through a hose to the outdoors. A tiny room had a tub and toilet compartment, with a pot in a box accessible to an outside door, through which the pot could be removed for emptying. She had

Jeannette, posed in front of the home she had built on sixty-four acres near Bogart, Georgia, in 1925, spent the interwar years organizing, lobbying, and lecturing for peace. The house burned during her second term in Congress.

a well drilled and a hand pump installed; there was no running water in the house. She considered the place quite comfortable; it was neither the first nor the last of her many ingenious housing ideas.

She was not alone. Her mother Olive lived with her most of the time. Her sister Edna was divorced, and Jeannette and Olive cared for Edna's two children, Dorothy and John, both under ten. Sometimes Edna stayed there, too. Often there were guests. Jeannette had to add two bedrooms and a loft to use as an office. When Olive and Jeannette first moved in, they were a little afraid of living alone in the woods, so Jeannette asked one of the black carpenters, who lived nearby, to come if he heard any commotion. She wondered why he looked so frightened; only later did she realize that if there were trouble he would be blamed. So they locked the door and heard every pinecone that dropped on the roof and squirrel that chased it. Later she stopped locking doors and slept well. She claimed it was the act of locking the door that triggered the fears, and she used the story to illustrate the flaws in national defense: the more worry and money we put into national defense, the more others fear us, and the more we fear them.

Caring for her sister's children was for several years in the 1920s the most important thing in Jeannette's life. She adored them. Forty years later, like any mother blaming herself for not handling things better, she mourned that she had shown too much favoritism toward John; Dorothy had resented it and was "mean" to John. When John died at summer camp at age seven, Jeannette was crushed. She continued all her life to cherish Dorothy like a daughter, worrying about her smoking, her heart condition, her personal problems.

In Georgia the Rankins lived a simple, rural life. Jeannette, who for years had paid meticulous attention to her clothes, often going so far as to wear "pink chiffon and marabou" to address a ladies' club, now went to the other extreme and slopped around the house in an old bathrobe. Dorothy went to public school. Jeannette bought a cow, and Dorothy learned to milk. Olive Rankin made butter, just as she had done in her first married days on Grant Creek.

Rural Georgia was a strange place for a radical, independent, single Montana woman to live. Jeannette liked her neighbors' quiet, unpretentious ways, but initially she probably did not fathom their deep conservatism. For instance in her first year there, 1925, the Georgia legislature considered a bill to forbid any public library or county school to purchase, or even accept as a gift, any book except the Bible, the hymnal, and the almanac. "Those three are enough for anyone," said the sponsoring legislator. "Read the Bible. It teaches you how to act. Read the hymnbook. It contains the finest poetry ever written. Read the almanac. It shows you how to figure out what the weather will be. There isn't another book necessary for anyone to read, and therefore I am opposed to all libraries." The bill failed to pass the Georgia House of Representatives, but only by fifty-seven votes to sixty-three.

Unemancipated for all practical purposes were African Americans, a people with whom Jeannette had had little contact. She was a little uneasy at first. They were not like her friend Mary Church Terrell, the cultured president of the National Association of Colored Women. But Jeannette had a genius for meeting people on terms of friendly equality, and people usually responded. One day she opened her door to a knock and found three or four black teenagers. Clothed in rags, they had walked six miles through an ice storm, looking for work. One had a frostbitten ear. They asked to come in to get warm. "I felt like a fool," said Jeannette. "Born and raised in Montana and didn't know what to do for a frozen ear. In the meantime there were these great big black boys sitting around the stove on my kitchen floor."

Jeannette was always interested in how people lived, their housing, their food, their employment. She went out into the fields, noting that the tiny farms aimed at little but subsistence. She wondered at people planting their potato peelings, having cooked and eaten the rest of the potato. She organized children's clubs. The girls had a "Sunshine" club, where she taught games, sewing, and parliamentary law. The boys met separately. All of them liked to visit her because she had one of the first radios in the neighborhood. She suggested swimming, but there was no pool, and no one could afford swimsuits. She helped the boys clear out and dam a nearby creek, and showed the girls how to make suits from some inexpensive natural-colored flannel Jeannette had bought from a nearby mill. When the girls balked at the ugly color, she taught them how to dye. These clubs were for white children only; integrated clubs would have been taboo.

She had a good friend her own age, a farmer's wife, "uneducated, ignorant but smart," with whom she was close. They drove back and forth to Atlanta in Jeannette's car for shopping. "It took the same time as it does now [in 1970], about an hour and a half." Later, the friend committed suicide, a blow to Jeannette, who was away in Washington at the time. She thought there was much illness in the community: polio, preventable birth defects, and depression.

Jeannette was not confined by rural life. She drove to Montana for the summers, stopping every hundred miles to buy a dollar's worth of gas, so as to get out and walk around and not go to sleep. She often made trips to New York and Washington. Grandmother could stay with children, and Jeannette had professional responsibilities. She spoke to peace groups, and she was vice-chairman and member of the executive board of the Women's International League for Peace and Freedom, which had grown out of the women's conference in Zurich in 1919. In Washington there was good friend Emily Balch, international secretary of the Women's International League, who would later receive the Nobel Peace Prize, but not, Jeannette would say ironically, until she had supported the Second World War.

She also had old friends in New York from suffrage days: Elisabeth Irwin, the progressive educator, and Mary Ritter Beard and her husband Charles, the historians. After Jeannette's second term, Charles Beard supported her in her revisionist theory of President Franklin D. Roosevelt's part in bringing America into World War II. A most rewarding friendship was with Katharine Anthony, the writer and collateral descendant of Susan B. Anthony, who lived with Elisabeth Irwin. Anthony traveled frequently to Georgia, and Jeannette visited Anthony and Irwin whenever she was in New York. Anthony had written articles signed by Jeannette when she was in Congress; now, under her own name, Anthony wrote two articles about Jeannette for the *Woman's Home Companion*, "My Gypsy Journey to Georgia," and "Living on the Front Porch," published in July and September 1926. Without mentioning Jeannette by name, Anthony described her idyllic surroundings in Georgia, where plain living and high thinking were practiced.

Most looked forward to were frequent visits with Fiorello LaGuardia. They had been good friends since their luncheon in 1917, when they were both congressmen elect, though they had had only five months to get acquainted before he left for the war in Europe. On his return he had married and then tragically lost his wife and tiny daughter to tuberculosis within a few weeks of each other. He was shaken; for months he raged around New York on binges. But, recovering, he returned to politics. By 1923 he was back in the House of Representatives, working for public power, pure food laws, equal rights for women, minimum wages, old-age pensions, workmen's compensation, child-labor laws, social security, regulation of utilities and the stock market—all Jeannette's issues.

Because they had such different personalities, the friendship might have seemed strange. The ebullient LaGuardia was full of laughter and loud noises and unexpected gestures; he liked music and wine and food. Jeannette was quiet and reserved, and her Anglo-Scots ancestry and youth in Montana had taught her little of music and wine. Fiorello had been born in Arizona; his father was an army bandmaster of Italian origin and his mother Jewish. But these differences were unimportant; Jeannette and Fiorello were alike in the ways that counted to both of them. Social workers at heart, they both believed that if only they worked a little harder, ran a little faster, they could make this world into a paradise. Intense and indefatigable workers, they were both pragmatic, nondoctrinaire, free-thinkers in religion and politics. They were both mugwumps; LaGuardia had made a remark similar to Jeannette's: he might run on the Republican ticket, but he did not run on the Republican platform. (Actually, his Republicanism was a reaction to Tammany Hall corruption.) Both could be impatient and irascible, though it was easier for LaGuardia, as a man, to get away with it.

Sometime in the mid-twenties Fiorello asked Jeannette to marry him. "You don't know how hard," he once told her sister Edna, his arm around Jeannette's waist, "I tried to get this gal to marry me." It is hard to imagine such a marriage, and they did not marry. In 1929 Fiorello married his supremely efficient secretary. Though he complained that he "lost a good secretary and got a bum cook," it was a successful marriage. The LaGuardias raised two children while his political fortunes increased. From 1934 to 1945, he served as mayor of New York, probably the best and certainly the best-known mayor New York ever had. But, unknown to most, the relationship between Fiorello and Jeannette continued. The two would dine together whenever they found themselves in the same city, New York or Washington. She received letters from him asking her to find Montana stones for his son's collection or scolding her for not coming to see him. "Here you were in New York, gave an interview to the newspapers, and you didn't come to see me. Don't you ever do that again."

During Jeannette's second term, Fiorello was a great support to her. He approved of her antiwar vote—he leaned toward pacifism himself—though they disagreed on military preparedness. His ebullience could often lift Jeannette's spirits, and her spirits sorely needed lifting in those dark days after her vote against World War II. "He was a great friend," Jeannette would say. "He said I was right about the First World War and he was wrong." She always spoke of him in terms she used for almost no one else, "my close personal friend."

CHAPTER ELEVEN

Peace Activist

_JC_

"WAR IS A CRIME."

FROM HER GEORGIA HOME base Jeannette Rankin worked right up
to the Second World War as a professional peace worker. For over
ten years she lectured, wrote, and organized while the United States
and other nations spent billions on armaments. She persevered
while Italy invaded Ethiopia in 1935, Germany and Russia per-
fected their military machines in Spain in 1936 during the Spanish Civil War, and Japan attacked China in 1937. Often she felt a
lack of accomplishment and personal despair; often she went unpaid. She was libeled as a Communist. A newspaper column about
her was headed "Up Pops the Devil." Still, she worked on.

In 1924 Jeannette went to Washington, D.C., to address the
Fourth Congress of the Women's International League for Peace
and Freedom (WILPF). There she advocated support of Salmon
O. Levinson's "outlawry of war" plan, which had found a champion in Senator William Borah. The Idaho senator had formally
introduced the idea in a Senate resolution in 1923, asking that
war be outlawed by making it a crime and that a World Court be
established to deal with such crimes. Fiorello LaGuardia introduced
an even more sweeping joint resolution advocating the outlawry
of war in the House in December 1925. (Neither passed, and
LaGuardia's resolution never even made it out of committee.)

Jeannette told the convention that hitherto all wars had been legal wars; there was actually a body of international law that legitimized war by laying down the conduct of war. "Instead of laws about war, we should have laws against war. War, though made illegal, might occur, but it would be branded as a crime, and the force of the world would be organized to deal with the criminal."

In 1925 she took a job as field secretary with WILPF, traveling, speaking, organizing. She spoke often to women and continued to emphasize the importance of women. "The work of educating the world for peace is a woman's job, because men are afraid of being classed as cowards." It would not be easy; any peace movement would be attacked as "socialistic" or "Bolshevist." But women should "stand by their guns," just as they had for the suffrage movement. "My family," she said, "has always been alarmed at the inclination I have to select unpopular causes, but at the present time I can see no more urgent cause . . . than outlawing war."

She tried to get the directors of WILPF to concentrate their organizing efforts in states with relatively small populations. She reasoned that working with smaller populations would cost less and would be equally as effective as trying to organize heavily populated states since the Senate controlled foreign policy and each state—regardless of size—had two senators. An added, if unspoken advantage to this plan for Jeannette was that these lightly populated states were mostly in the West, which would put her in familiar territory. She suggested that WILPF employ two units, each with two field workers and an office secretary, to cost about $1,000 a month. (Her own salary was $250 a month, plus $100 for travel.) But the board told Jeannette that she herself would have to raise the $6,000 that one unit would cost for a six-month trial. Since she could not raise funds and organize too, she resigned.

She withdrew to Georgia, where she organized a local peace group, planted peaches and pecans on her small farm, and cared for her niece. She visited Montana and spurred on Wellington's political ambitions; in 1928 he received the Republican nomination for governor but lost the election. In 1929 Jeannette was ready to reenter peace work full-time. The timing seemed propitious; after all, the United States had joined most of the world's great powers in ratifying the Kellogg-Briand Pact, which outlawed "offensive" or "aggressive" war as an "instrument of national policy." Peace organizations hastened to capitalize on the largely symbolic event, and one, the left-wing Women's Peace Union (WPU), asked Jeannette to lobby for the Frazier amendment, which was intended to implement the Kellogg-Briand Pact by prohibiting the United States government from appropriating any money to the military. Proposed by North Dakota senator Lynn Frazier, the proposed amendment was a constitutional amendment—to pass it would require support of a two-thirds majority in both houses of Congress and ratification by three-quarters of the states. Jeannette was "thrilled" to get into action again; she had "been in the country long enough."

The WPU's sole goal was the passage of the Frazier amendment, which declared: "War for any purpose shall be illegal, and neither the United States nor any state, territory, association or person subject to its jurisdiction shall prepare for, declare, engage in, or carry on war or other armed conflict, expedition, invasion, or undertaking within or without the United States, nor shall funds be raised, appropriated, or expended for such purpose." A radical redirection of foreign policy, the amendment never even made it onto the Senate floor.

"The Senators and Congressmen were friendly, cordial, and brutally frank," Jeannette reported back to the WPU's central committee. Burton K. Wheeler, now senator from Montana, had told his old friend that not only was the Senate uninterested in the Frazier amendment, it was also uninterested in the largely symbolic Kellogg-Briand Pact, though all but one senator had voted for it. Jeannette then traveled to Columbus, Georgia, to ask the Georgia state legislature to send a memorial to Georgia's two senators in support for the Frazier amendment. While the Georgia legislators also were polite, they, too, adamantly opposed the amendment. In fact as a result of Jeannette's overture, the legislature adopted a resolution condemning the Frazier amendment and asking Congress to resist "every effort to abridge or qualify the right of America to defend herself in time of national stress."

It did not take Jeannette long to decide that the Frazier amendment was too utopian. She thought the WPU was working at the wrong level; they should start developing peace sentiment at the grass roots. But the WPU, knowing Jeannette's habit of making her own decisions, had made her sign an agreement to do nothing but work for the Frazier amendment. So for six months, she compiled material and wrote speeches, interviewed twenty-two senators and fifty representatives, and went out on lecture tours.

She then went to work for the Washington, D.C., based National Council for the Prevention of War (NCPW), a middle-of-the-road organization that brought together several dozen participating societies of national scope: church groups, women's clubs, educational associations, a few farm and labor groups, even the Veterans of Foreign Wars. At first, at least, NCPW director Frederick J. Libby was delighted with Jeannette. He remembered her hiring in his memoir, *To End War* (1969), as a "a giant stride forward. The Hon. Jeannette Rankin, famous as the first congresswoman . . . headed the [legislative] department. Brilliant, dynamic, temperamental, she was loved and honored by her former colleagues in Congress." But Jeannette's relationship with Libby, though it lasted ten years, was never easy. While Libby hired excellent staff, he expected teamwork under his direction, and Jeannette, of course, liked to run her own show. Libby, for his part, said he had a "Quaker concern," a "strong conviction that God had shown me how we could prevent America's involvement in another war." This mandate from God made him hard to work with.

A former congregational minister turned Quaker, Libby had founded NCPW single-handedly and raised nearly all of the organization's money himself, soliciting donations from participating organizations and wealthy individuals. In good times NCPW had had a budget of more than a hundred thousand dollars a year, but by the time Libby hired Jeannette, the stock market crash of 1929 had hurt NCPW's finances. Although Jeannette's salary was a nominal $150 a month, at the time of her hire NCPW had no money, so she worked for expenses. Later, as the Depression worsened, she even paid her own expenses. She worked for NCPW for ten years, part of the time with the Georgia Peace Society, much of the time lobbying Congress, and often on the lecture trail.

Her Georgia work was an interesting and ultimately frustrating experiment in grass roots organizing. In Georgia Jeannette wore two hats, one as a field worker for the NCPW and the other as secretary of the Georgia Peace Society, a group she had organized in 1928 with thirty-five members of the University of Georgia faculty. The group sponsored several conferences on the "Cause and Cure of War" and passed out peace propaganda at state fairs. It was well received for several years, the main newspaper of the district, the Macon *Telegraph*, commenting approvingly on its activities.

As long as the Georgia Peace Society thought of itself as a study group and confined itself to innocuous efforts such as holding conferences, the "respectable" part of the community accepted it. But Jeannette wanted action, particularly because, by happenstance, in this case, local action could have larger ramifications. The United States representative from Jeannette's district was Carl Vinson, ranking member of the House Naval Affairs Committee, and after 1933, its chairman. He was a great advocate of heavy military expenditures and an enlarged navy. Jeannette hoped Vinson could be convinced to change his position—or be replaced by someone less bellicose.

With this goal, even before taking the position with NCPW, Jeannette had entered Georgia politics. She worked from her house, with no telephone, no secretary. She paid for her own gas and stamps. Her first move was to build peace sentiment in the district, and in 1930, while simultaneously working for NCPW, she toured it, driving 250 miles and making thirty-one calls, visiting newspapers, ministers, everyone she could think of. She even lunched with Carl Vinson, who had no illusions: "What you are doing is getting a lot of these people [stirred up] so they will write . . . next winter when the Navy bills come up."

Vinson planned to introduce a $616 million naval building program, which Jeannette naturally opposed. She argued that there was no proof of necessity for such a large expenditure, that it violated the agreements of the London Naval Conference of the year before, and that it cost too much money considering the poverty of the United States Treasury. She organized a postcard campaign against it, which generated some opposition—159 postcards from sixty-two different towns in the district. The Macon *Telegraph* said, "It is absurd for a nation with a tremendous deficit to go spending money on 'shooting irons' when it will have to buy bread for a great many of its family." Vinson seemed to heed the opposition in his district, and the bill was not reported out of committee.

When the Democrats came into power in 1933, however, and Vinson became chairman of the committee, he was one of the strongest militarists in Congress. In 1934 his bill for a greatly enlarged Navy became law. Jeannette immediately began plans to defeat him in the Democratic primary in 1936. (In the solidly Democratic state of Georgia, winning the Democratic primary was tantamount to winning the election.) In summer 1934 she organized the district precinct by precinct with a member of the Peace Society in charge of each. She had booths at county fairs, children's parades, bands, and trucks with sound systems. She passed out literature and mailed letters. It was the suffrage campaign system all over again.

Some of the propaganda probably offended people. Banners proclaimed: "Join the Navy and See the Next War" and "We Want War," (three clowns with profits spilling out of voluminous pockets). A children's banner read "War Will Make Us Lame, Blind, Orphans, Armless, and Humpbacked." And Jeannette may not have been the best messenger—although she was the only one available—for although she felt at home, her western accent and manners and Montana license plates branded her a carpetbagger. Still, she proceeded with her work relatively unhindered until late fall 1934, when she gave two peace lectures at Brenau College, a small, expensive women's college in Gainesville, Georgia.

In introducing her talk at Brenau, H. J. Pearce, Jr., vice president of the college, professor of history, and son of the college president, said he wished Brenau could establish a "Chair of Peace," to which he would nominate Jeannette Rankin as the first recipient. Pearce's generous introduction was misinterpreted, and the suggestion of a peace chair created a furor. The Atlanta post of the American Legion protested and passed a widely publicized resolution opposing Jeannette's appointment to a "Chair of Peace." "Pacifists [were] closely akin to communists," they proclaimed, and "no good could come . . . [from allowing Jeannette] to preach un-American doctrines to the young womanhood of the South."

Vociferous attacks on her character and politics—and continuing allegations of communist sympathies—continued for another year; Jeannette remembered the assault as the worst experience of her life. Personal attacks were not uncommon in a reformer's life, and Jeannette was not the only person with unpopular opinions to be accused of communism in the 1920s and 1930s. In fact the 1920s saw the development of a full-blown "red scare," and almost every reformer Jeannette admired, from Jane Addams to Fiorello LaGuardia, was accused of sedition during this period.

One source of misinformation was the four-volume Lusk report, published by the New York State legislature under the title *Revolutionary Radicalism* (1924), which claimed to expose subversives. Fear of a communist revolution only increased with the advent of the Great Depression and the concomitant rise of militant trade unionism. The year 1934 saw the publication of the influential *Red Network: A Who's Who and Handbook of Radicalism for Patriots,* by Elizabeth Dilling. An antiradical diatribe, *The Red Network* listed "460 Communist, Radical, Pacifist, Anarchist, Socialist, I.W.W. controlled organizations" and their 1,300 leading members. Jeannette was listed as "nat. com. ACLU; nat. comm. Berger Nat. Found.; assoc. sec. N.C. for P.W.; Wom. Peace Union 1929; lobbyist against National Defense legislation; her People's Coun. affiliation exposed in Lusk Report."

The description of Jeannette was rather short and mild compared to some. The four most dangerous people in the world, according to Dilling, were Gandhi, the nonviolent worker for Indian independence; Glenn Frank, the mildly liberal president of the University of Wisconsin; Jane Addams, who had received the Nobel Peace Prize in 1931; and Albert Einstein. She objected to Einstein on three counts: his pacifism; his daughter's marriage to a Russian; and the absurdity of his unintelligible theory of relativity. Jeannette's friends Burton K. Wheeler of Montana, William E. Borah of Idaho, and Fiorello LaGuardia of New York were also listed.

In its campaign against Jeannette Rankin, the American Legion distributed copies of *The Red Network*'s description of Jeannette across Georgia. Trying to counteract its effect, Jeannette issued a statement clarifying her affiliations. She was an honorary member of the American Civil Liberties Union (she had been a founding member) and a member of the national committee, but took no active role in it, mostly because she was rarely in New York. It was not a "communistic" organization but defended the right of free speech, free press, and free assembly. Its director was not a Communist, and one of the names on its letterhead, along with hers, was that of a dean of the University of Georgia.

She was unaware that any Communists were connected with NCPW or its thirty participating organizations, mostly church groups. She denied telling high school audiences that they should be ashamed to wear the uniform of the United States although she did object to high school Reserve Officers Training Corps. Her sole connection to the Victor Berger Fund was that she had made a five-dollar donation. (A socialist, Berger had won election to Congress in 1918 from Wisconsin. Congress refused to seat him because of his socialist affiliation. His district had reelected him, and Congress again refused to recognize him.) The college trust-ees accepted Jeannette's statement—though she was to do no more lecturing—and Vice President Pearce said it was only because he and his two brothers were members of the American Legion and the national commander was a friend of his that he was forgiven.

In the meantime the Georgia newspapers, particularly the Macon *Telegraph*, which previously had been friendly to Jeannette and the Peace Society, and the Macon *Evening News*, kept snip-ing. An editorial on the Brenau controversy, for example, was titled "Enough of Jeannette." The newspaper attacks came to a head in October 1935 while Jeannette was attending meetings of the Georgia Peace Society in Sandersville, in Vinson's district, to organize for Vinson's defeat. Attendance at the meeting was very low, and later she discovered that anonymous letters in Ameri-can Legion envelopes, attacking her as a Communist, had been sent to Sandersville residents.

While the meeting was in progress, the Macon *Evening News* ran an October 10 column by "Veterans Corner" reporter Bill Janes titled "Up Pops the Devil." He wrote that attendance at Jeannette's peace meetings would come to nothing when people found out what she stood for, and she would have to move on. He continued, "Jeannette Rankin was branded in the courts of Atlanta as being a rank Communist and was accused of belong-ing to several such organizations. She was fired from the faculty of one of the South's finest schools, Brenau, for forming a so-called Chair of Peace, and advocating Communistic ideas in our schools." On her return to her boardinghouse in the late after-noon after the meeting, Jeannette picked up the afternoon pa-per, saw the article, and, horrified, showed it to her landlady. "Look what they're saying about me," she said. "Well, isn't it true?" her landlady responded.

Devastated, Jeannette decided to sue to clear her name. While other reformers may have learned to ignore vituperative attacks, Jeannette never had. Besides, she reasoned, if people believed these things about her, her effectiveness in Georgia would be reduced to nothing. The timing was particularly bad because it undercut Jeannette's ability to organize a challenge to Vinson in the Democratic primary eleven months away. Although the ACLU advised against the suit, and Wellington thought the issue unimportant, Jeannette was determined to pursue it. Finally the ACLU agreed to advance five hundred dollars, and she filed in April 1936 against William Janes and the Macon *Evening News,* asking for fifty thousand dollars in damages.

Meanwhile, she continued to try to organize a campaign to defeat Carl Vinson for the Democratic nomination. It was impossible. Two prospective candidates declined to run against him, because of lack of finances, they said. The young man who finally agreed to run made his decision too late to certify, and he had to pursue a write-in campaign. Students from Duke University Emergency Peace Action came to help, but they lacked transportation. In September 1936 the Democratic Party renominated Vinson with thirty thousand votes, ten thousand more than he had received in 1934. Jeannette reflected that her campaign had actually helped him. Trying to arouse people from apathy, she had only "aroused her enemies." As for her lawsuit, it did no good at all. It was nominally settled in her favor (the paper paid her a thousand dollars and court costs and printed a retraction), but not until November, seven months after she filed it and three months after the Democratic primary.

At the same time Jeannette had been unsuccessfully organizing in Georgia, she was also spending considerable time on the lecture circuit as part of her work for NCPW. This work was scarcely less frustrating. She would work in a city for three days, speak at five organizations' meetings, interview a dozen people, get some publicity in the newspapers, and then go on to the next city. For instance in two days in Seattle in 1932 she spoke at an American Association of University Women luncheon, at a tea at the Young Women's Christian Association, at a public dinner, and another luncheon.

NCPW sent out thousands of leaflets, picturing Jeannette looking quite elegant in a sleeveless black evening gown, with pearls, and a (borrowed?) fur cape thrown over a chair. During World War I, the pamphlet said, "the sorrow and tragedy of many homes burnt their way into her soul. . . . Miss Rankin will be glad to confer with local leaders on organization and action for peace promotion. She is an expert organizer." Although she did it superbly, Jeannette believed lecturing to be unproductive; it was preaching to the already converted, "talking to yourself," she called it.

She spent the summers of 1931 and 1937 in Europe, studying depressed conditions and rising militarism in Germany, social experimentation in Sweden, and British attempts to avert the war. Libby, proud of the extended travels of his youth, could often find money to send staff to Europe when he could not pay salaries. While Jeannette was in Europe in 1931, Japan invaded Manchuria without declaration of war and in obvious contravention of the Kellogg-Briand Pact that Japan had signed three years before. The next few years would prove Wheeler's remark, that nations considered the pact a scrap of paper.

More fulfilling to Jeannette was direct political organizing and lobbying. In 1932 Jeannette organized a motorcade to Chicago where both the Republican and Democratic parties were holding political conventions. Composed of young women and college students, the automobile parades stopped along the way to gather more adherents and drove into Chicago with banners flying. Both parties gave lip service to peace, endorsing the World Court and international reduction of arms. Indeed, in spite of military flourishes across the oceans, there was growing peace sentiment in the United States. An influential book was H. G. Englebrecht and T. C. Haniger's *Merchants of Death*, first published in 1934, which blamed war on munitions makers and other industrialists that profited from it. Jeannette always believed profit to be the main cause of war. The Senate appointed the Nye Munitions Investigating Committee to investigate the charges. Jeannette helped develop material for the committee, worked with congressmen, and, on her lecture tours, supported the committee's findings—that weapons manufacturers indeed had profited excessively and perhaps bore partial responsibility for the United States entry into World War I.

She testified for the 1938 Ludlow amendment, which would require Congress to secure the approval of a majority of states before declaring war (excluding invasion or insurrection). She herself would have gone a step further and had the issue referred directly to the people. Whether they would decide differently from their representatives was questionable, but she believed (as she had said earlier about suffrage) that expressing themselves would make people think the issues through. She said, in those early New Deal days when little pigs were killed to bring up prices,

"They let the farmers vote on whether or not they want to kill little pigs. Why shouldn't the fathers and mothers vote on whether they want their sons killed?"

She spoke against the McSwain bill in congressional committee, which proposed to take profits out of war by establishing monetary ceilings on certain military products. She thought it well meaning but misleading. Jeannette, who characterized war as a "rich man's war fought by poor men," thought it possible to take the profits out of war, but not by any scheme proposed by rich men. Her idea was that once war was declared, Congress should create a new medium of exchange—fiat money—good only for the duration of the war. At the end it would be worthless, so no long-term profits could be made. She also suggested that everyone should be paid thirty dollars a month (a private's pay), beginning with the president and Congress. "But Congressmen," she said, "should be especially honored by being allowed to carry the flag in battle."

She suggested combining the Departments of the Army and the Navy (as they eventually were) with defense the only goal. She published a detailed discussion of the inefficiencies of the army and navy in *Congressional Digest*. She said the United States could not afford naval expansion when school budgets were being cut; the country had not recovered from the Depression. Nor did it need to expand its navy; planes and artillery could protect the shores of the United States. A navy was needed only to carry war to foreign shores. "My idea of defense is the kind we have between the United States and Canada, but if anyone is afraid and wants defense, then it is perfectly all right to let them have defense until we get them to the place where they are not afraid."

One of her few successes was a limited one; she played a role in the passage of neutrality legislation, spearheaded by her friends Senator Gerald Nye of North Dakota and Representative Maury Maverick of Texas. The bill prohibited the sale of munitions and extension of credit to belligerents and forbade American citizens to travel in war zones or on vessels of belligerent countries. Jeannette and the NCPW opposed the provision giving the president power to invoke the legislation at his discretion but otherwise thought it a good bill. Similar legislation had passed the Senate, but in the House it was tied up in the Foreign Affairs Committee. Jeannette, however, saw a chance to get it reported out. She was in the office of the chairman, with a number of representatives, and she suggested that if they put some limitation on the bill, say six months, it might be reported out. Her suggestion was adopted, the bill sent to the House within the hour, and the House accepted it by a voice vote. This temporary measure was to be renewed in 1936 and, again, with even stronger provisions in 1937. It was not the bill Jeannette wanted, but it was a step.

Hoping to get a stronger bill passed in 1936, Jeannette decided to make a speaking tour in eastern Tennessee, the district of Sam McReynolds, chairman of the Senate Foreign Affairs Committee, not to defeat him, but to influence public opinion in his district. It was Jeannette's old technique of carrying the issue to the grass roots. Despite an early snowstorm in the Appalachians, she toured all ten counties, speaking at luncheons, teas, labor meetings, business meetings, churches, women's clubs, high schools, on radio, and even at a religious revival meeting. Buttering her remarks with flattery, she told people how much influence Tennessee had in international affairs, since their Cordell Hull was secretary of state and Sam McReynolds chairman of the Foreign Affairs Committee. She thought she accomplished something because later McReynolds supported a stronger neutrality bill, which passed in 1937. It included a "cash and carry" provision for belligerent nations (this forbade loans to belligerent nations under the theory that United States bankers had pushed the country into World War I to rescue their loans to the Allies), prohibited American travel on belligerent ships, and forbade American merchant vessels to carry munitions to warring parties. These provisions, however, had to be invoked by the president, and when the time came President Roosevelt would not do so, which allowed private American ships to continue to carry arms and munitions to belligerents at their own risk. Jeannette was sorry she had not been able to get discretionary presidential powers removed from the acts.

By this time Italy was in Ethiopia, Germany and Russia were interfering in the Spanish Civil War, and Japan had resumed military operations in China. Peace societies organized a cooperative Emergency Peace Campaign in 1936, bringing in workers of all shades of opinion. They concentrated on college campuses; Jeannette's assignment was Duke University in North Carolina, where she gave a series of lectures at the Institute of International Relations on "Organizing Public Opinion."

In 1937 she spent the summer in Europe and was shocked by the rise of German militarism. On her return to the United States, she was again alarmed at the increase in war sentiment. After President Roosevelt's "Quarantine the Aggressor" speech in October 1937, in which he said the United States must oppose treaty violations and quarantine the war makers, she felt, that by insisting on naming aggressors and taking action against them, he was preparing public opinion to take sides. This was not implementation of the long-dead Kellogg-Briand Pact; rather, it was making a prospective future war into a "holy" war. In November 1938 she published an article, "Beware of Holy Wars," in *World Outlook*, a little church magazine.

She testified again on naval affairs in 1938 and 1939, asking how naval expenditures could be justified in the name of defense. How could we afford battleships when the nation still had, in the president's words, "one-third of a nation ill-fed, ill-clad, and ill-housed?" She protested fortifying Guam, because of the island's location in the Japanese power sector. She correctly foresaw that "Guam would more readily become a hostage in enemy hands than a salient in ours." Fortifying Guam would offend Japan. "Guam will not deter Japan. Why make a threat, especially when it is ineffectual?" It would be no comfort to her to be able to say, when in 1942 the Japanese occupied Guam, "I told you so."

Jeannette was spending more time in the halls of Congress and giving more serious thought to the issues than most congressmen. Drew Pearson, an internationally syndicated columnist, wrote in April 1935 that as a lobbyist Jeannette was having even more effect than as a congressman. Nevertheless, Jeannette was becoming increasingly dissatisfied with her job at NCPW. Her relationship with Libby had deteriorated; she felt he did not consult her on policy and gave her insufficient credit for her skill in congressional lobbying. Libby ran NCPW as if it belonged to him, which he believed it did. And now that military sentiment was increasing, the economy not fully recovered, funds for peace decreased. Jeannette often went unpaid. She wrote Libby:

> Am living in true Georgia fashion. No money. The stores are "furnishing" me with food and gas. They say, "It's been so long since we had any money we done got used to it." Please don't think I can get used to it. I've no doubt money is slow in coming in but if you can send me some or put me on a weekly payroll it will help a lot. It hurts my spirits so to be so broke.

By 1937 NCPW deficit was forty thousand dollars. Libby asked Jeannette to work full time at half salary; she countered with an offer to work half time at half salary. Libby should have accepted; Jeannette always worked more than full time anyway. Instead he asked her, on a six-month unpaid leave of absence, to organize a Colorado Peace Society such as she had done in Georgia. She would not. "My day for doing the spade work, as I did in Georgia, is past," she wrote.

Besides her disagreements with Libby, there was tension in the office. It was so bad that thirty years later she refused to talk about it. Clearly coworkers found Jeannette difficult to work with, in part because no one else could keep up with her. While other peace workers might take time to go to a concert or a baseball game or a movie, Jeannette tended to feel such actions betrayed a lack of dedication. If only they would all work harder, Jeannette believed, they would see some results. Some suggested if she was so dedicated she could work for nothing; they knew her brother was wealthy. Jeannette considered this an insult.

And she still had her bad temper. The final straw was a petty one, a speech written for her by the educational secretary, containing a sentence in disagreement with Jeannette's views. Jeannette asked that the sentence be taken out, but the writer refused, saying it was a balanced sentence, and the paragraph was a balanced paragraph, and the speech was a balanced speech: no doubt the entire balance would be destroyed if one sentence were eliminated. Jeannette went ahead and gave the speech and left out the sentence. There were recriminations in the office, and Jeannette was glad of the excuse to leave. She did not make a full break, however, but took on several little jobs at Libby's request. She lobbied, successfully, for retaining the existing "cash and carry" provision and testified, in 1940, to the House Naval Affairs Committee against battleship construction. Then she went to Montana to explore political possibilities there.

CHAPTER TWELVE

Again Congresswoman: Pacifist

"THE WORLD IS IN A CRISIS . . ."

IN 1939 JEANNETTE saw a political vacuum in Montana that she thought might make it possible for her to be elected again to Congress. The situation had resulted from the machinations of her old friend Senator Burton K. Wheeler to destroy political rival and Roosevelt loyalist Jerry O'Connell.

O'Connell, Democratic representative from the western First Congressional District, was a young radical such as Wheeler had been twenty years earlier. And he was a Roosevelt New Dealer through and through. Wheeler, for his part, had grown increasingly conservative and in 1937 had broken with the Roosevelt administration over Roosevelt's "court-packing" scheme. The "nine old men" on the Supreme Court had been busy nullifying the New Deal, declaring its measures one after another unconstitutional, so Roosevelt decided to appoint enough friendly justices to have his own way. Wheeler, remembering the intolerance of the World War I years, believed the courts were the bulwark of American liberties, and he led a successful fight against tampering with the judiciary. Roosevelt responded by pointedly building up O'Connell with patronage and favors while ignoring Wheeler.

Thrust to the fore, O'Connell threatened in 1937 to challenge Wheeler for the Senate in the 1940 elections. Worried that

O'Connell might make good his threat, Wheeler decided to take preventive measures. In the 1938 House election, he backed the political unknown Payne Templeton from Flathead County against O'Connell in the Democratic primary, and then, after O'Connell squeaked out a victory, threw his support to O'Connell's Republican challenger, Jacob Thorkelson, a political novice from Butte. Political pundits predicted O'Connell's victory over Thorkelson, Wheeler's consequent loss of influence, and O'Connell's succession to Wheeler's Senate seat in 1940.

It was a dirty campaign. Company newspapers would not report O'Connell's speeches but quoted those made against him. The railroad unions came out against O'Connell despite O'Connell's pro-labor record. They owed Wheeler (who chaired the Interstate Commerce Committee, which regulated the railroads) a favor. A friend of Wheeler's, Dr. Francis Townsend, progenitor of the popular Townsend Plan to stimulate the economy by giving every old person two hundred dollars a month (a precursor to Social Security), came out for Thorkelson in defiance of his own organization, the Townsend Foundation. Somehow, the Democratic state committee could not find money for O'Connell's campaign.

The Catholic Church opposed O'Connell. He had supported the loyalist regime in Spain during the Spanish Civil War; the Church—which had supported the fascists—insisted he recant, and he would not. The freedom of the Spanish working people was involved, he said; he reminded people that his Irish miner father had been shot down in Butte, striking for better conditions. The Bishop of Helena publicly criticized O'Connell for his divorce and remarriage, and in the closing days of the campaign the Catholic Church organized a pulpit and telephone campaign against him. In the face of opposition from the Church, the Company, and the Wheeler-dominated Democratic organization, O'Connell garnered 45 percent of the vote, losing the election to Thorkelson 41,319 to 49,253. Wheeler had not underestimated the political appeal of the young liberal.

Thorkelson quickly lost credibility during his time in Congress. Anti-Semitic and undiplomatic, he soon became an embarrassment to most Montanans. Best known for his diatribes against Jews and the New Deal and for his calls to revise the United States Constitution, his reelection in 1940 was unlikely. O'Connell would try to make a comeback but would have hard going. If neither Thorkelson nor

O'Connell could be elected, a political vacuum would be left that a smart politician could rush in to fill. That would be Jeannette.

Some Montanans believed Wellington "maneuvered" Jeannette into running for Congress, a forgivable misunderstanding. They had seen Wellington maneuvering all over the state and knew nothing of Jeannette's dedicated work for peace elsewhere. In fact close as she was to her brother, Jeannette went her own way. For instance, she twitted him a good deal when he became a Christian Scientist. She encouraged their sister Edna to work in the birth control movement while Wellington, embarrassed by Edna's activities, insisted that she leave the state. They held widely divergent economic philosophies. While Wellington was getting rich buying up ranches as they went on the market during the Depression, Jeannette had been living in self-imposed poverty in Georgia. Wellington was becoming more conservative, Jeannette more radical. It was about this time that she began to talk of the "stupid money system."

Few people lived through the Depression without being changed in some way. Looking at the situation through humanitarian eyes, Jeannette began to wonder seriously about the economic system. She looked into all the panaceas offered to cure the Depression and wrote to most of their proponents. Dr. Francis Townsend, a California physician, attracted millions of followers by advocating for old-age pensions. Novelist and social crusader Upton Sinclair promoted the creation of large state-run alternate economies based on the barter system. Technocrats wanted to do away with money altogether and turn the economy and government over to technological experts, who would run it scientifically. Louisiana politician Huey Long wanted to "make every man a king" by limiting the amount of money any one family could have and guaranteeing every family a minimum income. The Communist Party advocated for the ultimate overthrow of capitalism and the creation of a classless society. Fascist groups, European and American, argued the Depression had been brought on by international bankers, whom, they said, were Jews. There was not only hunger but also hate in the land.

In investigating options to the free-market economy, Jeannette encountered the theories of economist William T. Foster, who had called for public enterprise with steep taxes on profits and inheritances. He wanted government guarantees of bank deposits, regulation of the security market, unemployment and health insurance. "If anyone still doubts that our economic difficulties are mainly mental, let him consider what would happen if the United States would declare war today. Billions of dollars would be poured into the economy. . . . Some day," he continued, "we shall realize that if money is available for blood-and-bullets war, just as much money is available for a food-and-famine war."

Then the wars in Europe began. President Roosevelt asked Congress for a defense appropriation of more than a billion dollars in May 1940. Chairman Vinson's House Naval Affairs Committee appropriations had already accounted for nearly that much. More jobs were created than people dreamed of. Farmers grew food, sold it, bought tractors. Factories hired people, who could then afford to buy more food. The pacifist Jeannette saw it took killing to bring prosperity. Certainly there was something wrong with the "stupid money system." She would like, she wrote, to abolish the profit system, if she could think of some peaceful way to do so.

Their growing political differences testify that Jeannette was not Wellington's pawn, but she was glad to have his political advice; he was, after all, an astute political observer with good knowledge of the state. She was also glad of his financial support. She later said about her second congressional campaign: "Of course I wouldn't run if Wellington hadn't approved, because he would have to pay for it." Her opening campaign, however, sounds like her idea, not his. She began in fall 1939 by speaking at high schools. Later, when people might say, "I thought she lived in Georgia now," others would say, "Oh, no. She spoke at my son's school last fall." She did not wait to be invited; she wrote principals and told them when she would be at their school; they could hardly refuse. She spoke at fifty-two of the fifty-six high schools in the First Congressional District, a western Montana district that included Bozeman, Butte, Hamilton, Helena, Kalispell, and Missoula.

By fall 1939 the Second World War had begun, and Jeannette talked to the students about war. Russia and Germany had signed a nonaggression pact that August, Germany invaded Poland on September 1, 1939, and three days later Great Britain and France declared war on Germany. Jeannette asked the students to write to the president and congressmen, urging them to keep the United States out of the war. She encouraged them to discuss the matter with their parents before writing and asked them to write often, but not more than once a week. They laughed when she said, "Don't tell them your age. I never do."

She spoke over the radio on the same themes. American shores cannot be successfully invaded; America should not succumb to Hitlerism (by which she meant militarism). Killing young men caused permanent injury to the country in addition to the self-evident personal tragedy such loss of life entailed. She traveled around the state during the winter and spring and in June 1940 announced her candidacy for the Republican congressional nomination. Thorkelson was running for reelection, but, she told voters, she could do more for them than he. After all, she had experience on her side. She had worked with and lobbied congressmen for twenty years, so she knew the rules, and she knew the players. She won the Republican nomination by 7,299 votes to 6,214. Wheeler could not prevent the Democrats from renominating Jerry O'Connell, though the defeat Wheeler had engineered for O'Connell two years earlier had deterred O'Connell from declaring for Wheeler's seat in the Senate.

Jeannette was now sixty, lively, charming, attractively dressed, with well-kept fluffy white hair. Said the Kansas City *Star* on June 10, 1940: "Thirty years of fighting for woman's suffrage, minimum wages for women, and peace have not made her a zealot. She is vivacious with a quick, nervous speech, adjusting and readjusting her horned-rimmed spectacles, she can cram her conversation with statistics without sacrificing any of her feminine charm."

Jeannette made her usual vigorous but good-natured campaign. A typical speech was one she gave in Helena:

> The first necessity in national defense is to have loyal citizens . . . education, health, and economic security must be available. . . . Facilities for communication and transportation and modern industries to develop our resources are needed to defend our Nation against all enemies, including such enemies as ignorance, disease, and poverty.
>
> We also need a highly modernized, mechanized military defense. . . . The most tragic problem is unemployment . . . [and] an increasing number of old people fearful of their future. . . . No adjustment of our economic institutions will be satisfactory unless based on the astonishing fact that an abundance can be made available. . . . There are people in the United States who, year in and year out, never taste wheat flour products, children everywhere who

would be happier with better woolen clothes, and yet Montana farmers are not producing to their full capacity. . . . Wasting is the crime, not spending. . . . By voting for me . . . you can express your opposition to sending your son to foreign lands to fight in a foreign war, and by voting for me you will also express your determination to prepare to the absolute limit to defend this country.

Not all of the campaign was on such a high level. Some of Jeannette's campaigners took advantage of the old smears on O'Connell: he was "Communistic" and a divorced Catholic. O'Connell's partisans retaliated with statements from the Georgia American Legion charging Jeannette with Communist associations. Company newspapers ignored the campaign; to attack Jeannette would only help O'Connell.

Railroad brotherhoods specifically endorsed Jeannette, which suggests Wheeler's influence as chairman of the Interstate Commerce Committee. Of course, Jeannette had always had good labor support but so had O'Connell, and his was much more recent. Prominent politicians endorsed her. Senator Robert M. LaFollette, Jr., of Wisconsin came out for her. That was another Wheeler connection; Wheeler had been the elder LaFollette's running mate in a Progressive third party try for the presidency in 1924. Senator Ernest Lundeen of Minnesota had Jeannette's Helena speech printed in the *Congressional Record*, along with many laudatory remarks of his own. Jeannette's staff mailed out thousands of reprints. Fiorello LaGuardia, now the famous mayor of New York City, wrote in a letter published in the *Montana Standard* on November 3, 1940: "[Jeannette Rankin] has the training, experience and understanding to intelligently serve the people of Montana . . . I know of no one who has kept in closer touch with economic, social, and political conditions in this country. . . . This woman has more courage and packs a harder punch than a regiment of regular line politicians." Even Norman Thomas, Socialist candidate for president, endorsed her, saying he was willing to forgive her connection with the Republican Party. Her staff thought it wiser not to use his letter publicly.

On Election Day, Jeannette won a stunning victory, garnering 56,616 votes, over nine thousand votes more than O'Connell's 47,352. As in 1916 Jeannette had achieved a Republican victory in a Democratic district and a Democratic year. Burton K. Wheeler, who

Jeannette poses in front of Wellington's home at Avalanche Ranch, forty miles east of Helena, in 1941, during her second term in the House.

had unquestionably helped her to victory, was himself reelected by a large margin. O'Connell's political career was ended. Jeannette was pleased but calm. "No one will pay any attention to me this time," she said. "There is nothing unusual about a woman being elected." In 1940 six women sat in the House and two in the Senate.

But there was much congratulation. Margaret Hinchley, the red-haired laundry worker and suffragist, wrote from New York. Ruth Hanna McCormick Simms wrote as well; the Ohio political boss's daughter had never lost her taste for politics. She, too, had had a term in the House as a representative from Illinois. A letter even came from Eugene Talmadge, Governor of Georgia, though he spelled her name "Janett."

A luncheon honoring both Jeannette Rankin and Burton K. Wheeler's wife, Lulu, was held at the Butte Country Club on November 14, 1940. One hundred fifty women attended the nonpartisan affair arranged by Jeannette's old friend and mentor, the veteran newspaperwoman and Democrat, Mary O'Neill, now eighty years old. O'Neill must have found the occasion a great pleasure. The meal was a fine one; Butte insisted on good food. Probably there were no cocktails; though prohibition had been repealed it was not the custom in Montana to have cocktails at ladies' luncheons. The women wore their best clothes, dark, mannishly tailored suits with colorful blouses, small-brimmed hats, gloves. Their gored skirts, wide enough at the hem for comfortable walking, covered the knees.

Lulu Wheeler spoke of her recent decision to join the America First Committee, a group that believed America must protect itself by building a strong defense before sending arms to other countries. Senator Wheeler, she said, frequently spoke at their meetings. Jeannette spoke on "The New Challenge to Women." The November 15, 1940, *Montana Standard* reported her speech:

> She said that every woman's first responsibility rests in producing and conserving life, not in destroying it in warfare. 'The world is in a crisis and every woman must select essential things to do, and do them immediately,' she said. 'If you have a sick baby, that baby must be nursed to health. . . . This is no time for anything except essentials. The essentials are life, liberty, and democracy. Women can do much in every-day life to safeguard these essentials. Women have a great power in America, through suffrage, and they can use that power for good.'

So Montanans had no doubt as to the stands of their recently elected officials. Both Representative Rankin and Senator Wheeler had strongly expressed themselves frequently and publicly as opposed to intervention in the European war. Both had been overwhelmingly elected.

Jeannette and the rest of the family then went to Wellington's ranch in Avalanche Gulch, east of Helena, to celebrate. There were snowstorms, and the thermometer plummeted to twelve below. Jeannette planned to drive to Washington, D.C., with her mother, so they went to Missoula to prepare for the journey. Reporting later to a friend about her trip, she wrote: "when the weather seemed to be clearing we decided it would be better to go on to Washington before it was too cold. It was a great mistake. We should have stayed in Montana, for every night there was a fresh snowstorm."

The two women, ages sixty and eighty-seven, drove through snowstorms in Montana, North Dakota, and Minnesota. The storms grew worse and the roads became impassable. They put the car on the train at Minneapolis and took the train themselves. They picked up the car in Pittsburgh, drove on to the small apartment at 2220 Twentieth Street in Washington, and settled in. Sister Edna McKinnon and her daughter Dorothy, age twenty, came for Christmas. Though Jeannette had a cold, there was lots of fun and laughter. It was a very merry Christmas despite the specter of war, yet the events in Europe, Africa, and Asia remained at the foremost of everybody's mind, and old friends had already begun to lobby Jeannette to vote for war when the time came.

One such, Maury Maverick, now mayor of San Antonio, wrote Jeannette shortly after her election: "God bless you and save you, oh me, oh my." They were old friends and had worked together on neutrality legislation six years earlier, he as congressman and she as lobbyist. Though Maverick had worked hard to prevent American involvement in the European war, he had agonizingly changed his position. He was delighted to see his old friend in Congress but apprehensive that she might destroy herself by voting against intervention. His letter continued:

> Only one thing I want to say: as a soldier of the last war I admired you for voting against war. I have not become old and rickety and crazy. I have lately done a lot of praying, meditation, and thinking. Honest Jeannette. And I have come to this conclusion: THE SITUATION IS ENTIRELY DIFFERENT. We may have to go to war and if we do let us go aggressively, let us fight it hard, let us win it—and if you have to, VOTE FOR WAR. No, Jeannette, I have not gone crazy. Germany IS a menace. This time Germany has a chance to conquer the world. . . . Whatever you do I'll always love you and I'll never bulldoze you or say anything mean . . . but don't stick to your ideas because you've had them since the last war. This situation IS different, I tell you.

Though Maverick's apprehensions were well founded, Jeannette still hoped war could be averted. Noninterventionist sentiment was strong, particularly in the West and Midwest. Many Americans felt cheated because their allies of the last war had not paid their debts. Some thought bankers and munitions makers had gotten the United States into the first war and that people had been victims of a confidence game by official propagandists.

A new wealthy noninterventionist organization, the America First Committee, founded in 1940, had supplanted the old poverty-stricken leftist and church-related peace groups. America Firsters tended to be rich, reactionary Republicans—Roosevelt haters, whose original motivation was their objection to New Deal domestic policies. Some were pro-fascist and anti-Semitic. Some, like Senator Burton K. Wheeler and his wife Lulu, were motivated by sincere opposition to intervention. But the reactionary cast of the America Firsters made the whole movement suspect to many liberals who might otherwise have been sympathetic. Jeannette never belonged to the America First Committee though she did address some of its meetings and had friends who were actively involved. Jeannette's old suffragist friend former congresswoman Ruth Hanna McCormick Simms was one of the America First Committee's large contributors.

Despite agitation by members of the American First Committee and liberal peace groups, the war was coming inexorably closer. On January 6, 1941, President Roosevelt recommended lend-lease of supplies to Britain and her allies and declared the right of people around the world to the "Four Freedoms": freedom of speech, freedom of worship, freedom from want, and freedom from fear. He submitted to Congress a $17 billion budget, of which $11 billion was for defense. Speaking of America as the "arsenal of democracy," Roosevelt explained that the Lend-Lease Act would authorize him to exchange munitions and military information with any country whose defense he deemed vital to the United States.

Wheeler called Lend-Lease "the New Deal's Triple A foreign policy, it would plow under every fourth American boy." Jeannette opposed it as one step closer to war. She would support unlimited expenditures for defense in the Western Hemisphere, but she was opposed to sending men to Europe to settle boundary and commercial disputes of the Old World. She felt Congress had abdicated its responsibility when it passed Lend-Lease legislation because the act gave the president power to exchange munitions and military information with other countries without congressional authorization. She did not believe the president should unilaterally be able to define the United States' vital interests. Twenty-five years later she believed her position was vindicated when Congress once again abdicated its responsibility by passing the ill-advised Gulf of Tonkin Resolution. That resolution—a response to alleged attacks on American destroyers by the North Vietnamese—authorized President Lyndon Johnson to "take all necessary measures . . . to prevent further aggression" and gave the president power independent of Congress to escalate United States involvement in the ultimately hugely unpopular Vietnam War.

When the Lend-Lease Act came before the House, Jeannette offered the following amendment: "Nothing in this act shall be construed to authorize or permit the President to order, transfer, exchange, lease, lend, or employ any soldier, sailor, marine, or aircraft pilot outside the territorial waters of the Western Hemisphere without specific authorization of the Congress of the United States." In support of her amendment she gave a major speech in February 1941 to the House: "The propaganda [in 1917] was exactly the same as the propaganda today: We had to aid England or we would be attacked; the Germans would be over here. We were told that if we would vote promptly and unanimously for war, Germany would fall. We were told that if we would vote for war no soldier would cross the ocean. . . . If Britain needs our material today, will she later need our men . . . ?" Though everyone knew the bill would pass unamended, she had some articulate support, including from her House colleague, Democrat James F. O'Connor of Montana's Second District. O'Connor noted in a passionate speech: "Every member of this Congress ran on a platform of stating that they would not vote to send our boys to fight on foreign soils anywhere; the President practically so stated." Nevertheless, the amendment failed by a vote of 82 to 137.

A few months later, on June 6, 1941, Jeannette had a little fun introducing a similar amendment to the 1942 Military Appropriations bill. It was a joke because she used the exact words of the 1940 Democratic platform: "That no appropriation in this act . . . shall be used to send our army or air forces to fight in foreign lands outside of the Americas and our insular possessions except in case of attack." This, too, failed to pass.

Month by month the tension increased. In March 1941—in another preparatory step toward war—Roosevelt created the National Defense Mediation Board to cope with strikes in defense industries. The board, which consisted of four union representatives, four employer representatives, and three from the federal government, was charged with trying to settle union disputes in businesses with defense contracts; at least labor would not be treated as cavalierly as it had been during World War I. That same month Congress authorized $7 billion to carry out the Lend-Lease Act. At the end of March, the Coast Guard took sixty-five Italian, German, and Danish ships lying in American harbors into "protective custody" after reports that German and Italian seamen had been ordered to sabotage and disable the vessels.

In April Germany invaded Yugoslavia. The United States arranged for air bases in Greenland. The Office of Price Administration was created. In May the United States took into protective custody French ships in American harbors. The Germans sank an American merchant vessel. Roosevelt proclaimed an "unlimited national emergency." The Office of Civil Defense was created, with Mayor LaGuardia as director. Jeannette took the occasion of Mother's Day to make another speech in the House. "There is a great deal of sentiment about mothers and wanting to give mothers what they wish. There is nothing in the world the mothers of this country would like on this Mother's Day so much as assurance that their sons are not going to war." (Applause)

In June Congress passed the Ship Requisition Act, which allowed the Coast Guard to seize for the war effort vessels that had sought safe haven in American harbors, and Roosevelt froze Axis funds in America. Germany invaded Russia, violating their non-aggression pact. In July Japanese assets were frozen, and Japan bombed an American gunboat at Chungking. In August the export of aviation oil to Japan was banned. Several United States ships were torpedoed by Germany. Selective service was extended to eighteen months. President Roosevelt and British prime minister Winston Churchill met at sea. In September Roosevelt pledged every effort to defeat Germany and ordered the navy to "shoot on sight" in American defense waters. In October Lend-Lease of $1 billion was offered to Russia.

In November Ambassador to Japan Joseph C. Grew warned of a sudden possible attack by Japan. Secretary of State Cordell Hull said relations were critical. Japan sent a special envoy to Washington and began prolonged negotiations with the state department. Jeannette said on the floor of the House: "I commend patience to them. If their talks serve to put off or avert a war, I hope they go on tirelessly. Here is an occasion for the much-derided diplomatic tea sipping and cake pushing to vindicate itself." Then, on December 7, 1941, Japanese bombers made a surprise attack on Pearl Harbor, destroying 25 percent of the capacity of the American fleet.

Jeannette and her sister Edna heard the news of the bombing on the radio Sunday evening. Jeannette had a speaking engagement in Detroit, and she took the train with a heavy heart. But on the way she heard that President Roosevelt would address a Joint Session of Congress at noon on Monday. She reversed her direction at Pittsburgh and returned to Washington during the night. Wellington phoned, asking her not to vote against the war; she had sufficient reason, he said, since the nation had been attacked. The phone rang again and again. Visitors arrived. To escape them Jeannette got in her car and drove through the Washington streets alone in turmoil and anguish, "driving to my execution," she remembered it. She arrived at the Capitol in time for the session, heard Roosevelt describe the "day that will live in infamy," the "stab in the back," and ask for a declaration of war. Jeannette tried to be heard during the short discussion, but Speaker Sam Rayburn refused to hear her ("and I have a voice that carries," Jeannette later said bitterly). Finally he ruled her out of order. When the roll call came, Jeannette cast her vote in one word, "No."

The House vote was 388 Yes, 41 not voting, 1 No. There were no "No" votes in the Senate. Senator Wheeler was unavoidably absent, said a colleague, but "if present he would vote Yes." As the session ended reporters and others pressed around Jeannette. There were hisses and boos. A group of young army officers loudly condemned her, and Jeannette told them they had been drinking. She called for help from a convenient phone, and police arrived to escort her to her office. Immediately she prepared a statement for Montana papers:

> While I believed, with the other members of the House, that the stories which had come over the radio were probably true, still I believed that such a momentous vote—one which would mean

peace or war for our country—should be based on more au-
thentic evidence than the radio reports now at hand.

Sending our boys to the Orient will not protect this Country.

We are all for every measure which will mean defense of our
land, but taking our army and navy across thousands of miles of
ocean to fight and die certainly cannot come under the heading
of protecting our shores. . . .

It may be that it is right for us to enter the conflict with Japan.
If so, it is my belief that all the facts . . . should be given to the
Congress and the American people. So in casting my vote today,
I voted my convictions and redeemed my campaign pledges.

She also wrote a paragraph as a reply to letters she knew she
would receive: "In the confusion of the war vote, many people
lost sight of the fact that an actual Declaration of War wasn't
needed to defend ourselves and to protect the Philippines and
other possessions from an enemy who had attacked us. A Declaration of War was required [only] to send men to die in Europe,
Africa, and the Far East." In other words, she reminded them,
she had never been opposed to defense, and the president had
authority to order troops to defend us in our own territory. For
that the approval of Congress was not needed.

Reaction to Jeannette's vote, in Montana and the nation, was
strong and hostile. Wellington wired: "Montana is 100 per cent
against you." The chairman of the Montana Republican Party
called on her to reverse the vote "to redeem Montana's honor
and loyalty." Many telegrams were vituperative, some obscene.
They called her "bitch," "old fossil," "Hitler aid," "disgrace and a
traitor." Some old suffragist colleagues wired that they were
ashamed to be women after her vote, that the best thing she could
do would be to get a job as a maid. One man wrote that all she
was fit for was an "undertaker's assistant, for women only." Another correspondent pointed out that she could have been absent, "like foxy Wheeler." Radio commentators spoke of her in
such scurrilous terms that prudent station managers often interrupted them with music.

Friends, however, rallied around and called at her apartment
the evening after the vote. So stricken that she could hardly speak,
she said, "I have nothing left but my integrity." Other letters
poured in expressing admiration of her courage. A few even
agreed; Montana was not quite 100 percent against her. Old friend

Mary O'Neill wrote a long letter of encouragement, and Belle Fligelman Winestine wrote that she had heard many words of approval. Even Wellington, his secretary wrote Jeannette only three days after the vote, was not "disturbed" any more; Jeannette had done the only thing she could do, he said, and she would be admired for it.

Other expressions of approval came from all over the United States. Roger Baldwin of the American Civil Liberties Union, wrote: "Integrity is a virtue in public life rare enough in a crisis to command admiration even among your opponents. You could only do what you did—and your act is heartening to all who cherish fidelity to principle and ideals." Fiorello LaGuardia wired, "With all your faults I love you still." The famous pro-war editor William Allen White, who had organized the Committee to Defend America by Aiding the Allies, wrote on December 10, 1941, in his Emporia, Kansas, *Gazette*:

> Well—look at Jeannette Rankin. Probably a hundred men in Congress would like to do what she did. Not one of them had the courage to do it.
> The *Gazette* entirely disagrees with the wisdom of her position.
> But, Lord, it was a brave thing: and its bravery somehow discounts its folly. When in a hundred years from now, courage, sheer courage based upon moral indignation is celebrated in this country, the name of Jeannette Rankin, who stood firm in folly for her faith, will be written in monumental bronze, not for what she did but for the way she did it.

People still puzzle as to why Jeannette put herself through the torture of that vote. She accomplished nothing, as she knew she would not; she ruined her political career, as she knew she would. And there did seem to be some differences, as Maury Maverick had written, between this war and the last, the issues, for instance, of Nazi persecution and the Japanese attack on Pearl Harbor. But, as she later explained many times, her opposition to the war had nothing to do with the issues but with the method. War never settled issues. As to her personal sacrifice, she knew it was nothing compared to the sacrifices demanded by war, which would leave people dead, lands ravaged, and economies ruined. Possibly, she believed, her vote might accomplish something; perhaps in some future crisis her vote would strengthen someone's courage. But even if it did not, even if her name would never be written "in monumental bronze," she was glad she stood firm. As a popular movie of the time, *Mr. Smith Goes to Washington,* had it, "Lost causes are the only ones worth fighting for."

Having cast her courageous vote, Jeannette had to wait out her term for a year with little to do. Her influence had been discredited, and the kind of constructive legislation with which she would ordinarily concern herself had no place in wartime. She opposed extension of civil service retirement benefits to the president and Congress. She believed that not until all citizens had retirement benefits should their elected representatives provide them for themselves. The Camas, Montana, *Hot Springs Exchange,* applauded her vote in a February 19, 1942, editorial: "We've got to hand it to Jeannette. She made us awfully mad a few months back . . . and hurt herself politically. . . . Still you must give her her just dues. . . . Now she has come out and has presented a bill for the repeal of the 'Grab Act.' She deserves a big hand."

She looked into the possibilities of obtaining war contracts for small businesses. She voted "Present" to applause on the resolution declaring war on Germany and Italy; it was, as she said, a mere technicality in a war already being pursued. She had an interesting colloquy with Secretary of the Interior Harold L. Ickes on the subject of public power. At a hearing of the Committee on Public Lands she argued that the sale of surplus power to private corporations defeated the purpose of the Tennessee Valley Authority: to assure that power generated by public resources was used for the public good. Why should a public agency sell its power to war profiteers?

"A war profiteer?" said Ickes. "Your questions all contain implications that make them almost impossible to answer without seeming to agree with the implications. If you mean a sale to a war industry: yes . . . I don't think they are all war profiteers."

"Well," said Jeannette, "we have heard more about the profiteers than we have of the others."

"Sin is always more interesting than virtue," replied Ickes.

Jeannette surprised liberals with a vote to extend the Dies Committee to Investigate Un-American Activities (later better known as the House Un-American Activities Committee). Established in 1938 and chaired by Representative Martin Dies of Texas, the committee set the pattern for anti-Communist investigations and practiced the same sort of red-baiting that had been used unfairly against Jeannette in Georgia during her work in the peace movement. A Missoula correspondent wrote: "It is my conclusion after having followed the antics of the head of that committee, that it is a disgrace to the Congress of the United States, that it has never during its existence accomplished a single constructive end in searching out the un-American; that it has consistently smeared and vilified both private citizens and members of the government; that it is biased in favor of the Axis governments, whose methods it uses." Jeannette replied: "That was a very difficult vote . . . On the Dies Committee are outstanding labor leaders. Voorhis of California is most trustworthy, also Casey and Healy. The reports of the Dies Committee have been unanimous. I have no word of defense for Dies. He is an enigma to me."

Astonishingly and most satisfactorily, she was asked by the United Spanish American War Veterans to give a Memorial Day speech at a Soldiers' Home. "My first real consciousness of war came when the older boys departed for the Spanish American War," she began. It is obviously a speech she wrote herself. It reflects her language and rhythm; the copy even has her own markings to remind herself where to pause and what to emphasize. We have fought for freedom, she told them, in the Revolution for freedom from the tyranny of the Old World, in the Civil War for freedom for a race, in the Spanish American War for freedom of oppressed neighbors, in World War I for freedom from the tyranny of war itself. But still we have no freedom from tyranny in Europe, the black race has not attained economic and political freedom, the Cubans are economically dependent on the United States, the Filipinos have not been freed, the war to end war was the forerunner of the present wholesale massacre in Europe, Africa, and Asia. In peace, she said, the women and men still living must make practical the ideal of freedom for which these honored dead had died.

She refused to take the X gasoline ration card, which she was allowed as a congresswoman and which would have given her preferential treatment and extra gas. (Still, three gallons a week was not enough, she said.) She thanked Wellington for sending new plates for her car; they were not very pretty, but she supposed we must not expect pretty things in wartime. Tired of the endlessly dreary war legislation, one day Jeannette even played hooky, the first time she missed a day during the session. She stayed home and covered a chair with tan-and-rose striped material and then went up to the apartment roof garden and sat alone for a long time.

Often it was hard to sleep. She wrote family in Montana:

> I am inviting a couple of Congressmen and their wives to dinner tonight . . . I did not go to sleep until 4 a.m. so am feeling very dull and stupid and now have to have a party tonight. I set the table last night when I could not sleep—literally not figuratively. I served the dinner figuratively. I tried to get a girl to help me, but I do not know whether she is going to turn up or not, so I have to be prepared to do it myself.

And she spent some time shopping:

> As usual when I have nothing else to do I spend money on clothes. I bought an evening dress. I do not know why since I have not had one on this winter, but it was for sale and is what I have been thinking about for a very long time. . . . I saw another dress in a shop and bought it and had lots of compliments on it, so I am pretty well decked out. . . . I have been attending towel sales and am going to send you my promiscuous collection of seconds.

Friends helped; a trip to New York helped. "I had a very difficult time getting things straightened from the time of the vote until I had a vacation with Katharine [Anthony] and Elisabeth [Irwin]," she wrote. The three old friends from the suffrage movement did the New York theaters and Jeannette especially liked Noel Coward's *Blithe Spirit.* Old suffragist friend Abby Crawford Milton (the last president of the Tennessee Woman Suffrage Association) came to Washington for a few days. But Jeannette got so low one week that she peremptorily ordered a New York friend to "come tomorrow."

Fiorello LaGuardia could usually lift Jeannette's spirits, and fortunately he was often in Washington on civil defense business. One Saturday afternoon Frances Elge, Jeannette's administrative aide, was working alone in the office when she was startled to hear the door burst open and let in Jeannette and Fiorello, laughing together like children. Once he phoned and asked her to drive him to the train. "It brightened things up to have an opportunity to talk to him," she wrote. But she worried. She had never seen him looking so tired and worn; he thought the war would last years yet.

Hard blow, on her birthday, June 11, she did not hear from Gertrude McNally, who in 1917 had called Jeannette "an angel in disguise" for her assistance to the women working at the Bureau of Printing. "She has never failed me before." Jeannette could only attribute it to her antiwar vote. Toward the end of 1942, her term over, she went to Montana for Christmas, leaving secretaries to pack up the office. Before she left she took the opportunity on the first anniversary of the declaration of war to ask her fellow congressmen some pointed questions as to how America entered the conflict. And she answered them, too, expounding on her belief that the Roosevelt administration had left Japan no choice but to attack the United States by invoking economic sanctions designed to strangle Japan's economy.

> A year ago, one of my Congressional colleagues, having observed for months the adroitness with which President Roosevelt had brought us ever closer to the brink of war in the Atlantic only to be continually frustrated in the final step by a reluctant Congress, seeing fate present the President on December 7, 1941, with a magnificent moral categorical, right out of the blue—a causus belli beyond all criticism, exclaimed in despair: "What luck that man has!"

But, Jeannette asked her colleagues and the world, "Was it luck?"

CHAPTER THIRTEEN

Retirement

JEANNETTE WENT TO Montana for Christmas in 1942. She wanted to see her mother and the rest of the family and talk politics with Wellington. Olive Rankin had become ill in Washington in summer 1941, and Jeannette had had to get a series of nurses to stay with her. She even had to do much of the nursing herself and go to Congress, too, for Olive Rankin had a hard time getting along with the nurses. Finally, Edna and a nurse took Olive home to Montana; Wellington met the train with an ambulance. Olive improved somewhat, and was to live six years yet, but she became increasingly feeble and her cantankerousness and obesity made her hard to care for.

Jeannette wrote her frequent long letters from Washington, which offer some insight into the family relationships.

> I just had a letter from [sister] Grace saying you enjoyed having Janet [Kinney, Grace's daughter, a Chicago physician]. I am kind of mad at Janet because she gave you all the time and I doubt whether she is planning to give me any. I wish Hattie would come home. [Sister Hattie Rankin McGregor was living in London, where bombs were falling.] Now that we are allies with England I should think she could get transportation. I suppose you are dividing your time between the lesson [the Christian Science lesson] and Chinese checkers, going from the sublime to the ridiculous.

From Montana, where Jeannette had gone to visit and to convince her mother to accept help from a neighbor, she wrote sister Hattie: "Wellington's ranch is very beautiful; he is continually making improvements . . . there is a little doe fawn. The cook in the cookhouse feeds her with a bottle and we all play with her." But the fawn was not nearly as interesting as sister Grace's five-month-old granddaughter, who "weighed 19 pounds. Her mother is very calm and takes good care of her."

Amidst the joys and trials of family life, there was always politics. The Rankin family political fortunes were sadly declining. Wellington had just narrowly lost the senatorial election. When Jeannette had voted at the end of 1941 against the war, she realized, of course, that she could not be reelected, but she encouraged Wellington from her post in Washington to run for the Senate in 1942 against Democratic incumbent Senator James Murray. She thoroughly explored possibilities and wrote him she did not think her vote would affect him adversely because he could forthrightly say he did not agree with her vote and had advised against it. That would satisfy her critics and yet he would get a lot of votes from her own followers. The Anaconda Company would try to control the Republican nomination, but she did not believe it could. As for Murray, Democrat Burton K. Wheeler would work against him because he was a wealthy Butte man friendly to Anaconda and a Roosevelt rubber stamp.

She discussed finances with Senator John Townsend of Delaware, who assured her that funds would be forthcoming for Wellington's campaign: "I had a long conversation with him and I think I convinced him you could be elected." She discussed the matter with the eastern Montana congressman James O'Connor, a friendly Democrat, who did not believe a Republican could be elected, and anyway, that the Company would nominate its own man. "It was very depressing, but when I analyzed it, I realized we could get the vote out, and it is just a matter of getting the people in the rural areas interested in the election." She talked with Senator Wheeler, who was more friendly than ever; it was not his Senate seat they were after. She hoped Wellington would canvass the situation in the eastern district very carefully as to the possibilities of electing a Republican senator. "I believe a Republican would have a good chance." Jeannette also gave Wellington advice that a good politician should not have needed, pointing out people he should cultivate and things he should do for them. For instance, she wrote on September 22, 1941, that Joe Martin, national Republican Party chairman (she had to remind Wellington of Martin's position) was going to be in Helena; Wellington must have him to the office and out to Avalanche Ranch if possible.

Jeannette gave Wellington campaign advice:

> I know your ideas and mine on campaigning are not the same, but I am thoroughly convinced you cannot win unless you go out among the people yourself and find out how they feel. . . . If you lose, in my opinion it is going to be because you do not campaign in the way people want a campaign run. I know you will think any campaigning I do will hurt you, but I cannot deliver votes without campaigning. By campaigning I mean quietly going around and talking with my friends. Your chances to win would increase tremendously if you would meet the people. Your aloofness is your greatest handicap.

And she kept him informed on what was happening in the Senate: "You asked for points for your campaign . . . The President is now signing agreements with other countries that are, in effect, treaties [without] . . . presenting them to the Senate or to the Congress as a whole. This you may consider of no importance, but I am just making the suggestion that one of the Senate's prerogatives is endangered." So the conferences had gone on through summer 1942. Wellington, who rarely wrote his sister a letter, would telephone frequently, often talking for an hour or more. (He was even to telephone Jeannette in India in 1948 to talk politics.) Jeannette replied in closely reasoned letters.

The outcome followed her predictions pretty closely. Wellington easily won the Republican nomination but lost in the general election by only 1,212 votes out of 170,514. This, except for 1920, was the closest he had ever come to winning the Senate seat. He was not the politician she was. He was aloof, even arrogant, though, in Jeannette's words, he could "pour on the charm" when he chose. Jeannette understood people better, she knew the complex technicalities of politics as well as he, and she was trusted. It is likely Jeannette did not realize, however, the hostility many Montanans had for Wellington, whose predatory land purchases, overweening ambition, political opportunism, and willingness to switch sides on important issues to curry favoritism (a quality that decidedly distinguished him from Jeannette) offended many Montanans.

Wellington's defeat after such a close race was a hard blow and left Jeannette at a crossroads. She realized she could not be reelected; she could not even get a job in some public organization. She was too prominent to put in the back room stuffing envelopes, and her antiwar vote made it impossible to use her up front. And she was sixty-three. So she returned to Georgia to establish a new home. The old house near Bogart had burned down while she was in Washington. The cause was said to be a kerosene stove explosion in the kitchen, but no one was living there. Whatever the reason for the fire, she had to build anew. So Jeannette, who often tried to think of better ways to house the poor, decided to experiment by building an inexpensive house of rammed earth. She had forms put up for a room fourteen by twenty feet, filled the forms with red clay dug on the property, and rammed the clay down and let it dry. There was a roof of saplings covered with tarpaper. But in April 1942 she abandoned the project half completed due to lack of help. (The shell remained standing under the pines thirty years later, having survived torrential rains, the occasional hurricane, and the occasional vandal.) In 1943 she moved into a three-room sharecroppers' cabin she owned on property about six miles southeast of Bogart on Mars Hill near Watkinsville, eight miles due south of Athens. She had bought the cabin and thirty acres, paying five hundred dollars in 1935 for a friend who then had lost interest.

She named her new home Shady Grove for its trees, particularly two magnificent water oaks in front. It was a gray asphalt-shingled house, ivy-covered, set up on blocks, crudely built but sturdy, already fifty years old. Just outside the kitchen door was a well with a hand pump. (Twenty years later the City of Athens extended a water line out that road, so in her extreme old age Jeannette was to have the luxury of one cold water tap in the house.) There was electricity. In the living room was an arched stone fireplace. She had a rack made for it: an iron rod supported at each end by an A-shaped frame. She could hang the *Sunday New York Times* over it, touch a match, and have instant heat, although glowing pieces of paper sometimes went up the chimney.

She bought secondhand oil stoves, rusty and broken but sufficient, for the kitchen and bedroom. A homemade tin bathtub stood in a tiny cubbyhole off the kitchen, not far from where the teakettle boiled on the stove. This room had an airplane chemical toilet and a shelf for a washbasin. Off the bedroom was another little cubbyhole, part closet, part bathroom. It had a railroad toilet, with a pit underneath. A twenty-gallon stone jug held water to be dipped out for flushing the toilet. A corner shelf with a cloudy mirror over it was just large enough for a washbasin. On the floor was an old-fashioned electric toaster to plug in on cold mornings to warm the feet. An electric skillet was enough for what little cooking Jeannette did, and there was a tiny refrigerator. For quick hot water she had an immersion heater. Dishes were washed in an elegant Indian brass bowl.

She built an annex with a southeast exposure and two big many-paned windows looking out into the garden. She planned the annex herself and worked with her black neighbors, who helped her build it. They showed her how to make a tamped earth floor. Jeannette took one end of a two-by-six plank and a helper the other; back and forth they would go, smoothing out the dirt and tamping it down. She floored it with tarpaper and covered it with rugs bought on her many travels to India. Old overstuffed furniture, the upholstery spilling its stuffing and the springs broken, was covered with pieces of Indian and Indonesian fabrics. She had a good electric heater in this room and spent most of her time there.

Montana remained home, too. Every May she would pack her car, pick up Sam, her dachshund, and drive the three thousand miles to Montana, and every fall she would drive herself back to Georgia. In the summers she was the guest of her brother, either in Helena at the Placer Hotel, which he owned and where he lived, or in the country at Avalanche Ranch. The hotel and ranch were comfortable but not sumptuous. Rankins were not ostentatious spenders. At Avalanche there was usually someone to cook and clean though sometimes the family had to do its own work. A neighboring friend drove to Avalanche to see Jeannette, who had come to the ranch early in the summer before the rest of the family, and found her, then more than eighty, down on her knees scrubbing the floor.

Jeannette's life in her second Georgia home was distinctly different than life had been in her first Georgia home. Unlike in the 1920s and 1930s, when mother Olive, niece Dorothy, and sometimes sister Edna lived with her in Georgia, Jeannette's family almost never came to visit her new Georgia home, though she often invited them. Dorothy did leave her small children there early in the forties while she visited her husband in the armed forces, and Edna came to Georgia in 1968 when Jeannette was ill and scolded her for the way she lived. No Georgians came to Montana.

In Georgia fall after fall she planted bulbs to bloom in the spring before she left for Montana. Each spring hundreds of daffodils would bloom under the lilacs, the spirea, the pear, peach, and crabapple trees. Around the iris, the ground was carpeted with blue myrtle and violets. A redbird often sang from the top of a chinaberry tree while a mockingbird flipped himself ten feet in the air up from the top of a pine and turned a somersault, singing all the while. When flowers were blooming there would be four or five vases in every room and always a vase or two of artificial flowers, with ivy cut from the inside walls of the house. (The ivy outside found its way through numerous cracks around the windows and came inside to grow, festooning the inner walls.) "I suppose I ought to cut it out and chink up the cracks," she would say, "but it amuses me, don't you know." Looked at one way, it was an enchanted cottage; looked at another way, it was a dilapidated cabin (black sharecropper housing) with a dirt floor and no plumbing.

Jeannette dressed to fit the house. Though she knew how to dress well and did so in public, at home she often just wore her old bathrobe. This explains the conflicting stories about her clothing. The fact is, she did not care, personally. If you called on her, and she met you at the door in muddy ski pants discarded years ago by some Montana relative and a ragged sweater, you knew you had been accepted. But in public she always took great pains with her dress. For instance one weekend she went to a friend's house in Athens. She knew people would be invited in to meet her, and she brought a nice silk dress but forgot dress shoes. She borrowed her hostess's high heels; they did not fit. "I can't walk in them," she said, "but I can sit in a chair and people will excuse it on account of my age, and I will look all right."

People could not understand why this famous woman, well along in years, who had a wealthy brother, lived the way she did. One magazine writer flew down from New York expecting to find an old southern mansion and had to be shown how to use the toilet.

But Jeannette felt she was comfortable; she knew most of the world's people lived in far worse circumstances. Her family said she was neurotic in her desire to appear poor, but Jeannette thought it only reasonable for a woman who had made a career as a champion of humanity to live simply. She saw herself as a living protest against establishment commercial values, the "stupid money system."

She was not actually as impoverished as she seemed. With the growth of the University of Georgia and the City of Athens, her land became valuable, and she sold some now and then for travel expenses. As an ex-representative she had a tiny government pension (which she had voted against), a small income from a little farm she owned in Montana, and a three hundred dollar a month annuity bought for her by Wellington. She had the luxuries she cared for—radio, television when it came in, a secondhand car, travel.

She was not alone. She had the Robinsons, a black family she met soon after she moved to Shady Grove. The three little boys did errands for her and did not go to school; the state did not enforce truancy laws for Negroes. Nevertheless, Jeannette informed the truant officer; he made one call on the family and nothing came of it. Still, the two oldest learned to read and write, went north, and got jobs. Wonder, the youngest, nearly illiterate, stayed in the neighborhood, married, and had three children of his own. Jeannette befriended them and they her.

She built them a concrete block house in the trees behind her house. Wonder and his wife Mattie finished it themselves, but Mattie did not care for a dirt-and-tarpaper floor, so when Jeannette was away Mattie had concrete poured. Wonder had a series of substandard jobs that paid substandard wages. Mattie cooked in Athens. When Wonder got home from work in the late afternoon he stopped to see what he could do for Jeannette. He carried in water (carried it some distance after the pump broke), filled the bathroom jar, the teakettles, and sometimes washed a few dishes. ("I have a good way with the dirty dishes," Jeannette said. "I hide them, and after a while Wonder finds them and says, 'Miss Rankin, look at this,' and then he washes them.")

Mattie was supposed to help with the housecleaning, but she did not do much, and, as Jeannette grew older and her eyes began to fail, cobwebs and dust accumulated in the corners. Jeannette would never throw anything away, so the shelves were cluttered with empty bottles, cans, and boxes. Once the children, roughhousing, broke a large mirror in the kitchen. Jeannette took the broken pieces and propped them on shelves behind old bottles; she said it gave a nice light effect. Then she rummaged in a trunk and brought out a piece of Guatemalan cutwork appliqué, made of many layers of different colored cotton, and hung it in place of the mirror.

The children loved her and she loved them. They stayed with her when they came home from school, since their parents were both at work, and she helped them with their reading and arithmetic. Jennifer learned to read on a big poster that hung in the kitchen: "In war truth is the first casualty." Sometimes the children were rowdy and made Jeannette nervous; she was then in her eighties. She spoke sharply to them once, and they stayed away for several days. She had to ask Wonder to tell them to come back. She kept photographs of them on her dresser and taped on her mirror was a note from seven-year-old Jennifer that had awaited her on the kitchen table when she came home from some trip: "Dear Jeannette Rankin: You is coming home tonight. I did miss you and I no you miss me. Stanley, Wonder, Mattie and Jeff and me miss you. We wrote you a letter did you right us a letter. We send you a picture and we send you a letter. Miss Rankin I did miss you. I love you all of us love you. From Jennifer. Love You."

Jeannette accepted responsibility for the family. She paid their emergency medical expenses and became angry when she thought the family was ill treated by the medical establishment. Once, when Wonder, suffering from severe pain in his head, went to the local hospital, the staff refused him nursing care, although they allowed his family to come and nurse him. Then, they claimed his pain was mental; later, they found impacted wisdom teeth. Extraction cured the pain, but Jeannette refused to pay the hospital bill until she could go to the management in person and "give them a piece of my mind." But if the Robinsons needed her, she needed them, too, and she was not above using money to control the relationship. Wonder wanted a deed to his house, but she said she would leave it to him in her will. "If I give you a deed somebody would get it away from you, don't you know, and then where would I be?" (She did leave the house to him and money in trust for the children.)

Five hundred yards down the road was another family that befriended Jeannette, this one white. Blanche Butler had been one of the members of the Sunshine Club, Jeannette's girls' club of the twenties. Jeannette took her noon meals with Blanche and her family, a hearty rural dinner, ham or chicken, potatoes, okra and tomatoes, coleslaw, pie and cake, buttermilk and iced tea. Because she insisted on paying, the Butlers charged her a dollar and offered her the use of their tub. The Butlers had a nice modern bungalow, and Jeannette had to admit their bathroom was more comfortable than hers. Other people kept track of her, too. Neighbors brought old newspapers for her to burn in her fireplace. Old friends, knowing she did not cook, dropped in with presents of bread, meatloaf, cake. She had friends on the faculty of the University of Georgia, some of them from Peace Society days, and she was often asked to lunch or dinner in Athens, which was only a short drive away.

She also busied herself with another of her ingenious housing ideas, this one a communal home intended for elderly women. In 1966 Wellington died and left each of his sisters seventy-five thousand dollars, so Jeannette had the money to work with. She wanted a cooperative home to belong to the women who lived in it, "one where they could manage on what money they had. They could arrange things for themselves, take turns cooking and doing chores, and care for each other when they are ill. The object is for each of them to help make a home—family style—for the others."

To this end she had built a round house, which she designed herself. She could not get a regular contractor, so she hired men and supervised the work herself. The main feature was an enormous round hall, circled by clerestory windows. Surrounding the hall, under the windows, were ten private bedrooms, each with a half bath. Kitchen and dining facilities and a large bathroom were in an annex to the rear. Jeannette planned to charge fifteen dollars a month rent, and when the building had been paid for she would give it to the occupants. It was a pioneering idea that some day might become a feature of old age housing, but Jeannette never found the old women to occupy it and became too busy with other projects to organize it. She rented it to students for a while, but most of the time it stood empty.

For nearly thirty years Jeannette made a home for herself at Shady Grove. During that time north Georgia changed rapidly. By the end of her life there most of the farms were gone, the pines cut down. Farm people now worked in small factories that made fabrics, overalls, or processed chickens. Even Jeannette's old enemy, the Anaconda Company, had a brass wire plant just outside Watkinsville. Yet, in spite of the changed character of the countryside, Jeannette continued to live undisturbed with unlocked doors. The neighbors were proud of the indomitable old lady. A visitor with Montana license plates stopped one day in 1965 at a service station near Watkinsville. "You know," said the attendant, "there's a lady from Montana living right down the road." "Yes," said the visitor, "I hope you're taking good care of her." Jeannette was then eighty-five. "Miss Rankin don't need taking care of," the attendant said. "Miss Rankin can take care of herself."

Take care of herself she did. She continued to speak out for peace and advocate for election reform, and she continued to travel. Jeannette could find money for travel when she had none for anything else. She told a friend, who pointed out that for four hundred dollars she could bring water to her house from a spring, that for four hundred dollars she could go to India. Occasionally, she sold some property to finance her trips, and Wellington was generous.

Until the last year of her life, she shuttled back and forth across the United States. Fiorello LaGuardia died in 1947 and so closed a chapter of her life. But there were still Katharine Anthony and Charles and Mary Ritter Beard in New York. The eminent historian supported her in her revisionist theories of America's entrance into the war, for Jeannette continued to believe that the president could have prevented the Japanese attack on Pearl Harbor. In Washington she occasionally saw Sinclair Lewis and his wife Dorothy Thompson. She blamed Dorothy for "helping Roosevelt get us into the war." She also said Dorothy should have overlooked Lewis's heavy drinking; he was a genius and Dorothy should have taken that into consideration. "All she was interested in was her own career." Strange talk from a feminist, but Jeannette was a complex kind of feminist. Also, her loyalties ran deep and strong, and she had known Lewis since 1916.

There were also old suffragist friends. Alice Paul lived in Washington at Belmont House, headquarters of the Woman's Party. So she had a lively intellectual and social life, and now she had time to range farther. She went to Mexico City in 1945, attending a

Pan-American conference with her old suffragist friend, Abby Crawford Milton of Chattanooga. While she was there the United States dropped the atom bomb on Hiroshima, ushering in a new kind of warfare. From that time on Jeannette believed more strongly than ever that the peace issue overshadowed all others. At that moment, however, she had no handle on the issue and spent most of the next fifteen years traveling and trying to find one.

Of all the places she visited Jeannette was most fascinated by India, in large part because of Gandhi's nonviolent campaign for Indian independence. She traveled to India seven times, sometimes for six months or a year, sometimes driving her own car from village to village. She had become interested in India first in 1917. After she had introduced a resolution for Irish independence, an Indian, Lajpat Rai, one of the pre-Gandhi leaders, introduced himself to her. She read Rai's books, *Young India* and *England's Debt to India*. She wrote her mother from Congress that she was "immersed" in India's problems and wrote Mary O'Neill of England's "stupidity" in not freeing India; sooner or later it would have to be done. She closely followed Gandhi's campaigns and was especially interested in his theories of passive resistance; perhaps pacifists could use such tactics. She thought it interesting that Gandhi acknowledged his debt to the American Henry Thoreau, who first advocated nonviolent civil disobedience; Thoreau had gone to jail rather than pay taxes to support a war, and Jeannette was later to try to emulate him.

So, when the war ended in 1946 and Jeannette scheduled a six-month world tour, she especially looked forward to a stay in India. She secured an interview with Nehru, the Indian leader and disciple of Gandhi. She wanted to meet Gandhi but felt she should not bother him; he was at the time trying to stop the bloody war between Moslems and Hindus. It would be a lifelong regret that she never met him, for she would not return to India until after he was assassinated.

In 1949 she went again to India to attend a world peace conference. Leaving from Seattle, she was pictured in the newspapers on ship deck in a light tweed suit and silk scarf, with matching turban. Gandhi, she said, "used spiritual power to solve modern political problems. Without violence he obtained the independence of India. India, with all its misery, is less depressing than modern Europe, because people are looking forward to an ideal, to build a new government based on understanding and good will rather than the threat of violence. . . . Civilization can be saved only by new ideals. If India has anything to give us in the way of inspiration, we should receive it gladly."

Her Ford rested in the ship's hold, and it took ten days to get it off the dock in Madras; she was late for the conference. Afterwards, she hired a driver and began a tour of the country. She soon found, however, that he "ran out of languages." She had hoped he would interpret and had not realized how quickly the language changed from village to village. He wanted to go home for Christmas, so she let him go and drove herself. She stayed with missionaries along the way; they sent her to other missionaries. When they did not, and she ran out of invitations, she located the missionaries and "just descended on them." Highlights of her trip included a visit to Santiniketan, the last home of the poet Tagore, and another at Sevagram, Gandhi's last home and site of his famous school and commune.

In 1952 she returned to India for nearly a year, settling down for some time at Almora, high in the northern mountains. She wrote frequent letters to her sisters. Nainital, the old English summer capital, looked like Wallace, "a little dressed up." (Wallace was a grimy mining town in a narrow canyon in northern Idaho.) The climb up to Almora is "longer than the Greer grade." (The Greer grade was a one-lane steep dirt road, with hair-raising hairpin curves, carved out of an Idaho mountainside.)

The goldenrods at Almora were fourteen feet tall. There were other American women, one of whom had brought four hundred books with her. Jeannette was living on one hundred dollars a month, "better than Georgia." She had bought a car; she hoped to sell it for a thousand dollars when she left. The trip had cost about thirty-five hundred dollars. Wellington had given her another thousand dollars, but she had not spent much of that. "You see I am rich."

When she went to Delhi she could stay at Constitution House for $3.50 a day. It was really for government people, but she could get in, whereas the Ambassador Hotel cost $6.00 a day. Even in India, though, her mind was on America. She was reading biographies of Will Rogers and Frederick Douglass. She was worried about the coming election. She was playing with the idea of a new way of selecting a president. "There is no choice now," she explained.

Jeannette became an inveterate world traveler during her retirement but always kept in close touch with her family. Wellington was the recipient of this picture of Jeannette, taken on a trip to Giza, Egypt.

In addition to her numerous trips to India, Jeannette also traveled to South Africa, South America, Iran, Turkey, Ireland, Europe, Hawaii, Indo-China, and Russia. All over the world people fell in love with Jeannette, who, in her sixties and seventies, was probably at the most attractive time of her life. She had a fresh, fair, unwrinkled complexion, a mass of softly waved white hair, and stylish clothes. She had a smiling self-confidence, relaxed now that she no longer had to fight congressmen, militarists, labor-sweating employers, suffragists opposed to pacifism, liberals angry because she voted for the Dies Committee.

She had an instant warm friendliness, and she was interested in everything. She liked to sit herself down in the lobby of a hotel, say the Taj Mahal in Bombay or the Placer in Helena (or Paris or Mexico City or Honolulu or Moscow) and hold court. People would stop to chat with her and then move on to allow someone else a turn. She always made contact with acquaintances wherever she went, and she knew someone everywhere. Sometimes her tours seemed like royal progresses, for she was much in demand for speaking, luncheons, tea parties, and dinners. Yet

she always met ordinary people as well. Sitting in a foreign waiting room, she would ask with age-old international gestures to
hold some young woman's baby. Soon the two women would be
nodding and smiling and understanding each other very well.

In Turkey she was invited into a home to speak to a neighborhood meeting and spoke sitting behind a curtain with the
rest of the women, with the men on the other side. In South
Africa she caused a small riot by going to court to observe pro-
cedures and sitting on the side of the room reserved for blacks.
In Teheran she spoke to a large group of women students,
with the president of the college translating. "I have not come
to Iran to talk," she said, "but to discover how people live and
the condition of women in Iran and what they are thinking about
world conditions and the problems that concern us all." In
Russia, where she went twice, once to a World Congress for General Disarmament and Peace, she told the astonished Russians
that they should disarm unilaterally. "Why talk about it? Just
disarm." Then people would not be afraid of them, and others
would disarm. She told them, with the little flattery she always
worked into a speech, that the Russians were the only people
who could do so since they were the only ones who controlled
their own military establishment.

Several times she was able to meet her sister Edna, who worked
in Southeast Asia for an international birth control organization,
the Pathfinder Fund. In Bangkok, Djakarta, and Bombay they
shared experiences and argued about the reasons for resistance to
birth control. Edna thought them to be religious and political, but
Jeannette believed economic interests underlay all others.

She enjoyed meeting Eamon DeValera in Dublin. She had
supported Irish independence since her first term in Congress.
In 1920 DeValera, leader of the movement and a fugitive from a
British prison, had toured America to raise funds for the cause.
The Butte Irish had given him a magnificent dinner (Butte liked
big dinners), and Jeannette sat next to him as a guest of honor.
Now, in 1962, he was president of the Irish Republic.

Jeannette wrote the American Embassy asking them to arrange
a meeting, but the embassy said DeValera was too busy to be both-
ered with tourists, so she wrote him directly. At once came an
invitation to lunch, and a car was sent for her. Unfortunately,
when they met she had a hard time making conversation. It had

been forty-two years since they had met in Butte, yet DeValera seemed to remember it all, and Jeannette could not. Finally she dredged up from her memory the Irish name of Judge J. J. Lynch, who had sat with her on the platform in 1917 when she addressed the miners. DeValera laughed and said, "Oh, Judge Lynch was on the other side. He was against Irish independence." After that the conversation went well, though Jeannette never understood how DeValera had retained an intimate knowledge of Butte Irish politics for forty-two years. After lunch when DeValera put her in his car to send her back to her hotel, he waved and shouted as the car went through the gates, "Remember me to Judge Lynch."

As much as she enjoyed her travels elsewhere, Jeannette always returned to India, visiting the country again in 1956, 1960, and 1962. Disappointed with Nehru's progress toward militarism, she did not ask to see him the last time. "All I could have said was, Why?" Her last trip to India was in 1970, when she was ninety. She had broken her hip but walked well with a cane. She attended a conference of her old peace organization, which she had helped found and for which she had worked, the Women's International League for Peace and Freedom. She enjoyed it, received a lot of flattering attention, was glad to see India again, but the people at the conference "were a lot of old ladies. The peace movement just talks to itself." Jeannette—in her travels and at home—had little patience for inward looking movements. She wanted to convert the world, not preach to the converted.

Although Jeannette did not campaign on horseback, as John F. Kennedy intimated in his 1958 McCALL's MAGAZINE article, "Three Women of Courage," she did like to ride. She is pictured here circa 1952 at Avalanche Ranch mounted on her sister Edna's horse, Whitetale.

CHAPTER FOURTEEN

Woman on Horseback

"THIS IS NO TIME
TO BE POLITE."

"JEANNETTE RANKIN WAS not a woman who shrank from hard and difficult tasks," wrote Senator John F. Kennedy. Gearing up for his presidential campaign he had published a book called *Profiles in Courage* (1956). When it was belatedly called to his attention that he had included no women, he published an article in January 1958 in *McCall's Magazine* lauding three women, one of them Jeannette Rankin.

Jeannette was pleased at the publicity, for she had been almost forgotten, but the article's inaccuracy amused and annoyed her. Kennedy had written: "Covering every inch of her vast Montana district, much of it on horseback, spending more time in kitchens and parlors than in meeting halls or political headquarters, she had entered without fear in the heretofore all-male world of politics." To cover "every inch," "much of it on horseback," was impossible, of course. She used automobiles, which she usually drove herself, and trains. She had spent time in "kitchens and parlors," but she had gone into meeting halls and political headquarters like anyone else. Responded the astonished Jeannette, "What kind of fool does he think I am?" But there was figurative truth in Kennedy's remarks. She was a woman on horseback, fighting for woman's suffrage, humanity, peace. And in the late 1950s, she

entered a period of furious activity that would end only with her
death fifteen years later. She protested the Vietnam War; she worked
out and propagandized a system of electoral reform; she befriended
dissident students; she became the heroine of the women's movement; she even considered running again for Congress.

She became a national heroine to those who opposed the Vietnam War although most of them opposed that particular war,
while she opposed all wars. The war itself raged without any declaration by Congress, its only authorization being the 1964 Gulf
of Tonkin resolution, which gave the president power independent of Congress to prosecute the war. Jeannette had worked
hard, but unsuccessfully, in the 1930s to prevent Congress from
abdicating its responsibilities in that way.

By 1964 she was speaking out wherever she could although she
found few audiences. In those early days of the war she was too controversial. A public television station in Atlanta would not allow her
on the air; a graduate assistant at a university was criticized for asking her to speak to his students. Jeannette sent small advertisements
to newspapers, asking women not to vote for candidates who supported the war, by "writing in the names of persons who are opposed to war—your own, if necessary." Bozeman, Montana's, *Gallatin
County Tribune* refused to run the ad, and the editor wrote Jeannette
politely on October 20, 1966, explaining his reasons: the war was
"the only way we have of combating communism, Miss Rankin."

She refused to pay the tax on her telephone bill because it
went to pay for the war. She hoped to be arrested and sent to jail
like Thoreau and Gandhi; instead the Internal Revenue Service
collected the tax directly from her bank account. Soon other
voices joined Jeannette in protesting the war. By 1965 senators
Ernest Gruening of Alaska, Wayne Morse of Oregon, Frank
Church of Idaho, and George McGovern of South Dakota all had
spoken out against the war, which Morse called immoral, illegal,
and impossible of success. And in April 1967, a half million students across the country took to the streets during the Spring
Mobilization to End the War in Vietnam.

Jeannette received much publicity that April, as well, for April
2, 1967, was the fiftieth anniversary of Jeannette's entrance into
Congress and her vote against World War I. She welcomed the
publicity because it dramatized the antiwar cause. In television
and newspaper interviews she said,

It isn't a question of war against Germany, Japan, or Vietnam. It's just that the whole system is very stupid.

War is nothing more than a method of settling a dispute but it has nothing to do with the dispute. In fact you never have the same issues at the end of war that were present at the beginning. Shooting a young man is no way to settle a political dispute. You cannot change opinion by force.

We drifted into this Vietnam War and we can drift out.

How can we get our boys home? Why the same way we got them over there, by planes and ships.

She kept appealing to the women: "We—women—should picket everything. This is no time to be polite." "Women remind me of the cows on our ranch in Montana. A cow has a calf and after a while some man comes along and takes the calf away. She bawls for a while, then goes on and has another calf." "If we had 10,000 women willing to go to prison that would end the war. We've had 10,000 women sit back and let their sons be killed."

In 1968 a number of activist women made plans to demonstrate on the opening day of Congress, calling their organization the Jeannette Rankin Brigade. Support came from the Women's International League for Peace and Freedom, the Black Congress, and Women Strike for Peace (an organization founded in 1961 to protest nuclear testing). Wearing black, three to five thousand women, including Jeannette, met at Union Station in Washington on January 15, 1968.

Instructions went out to the marchers to keep the peace, for police had invoked an 1882 law forbidding demonstrations on Capitol grounds. Though it had never been applied, it had recently been amended to carry a fine of up to five thousand dollars and a jail sentence of up to five years. Police stood by, prepared for mass arrests, with detention centers set up for five hundred demonstrators. The women marched from Union Station to Union Square, across the street from the Capitol, where they held a peaceful rally. There were no arrests, and later the brigade sued for not having been allowed access to the Capitol grounds. The Supreme Court later ruled that they had been denied their first amendment rights—a decision that now makes peaceful demonstration legal in that area.

Some activists, though, objected to the overly peaceful aspects of the march, feeling that women should not have followed police

Jeannette met with Senate Majority Leader Mike Mansfield of Montana on January 15, 1968, after leading the three- to five-thousand member Jeannette Rankin Brigade on a peace march protesting the Vietnam War.

regulations so docilely. Certainly, that was no way to put "10,000 women in jail." Others objected to Jeannette's symbolic leadership because of her generalized pacifism. But Jeannette thought the peaceful aspects of the march brought out women who otherwise would not dare participate, and the bringing together of women of different views was worthwhile. It was the grass roots approach that Jeannette had always advocated. This aspect of the march was nationally noted. "On the opening day of Congress," wrote columnist Mary McGrory in *America*, on January 27, 1968, "Miss Jeannette Rankin, a sensible but redoubtable spinster, led five thousand women through a day of marching and remonstrance that did much to restore respectability to dissent."

As the protests continued, public opinion turned against the war, and Jeannette received many invitations to speak. "Can you imagine? I'm respectable!" she said, much amused. She was televised nationally on the David Frost and Merv Griffin shows, locally in Georgia and New York, and frequently interviewed by the press. In October 1969 she spoke to fifteen hundred students at the University of Georgia at one of the antiwar moratoriums then sweeping the country. She opened the demonstration by ringing the old campus bell, which previously had been rung only when Georgia won a football game. Pulling vigorously on the rope, she was nearly swept off her feet. She spoke of the war and of electoral reform, which was the first step toward changing foreign policy. The American people could not make their voices heard because industrial interests that profited from war dominated both parties. But she was optimistic. "Every child today knows physical laws that were unheard of 100 years ago. Now they are learning moral laws, that it's wrong to hate and kill." Fifteen hundred students rose and cheered. "This is really something for a conservative place like Georgia," said one.

She began to attract a number of dissident students, some responsible and others not. Reita Rivers, a graduate student in history who became part-time secretary and full-time friend, helped her write letters and pamphlets and arranged for their printing and mailing. They kept no accounts; once in a while Jeannette would think to give Reita a check for a hundred dollars. Reita was a good example of the many brilliant and loyal aides Jeannette managed to find. Others did not work out so well. Jeannette suspected one young friend who had come to stay with her of taking drugs. Despite her repeated requests that he leave her home, he stayed on. Finally she had Wonder pack his things and dump him at the bus station.

She rented the roundhouse to some members of Students for a Democratic Society. They left it a mess, destroyed some of it. One was arrested for burning down the ROTC building. He told Jeannette he was innocent, so she tried to give bond for his bail only to be told that a woman could not give bond in Georgia. Then, according to Jeannette, the authorities told the student that if he would plead guilty they would put him on probation. He pled guilty and was sent to jail. Jeannette was disgusted with the whole affair: the duplicity of the authorities, the fact that they would not accept her bond, and with the student, who, she decided, probably was guilty. "I can't see what good it does the peace movement to burn down the ROTC," she exclaimed.

There was an arrest in May 1969 at the roundhouse on marijuana charges. Several ounces were found. Jeannette was indignant, telling the reporter who interviewed her for the story that appeared in the May 29, 1969, Athens *Daily News*: "When it's something important, like poverty where is the law? But if it's something like pot, they are right on the job. They said I was running a 'hippie hangout.' I don't know what a hippie is. I thought the sheriff was a friend of mine." In truth, the sheriff and his wife were friends of hers. They kept an eye on the neighborhood, and no doubt it was more for her own protection than anything else that the students were removed. Many of her neighbors who might not have approved of her ideas were quietly protecting her. The roundhouse remained empty after that.

In spite of her disclaimer, Jeannette was well aware of "hippies." She thought there was "something the matter" with a young person if he did not have a "little of hippie in him." The movement's ideas of peace and love and disdain for material things were precisely her own. She did not approve of drugs, though. She did not approve of anything mind-clouding, not drugs nor alcohol (though she liked a glass of sherry in the evening), not mysticism nor romanticism nor even cynicism. "It is too bad," she said, "that the young people are not more responsible." She understood why they dropped out of school but not why they dropped out of society. She herself never rejected society. Even at its worst she tried to improve it.

Preoccupied with electoral reform since the 1950s, Jeannette became increasingly convinced in the late 1960s that society needed a new electoral system, so that government would more nearly reflect the wishes of the people. A new system would allow the people to express their wish for peace; the present system, she felt, was dominated by interests that profited from war. She advocated two reforms: preferential voting for president and multiple member congressional districts.

Preferential voting, advocated in the twenties and thirties and tried in city elections in the west, had been found at that time to be too cumbersome and expensive. The reasons, Jeannette thought, were that people had not been educated to it, and it had been too difficult to count. It could work in the 1960s, she believed, because people were better educated and computers could do the counting. In her vision, voters would express their first, second, third, fourth, and fifth choices for president. If a voter's first choice lost, and no candidate received a majority of first choices, the voter's second-choice vote would be counted, or even the third. Thus, voters would not have to choose between two candidates preselected for them by powerful interests but could vote for the candidate who best represented their views.

Multiple-member congressional districts would give minorities opportunity for representation. In a single-member district, the majority elected the representative, and if there were twelve districts in a state, all twelve people elected would likely represent the majority opinion. Even a 49 percent minority would have no representation at all. If that same state were divided into four districts, however, each district to elect three members and each voter to vote for three candidates, one or more representatives would probably come from an ethnic, ideological, or political minority. The idea harkened back to her 1916 congressional victory, which she felt she owed to the at-large election of the two representatives.

In 1969 she was invited to speak to the House Judiciary Committee, then considering a bill calling for the direct election of the president and vice president. Jeannette had once advocated such a measure, but by 1969 she thought that this would give voters no more choice than they currently had because political candidates, with tremendous financing, were sold on television like soap. She told the committee so in forceful language, while standing. They had asked her, in deference to her age, eighty-eight, to be seated. "No thanks," she said, "I fight better standing up."

A lifelong advocate of democracy, she said in the late sixties that she could not sincerely advise anyone to vote. "There is no choice." Her own votes for the last twenty years of her life show much ambivalence. She voted for Dwight D. Eisenhower in 1952, though she had written her family that she was "interested in Wellington's relations with Eisenhower, and was glad she wasn't home, as she 'might express a grudge against Ike and spoil Wellington's pleasure'." In 1960 she voted for Richard M. Nixon, who had served as Eisenhower's vice president, because she thought that Ike, a military man himself, might have taught Nixon how to handle the military. Eisenhower, after all, had said, early in his presidency: "Every gun that is made, every warship launched, every rocket fired, signifies in the final sense, a theft from those who hunger and are not fed, those who are cold and are not clothed. This is not a way of life at all. Under the cloud of threatening war, it is humanity hanging from a cross of iron. Is there no other way the world may live?" Then, in his valedictory speech, he had warned the country against the "military-industrial complex." This was

Jeannette's kind of language and what she had been saying for fifty years.

In 1964 she voted for Barry Goldwater, primarily because she could not stand Lyndon Johnson. Johnson had been "Roosevelt's flunky" when she was in Congress, and he was militaristic. She did not believe Goldwater was as reactionary as he was painted; the public was being brainwashed, she said. But at the same time she campaigned in Montana for the election as governor of R. R. Renne, a moderate Democrat and former president of Montana State University. (Renne narrowly lost, and she blamed it on poor organization; she said a postcard campaign would have elected him.) In 1968 she supported Eugene McCarthy, the liberal Democrat, but he was not nominated. She considered Humphrey militaristic and again voted for Nixon. By 1972, however, she decided that Nixon had learned nothing from Eisenhower and voted for George McGovern.

In 1968 she toyed with the idea of running again for Congress, "to have someone to vote for." Montana's First District incumbent Arnold Olsen was vulnerable; she might have won. In the end she did not run; old age was creeping up on her. Her tic douloureux became frequent and severe. She had put up with this terrible ailment, all the while living life to its fullest, for at least fifty-five years. Alcohol injections had brought no permanent relief. Half a dozen aspirins night and morning helped prevent an attack. Niece Dorothy would see her off to the plane on some round-the-world trip and stuff bottles of aspirins in her raincoat pocket, but Dorothy was one of the very few who knew of the problem.

Jeannette never talked about her ailments; she rarely saw a doctor. She was not a Christian Scientist like some of her family; she just did not like to take the time or admit to a weakness. So it was with surprise that one dark rainy Sunday evening Dr. Roy Ward, the Watkinsville general physician, received a phone call from someone in such pain she could hardly speak. He finally ascertained it was Jeannette, whom he had met only once before. Yet he remembered seeing her at a state fair, handing out pamphlets, when he was a boy. People had said she was a former woman congressman, and he had been impressed, not knowing there could be such a thing. And only a few days before the phone call he had seen her on television, with a picture of her "primitive cottage near a backwoods Georgia town."

Jeannette was very old, he knew. He was afraid she had had a stroke and would die. "And it would be in the newspapers all over the world that the famous Jeannette Rankin, former Congresswoman, suffrage leader, peace activist, had died because she could not get medical attention in this little backwoods Georgia town." He called an ambulance and alerted the Butlers at the crossroads to watch for it. He himself drove the several miles and arrived at Shady Grove just as the ambulance did; the Butlers and other neighbors were there, too. Jeannette, perfectly dressed, composed, and smiling met them at the door, saying "Whatever is all the commotion?" Dr. Ward was furious, of course, although relieved; later the two became good friends.

She went to Atlanta for an operation to sever the nerve and stop the pain, but afterwards her eyelid and the whole right side of her face drooped. She was sensitive about it, and always turned her good side to the camera. Other people did not think it was unsightly. In April 1970 she broke her hip in a fall on Watkinsville's Main Street. She said it was a most painful thing, but was amused that, in a daze of pain, she heard someone say "My God, what's that?" "Pick it up, pick it up, it's her wig," said someone else. She realized she must look grotesque without her wig. She had very little hair of her own left. She recovered from the accident and walked well with a cane, which she used more as a precaution than as a necessity. She was still in a wheelchair, however, on her ninetieth birthday, June 11, 1970, but able to enjoy every minute of a birthday party thrown for her in Washington.

Jeannette had her share of human vanity, possibly a little more (as public figures usually have), and she loved public kudos. She had been thrilled with her first award, an honorary doctorate of law from Montana State College in Bozeman in 1961, at a time when she had been nearly forgotten, and, if remembered, considered too controversial to recognize. In 1964 her own alma mater, the University of Montana, gave her and Wellington its distinguished alumnus award. Now, in 1970, two hundred people were honoring her in the nation's capital.

At the head table with her was Majority Leader Mike Mansfield, Senator Lee Metcalf, Representative Arnold Olsen, ex-Senator Burton K. Wheeler, Montanans all, and Democrats. All had once represented Jeannette's first district, a hard one to represent, they said, because of its variety. It was a Democratic district, too;

Jeannette was one of very few Republicans to be elected from it. Republican former governor Tim Babcock was there, though she had campaigned against him six years earlier. There were old friends, Ernest Gruening of Alaska, who had voted against the Gulf of Tonkin Resolution, and former senator Gerald P. Nye of North Dakota, a progressive Republican with whom Jeannette had worked for neutrality legislation and munitions investigation in the thirties. Representative Patsy Mink of Hawaii had come, reluctantly leaving Hawaii's annual King Kamehameha celebration. Most of these people were doves, opposed to the Vietnam War, so Jeannette was in friendly company, but a prominent hawk, Senator Margaret Chase Smith of Maine, gave the best tribute of the evening: "Perhaps I am a hawk, but I salute Jeannette Rankin as the first of the doves. Senate doves just shot down the Byrd amendment. Even I voted against it. Perhaps it was Jeannette Rankin's influence on such a stubborn hawk as I have been known to be." (The Byrd amendment would have increased the president's power to prosecute the war even more independently of Congress.)

Senator Metcalf summed up Jeannette's career: despite her age, he said, she not only bridged the generation gap, she "had jumped over a couple generations and is now shoulder to shoulder with the youngsters of today who are seeking peace." He continued:

She was far ahead of her time in other areas. . . . She spoke for disarmament. . . . She spoke for the consumer. . . . She spoke for child welfare, of industrial and labor problems, of economic maladjustments, their need for raw materials, the interdependence of all nations in distribution of the world's goods, the pressure of growing populations, social injustice, racial injustice. She believed in freedom for our First American—the American Indian—and of his need for recognition and education. She was interested in the development of public lands, including our national parks. Her advocacy of the direct election of the Presidency is a matter of public record. These all sound like a reading of the calendar of the issues before Congress today.

Think of the proposals Miss Rankin espoused that have become part of the body of American law: suffrage for women, support for dependents of an enlisted man, free postage for members of the armed forces, granting to American women married to aliens the right to retain their citizenship, the creation of a water-power board. . . .

The tributes concluded, Jeannette, glowing, rose from her wheelchair. She was attractive and vigorous, wearing her best wig freshly set and a gold dress made of Indian sari cloth. She used the occasion, as she now used every occasion, in meeting halls and "kitchens and parlors," to push electoral reform.

And so she continued to work into her nineties despite with increasing difficulties. She could not see well and wrote phone numbers with a heavy black crayon on index cards though she could remember most of them. She walked with a cane; weeds took over the gardens. Seeing how fragile she was in her uncomfortable home, a Georgia university professor and his wife offered her a home with them for the rest of her life. But, of course, independent Jeannette could not accept. She had to do something, however, and somewhat against her wishes she bought a retirement home at Carmel, California, near her sister Edna, and now she flew there every summer. It was a place to die, she said, writing one friend, "Come and see me in my death house." The home offered what Jeannette laughingly called "perpetual care," so she really had no further worries. Her little studio apartment was unfurnished, so Jeannette, three thousand miles away in Georgia, had to hire an interior decorator. He bought simple modern furniture and sent pictures of the apartment to Jeannette in Georgia, along with the bills, which she embarrassedly tried to hide from her secretary. Poor Jeannette felt foolish spending two thousand dollars on mere furniture.

She spent very little time in California. She was beginning to receive much attention and accepted all invitations for newspaper, magazine, and television interviews and speaking engagements. No matter how tired she was she could summon up smiling energy to address a meeting, be it only two or three people or hundreds. The new women's movement paid tremendous attention to her, for she was an ornament to it, a fact she well understood. This energetic "oldest living feminist" dressed in bright prints, with skirts just below the knees, had good legs, and wore black high heels. For a time, while she still had some hair, she had dyed it a soft auburn, but toward the end of her life, she took to wearing an ash-blond wig with a soft feathery cut. It took years off her age.

Her bad temper and her quirky brand of feminism got in the way of her relations with the leaders of the movement, however.

"She was positively nasty to some of them," a good friend reported. For one thing, they tended to treat her as a treasure instead of as an active person who could do things and make decisions. For another, she believed they were much too interested in money and status. "What kind of a job do you want?" she asked one horrified young woman who advocated for women's acceptance in the workplace, "cutting off chicken heads?" That was how Wonder Robinson made his living. "What is money?" she asked. "Nobody can tell me what it is." She had been asking that question for sixty years. "Why do they want to get involved in the stupid money system?" "I live without money," she said, not quite accurately. "I have one cold water tap in the house, a dirt floor in the living room, a two-burner hot plate, an electric fry-pan, an electric heater, and an electric blanket."

She thought the movement was poorly organized. There were too many leaders talking to one another. Too many meetings. They should pull women in from the grass roots, give them tasks to do for the movement. "Don't give them a book to read," she advised. "Give them something to do. . . . We never got anywhere in woman suffrage until we went out on the streets and began to speak and demonstrate. . . . Meetings don't convince the unconvinced, the ones who don't come to meetings." But her main quarrel with the women's movement was that it was not now her issue. The one burning issue now that nations had atomic weapons was peace, Jeannette believed, and the splendid energy that went into the women's movement was simply misdirected.

Yet, she still favored women's issues. The Equal Rights Amendment was not only just, but for the good of society. She still cited her early mentor Benjamin Kidd's view that women, because they nourish children for so many years, are less concerned with immediate gain and think more of the future, not only for themselves but for the society in which their children grow and will have to live in their adulthood. Men's violence was the result of their tendency to translate their emotions into immediate unthinking action. "Men have progressed as much as they could without the help of women," she said in a newspaper interview in 1972. And she laughed until the tears ran down her face at the quip of one of her young friends. They were talking about putting fluoride in the water, and the young woman said, "I know what they should put in the water: estrogen."

If people asked Jeannette about sex, she would say, with a twinkle in her eye, "Never having married, I wouldn't know about such things, would I?" But Jeannette had been a social worker, helped raise children, knew intimately people with all sorts of life styles, had observed teeming life all over the world. She knew about sex, and she was not afraid to talk about it. Way back in 1918 she had told male colleagues nervous at naming "communicable disease," "If you mean syphilis, why don't you say so?" In 1970 she could discuss with anyone the clinical details of birth control, the pill, the diaphragm, the IUD. Her young student friends never toned down their raunchiest jokes; there was nothing you could not say to Jeannette.

She took every chance she had, in every interview, to speak for electoral reform. "Governments make war and governments can make peace, and it is only by working through governments that we can stop war." People had no choice, but if a people truly had choices they would vote, participate in society, would become aware of their responsibilities and educate themselves for them. They would feel like citizens, as the pioneers had, when everyone had a part in developing the country. People who have no choices fall into apathy. She would speak of Gandhi, of his ideals of truth and nonviolence.

> A person can be shot, but an idea cannot. . . . It is the same passion for the ideal [Benjamin Kidd again] which a mother expresses in her love for her children which we must achieve and maintain if we want our ideals to mature and flourish in society: self-control, compassion, honesty, integrity and love must be maintained in our minds, incarnated through our daily actions and living, and patiently maintained in adversity. . . . We must end violence in our hearts and in our dealings with each other; and then we can resolve our domestic problems and will have found an alternative to war.

Those words sound saintly, but Jeannette was not saintly; she was no Gandhi. She was subject to anger and irritability. She herself told the story of the time she "lost" her pacifism. A strange cat had wandered into her house, through the back door that nearly always stood open, a yellow cat much like her own. Not seeing well, and thinking he was hers, she let him stay. Later she realized her mistake and picked him up to put him out. But he had established territorial rights. He bit her. "I lost my pacifism," she said. "If I could have killed that cat I would have."

In all her interviews and public appearances she was full of brave words, but privately at ninety-one she said, "It's hard to push and push and push and never get anywhere. A person begins to get tired of it." Nevertheless, she continued to push. She went to Hollywood to appear on the Merv Griffin show and back to Georgia for a national meeting of the War Resisters' League, at which she received a plaque honoring her efforts. She stayed to lobby the Georgia legislature, which faced the challenge of redistricting after losing two House seats following the 1970 census, and urged them to adopt multiple-member districts. One Sunday evening with the help of a young student friend to do the dialing she spoke on the telephone to state legislators across Georgia. The next day she followed up with letters. Visiting the legislature in person, she was lionized. Governor Jimmy Carter canceled appointments and talked with her for an hour. She was pleased. "Though I know," she said, "that they're only interested in my historicity."

Late in 1971 she acquired the full-time help of a dropped-out law student, John Kirkley. He was a restless and disturbed young man looking for answers. He had met Jeannette several times, heard her speak, and one day he suddenly asked himself, "Can a woman be a guru?" He drove out to Shady Grove and pitched his tent under the huge oaks in the front yard. Two days later she allowed him to move in. "It was like living in a temple," he said— but he did make some changes to make the temple more comfortable. He did all the cooking, cleaning, and secretarial work, drove the car, scheduled meetings, made travel arrangements, helped her dress, and took care of her every wish. In return she paid his school debts, more than three thousand dollars.

Friends were alarmed at the situation and kept warning her that she was being "taken in." Jeannette was angered. "Do they think," she said, "that I can be taken in by a 29-year-old boy? Of course he's using me, but I'm using him, too. . . . And at 91 I do as I please with my money." With his help, the last year and a half of her life became nearly as busy as those of the suffrage years. She looked frail, could hardly see, tired easily, drooled a little, and her speech was becoming slurred. But she gloried in her active life. For instance in January 1972 she appeared in New

York on a local television show hosted by women's rights leader Gloria Steinem. She went back to Atlanta for a meeting, did a television interview, lunched with Shirley Chisholm, the black representative from New York whom Jeannette supported for the presidency, and attended a large banquet in the evening.

On the morning of February 12, 1972, she made the opening speech in Nashville at the Southern Women's Conference on Education for Delegate Selection. Immediately after the speech Kirkley picked her up, literally, from the platform, announcing to the startled women, "behind every great man they say there is a woman. Behind this great woman there is a man. And I'm the man." He rushed her to the plane, and that evening they were in New York at the regional conference of the National Organization for Women, which called Jeannette "the world's outstanding living feminist" and made her the first member of its Susan B. Anthony Hall of Fame. She made an acceptance speech, held a series of conferences, and spoke at Barnard College.

On March 4 she gave the opening address at the Georgia Women's Political Caucus in Atlanta and then went to New York, where she made the principal address at the fourth annual meeting of the Jeannette Rankin Rank-and-File, an outgrowth of the 1968 peace march. She taped an interview for the television show "Today's Woman" and oversaw an experimental testing of the preferential ballot system in a Westport, Connecticut, junior high school. Then came a great pleasure: on March 14 she spoke at the Montana state constitutional convention, being held at the Capitol in Helena. There she stood, nearly ninety-two, in the same House of Representatives chamber in which, sixty-one years before, she had asked for votes and received violets. The hall was filled with progressive delegates; they would produce a new state constitution that would be praised all over the country.

She spoke to them of the danger to Montanans of the Intercontinental Ballistic Missile sites located in the state. The more heavily populated centers of the country, she said, considered Montana to be expendable; it would be one of the first targets in case of war. She warned against trying to combat communism by killing young men. "If we're so afraid of Communism why did Nixon go to China? . . . We spend over half of our peace time money getting ready for the next war." She talked of the preferential vote. "We're in a box, and don't have a chance."

She went to dinners and receptions and spoke on television. Then it was back to New York for another speech. Stopping en route in Syracuse she told newspaper interviewers she hoped to see preferential voting accepted before she died. She also spoke at Le Moyne College in Syracuse and the University of Massachusetts. But she was failing. In Georgia summer was coming on, so it was time to go to California. She wanted to drive across the country, as she had done countless times since 1913. So they packed the car, and John Kirkley drove her the three thousand miles to Carmel. She tried to persuade him to go back to law school. She had her sister and other relatives nearby, and reluctantly he left her.

She was having trouble speaking and swallowing. She spent the summer working with a therapist, and there was some improvement. She thought of studying Spanish; perhaps that would exercise her recalcitrant throat muscles. In September 1972, along with other ex-congressmen, she received a questionnaire from Ralph Nader, the consumer advocate. A group of his young people was studying Congress, and they wanted informed opinions. The opportunity was too good to miss. She asked to speak with the group in person and flew back to Washington. Nader reported in his syndicated column: "We're all younger as a result. Her stamina behind her ideals is absolutely staggering. What an example for millions of young people today. For the students in their early 20's, listening to her talk that day, a comparable commitment on their part would extend until the year 2042. 'A 40-hour-a-week job isn't worth doing,' she says. Jeannette Rankin is young forever."

She had accepted an invitation to receive an award at an American Civil Liberties Union dinner, but she was too ill. On the way back to Carmel she stopped for a week in Georgia. Too tired to open up her home, she stayed with her friend Reita Rivers. Her speech was worse; she could not eat in public because of the difficulty of swallowing. After a rest, however, her spirits improved. She would go out to Carmel but made plans for "when I come back to Shady Grove."

But she had made her last public appearance. In spite of loving care and good medical attention, she was getting weaker and could scarcely be understood. Yet she wrote friends that she was thinking of buying a trailer and "just wandering around the country." She read (or had read to her) a recent article in *Life*, by Colin Simpson on the torpedoing of the *Lusitania*, an act that had inflamed the public before America entered World War I. The article demonstrated that it was not as simple an act of aggression as had been assumed. "If the country had known about the *Lusitania* we would not have gone to war in 1917. We are just as ignorant now as we were then." She was bitterly disappointed in the election: she had voted for George McGovern.

Physical infirmities became worse; soon not even her friends could understand her. The magnificent throat muscles that had done yeoman service for sixty-three years no longer worked. She could not write either; a stroke had paralyzed her right arm, but she was learning to use her left. The good mind continued; she enjoyed having the news read. She watched the unfolding Watergate scandals on television. She listened to others talk and made her enthusiastic approval or disapproval known. The time of dying was mercifully short. The end came in her sleep on May 18, 1973, twenty-four days short of her ninety-third birthday.

Essay on Sources

THIS BIOGRAPHY IS BASED on extensive interviews and correspondence with Jeannette Rankin between 1965 and 1971, as well as the author's interviews and correspondence with people close to Jeannette Rankin and her family including Vernon Edenfield, Rosalie Daggy Miller, Pearl Goodall, Jessie Marsh, Blanche Butler, Roy Ward, Grace Stone Coates, John Kirkley, Reita Rivers, and Belle Fligelman Winestine. Much of this material has been donated by the author to the Merrill G. Burlingame Special Collections, Montana State University Library, Bozeman (hereafter MSU).

The author also relied on other interviews conducted with Jeannette and the reminscences of those close to her. These include Jeannette Rankin's interview with John Board, in the collections of the Montana Historical Society Archives, Helena (hereafter MHS); her interview with Malca Chall, Suffragists' Oral History Project, Bancroft Library, University of California, Berkeley (hereafter SOHP); her interview with Katrina R. Cheek, transcribed in "The Rhetoric and Revolt of Jeannette Rankin" (master's thesis, University of Georgia, Athens, 1969); and her interview with Hannah Josephson, SOHP.

In addition, the author researched in Jeannette Rankin's personal papers, which were carelessly collected and even more carelessly preserved. Some of the papers used by the author are no longer available, including a collection on Jeannette's early life before going into politics, which was also used extensively by Ronald Schaffer for his doctoral thesis, "Jeannette Rankin, Progressive-Isolationist" (Ph.D. diss., Princeton University, 1959) and Ronald

Schaffer, "Montana Woman Suffrage Campaign, 1911–1914," *Pacific Northwest Quarterly*, 55 (January 1964), 9–15.

Another collection, mostly concerning her second term and later life, was originally in the library at the Maureen and Mike Mansfield Library, University of Montana, Missoula, but at Jeannette's direction was removed and shipped back and forth from Montana to Georgia for use by graduate students. Most of these papers were seen by the author in Great Falls and Helena, Montana, and Watkinsville and Athens, Georgia. After Jeannette's death what remained of this collection was deposited in the Schlesinger Library, Radcliffe Institute for Advanced Studies, Cambridge, Mass.

A third collection, concerned mostly with Jeannette's first term, was donated to the MHS archives by Belle Fligelman Winestine, along with Winestine's own papers. Winestine was Jeannette's first term administrative assistant. Also in the MHS archives are the Wellington Rankin Papers.

A final collection of Jeannette Rankin papers resides at the University of Georgia Library, Athens. This collection consists primarily of newspaper clippings, photographs, and some correspondence.

Jeannette's public positions during her terms in Congress can be gleaned from the *Congressional Record*, 65th Congress (1917–1919) and *Congressional Record*, 77th Congress (1941–1943). And, of course, Jeannette's own writing proved invaluable. Among many other pieces, Rankin's published writing includes "Why the Country Folk Did It," *The Woman Voter*, December 1911; "How Suffrage was Won in Montana," presented at the Forty-sixth Annual Convention of the National American Woman Suffrage Association, Nashville, Tenn., November 11–17, 1914 (available on microform); "Two Votes against the War," *Liberation*, March 1958; "On War and Non-Violence," in Don Lawson, *Ten Fighters for Peace* (New York, 1971), 82–97; and pamphlets including *Case for a Direct Preferential Vote for President* and *A Statement on Electoral Reform*.

The work of two historians proved particularly invaluable, and their research informed this book throughout. The first is Ronald Schaffer, author of "Jeannette Rankin, Progressive-Isolationist" (Ph.D. diss., Princeton University, 1959). The second is Ted Carlton Harris, author of "Jeannette Rankin, Warring Pacifist" (master's thesis, University of Georgia, Athens, 1969); "Jeannette Rankin, Suffragist, First Woman Elected to Congress, and Pacifist" (Ph.D.

diss., University of Georgia, Athens, 1972); and "Jeannette Rankin in Georgia," *Georgia Historical Quarterly*, 57 (Spring 1974), 55–78. The author is particularly indebted to Harris for material he shared about Jeannette's Georgia peace campaign, described in chapter eleven.

Other work on Jeannette Rankin referred to by the author includes Joan Hoff Wilson, "'Peace Is a Woman's Job . . .': Jeannette Rankin and American Foreign Policy: The Origins of Her Pacifism," *Montana The Magazine of Western History*, 30 (January 1980), 28–41; Joan Hoff Wilson, "'Peace Is a Woman's Job . . .': Jeannette Rankin and American Foreign Policy: Her Lifework as a Pacifist," *Montana The Magazine of Western History*, 30 (April 1980), 38–53; John C. Board, "The Lady from Montana: Jeannette Rankin" (master's thesis, University of Wyoming, Laramie, 1964); Katrina R. Cheek, "The Rhetoric and Revolt of Jeannette Rankin" (master's thesis, University of Georgia, 1969); Hannah Josephson, *Jeannette Rankin, First Lady in Congress: A Biography* (Indianapolis, Ind., 1974); and Kevin S. Giles, *Flight of the Dove: The Story of Jeannette Rankin* (Beaverton, Ore., 1980).

Late-life tributes and popular articles about Jeannette Rankin include Nadine Broznan, "Crusading Forerunner of Women's Lib," *New York Times*, January 24, 1972; John F. Kennedy, "Three Women of Courage, " *McCalls*, January 1958; Lucy Justus, "First Woman in Congress Still a Pacifist," *Atlanta Journal and Constitution Magazine*, May 7, 1967; "She Campaigns for Change," *Atlanta Journal and Constitution Magazine*, February 13, 1972; Elizabeth Frapollo, "At 91 Jeannette Rankin is the Feminists' New Heroine," *Life*, March 3, 1972. Insights into how Jeannette's childhood may have shaped her adult life were gleaned from one of the few second-wave feminist books Jeannette liked: Caroline Bird, *Born Female: The High Cost of Keeping Women Down* (New York, 1968).

For information about Jeannette Rankin's work as a social worker and the Washington suffrage campaign, the author conducted research at the University of Washington Libraries, Seattle, including the Nellie M. Fick Papers. For additional information on the Washington state suffrage movement, the author turned to C. H. Bailey, "How Washington Women Regained the Ballot," *Pacific Monthly*, July 1, 1911; Stella E. Pearce, "Suffrage in the Pacific Northwest," *Washington Historical Quarterly*, 3 (April 1912), 106–14; T. A. Larson, "The Woman Suffrage Movement in Washington,"

Pacific Northwest Quarterly, 67 (April 1976), 49–62; James W. Montgomery, *Liberated Woman: Life with May Arkwright Hutton* (Spokane, Wash., 1974); and Abigail Scott Duniway, *Path Breaking: An Autobiographical History of the Equal Suffrage Movement in Pacific Coast States,* (1914; reprint, New York, 1970).

On suffrage nationally, the author used the following material: National American Woman Suffrage Association, *History of Woman Suffrage,* by Elizabeth Cady Stanton, et al. (Rochester, N.Y., 1922); Carrie Chapman Catt and Nettie Rogers Shuler, *Woman Suffrage and Politics: The Inner Story of the Suffrage Movement* (New York, 1923); National American Woman Suffrage Association, *Victory, How Women Won It; A Centennial Symposium, 1840–1940* (New York, 1940); Harriot Stanton Blatch, *Challenging Years: The Memoirs of Harriot Stanton Blatch* (New York, 1940); Mildred Adams, *The Right to Be People* (Philadelphia, Penn., 1967); Alan P. Grimes, *The Puritan Ethic and Woman Suffrage* (New York, 1967); Eleanor Flexner, *Century of Struggle: The Woman's Rights Movement in the United States* (Cambridge, Mass., 1959); William L. O'Neill, *Everyone Was Brave: The Rise and Fall of Feminism in America* (Chicago, 1969); and Elizabeth A. Taylor, "The Woman Suffrage Movement in Florida," *Florida Historical Quarterly,* 37 (July, 1957), 42–61.

On the Montana suffrage movement the author used Mary Long Alderson, "Woman Suffrage in Montana," unpublished typescript, 1904, MHS; Mary Long Alderson, "Women Suffrage in Montana, 1904: A Half Century of Progress for Montana Women," circa 1935, MHS archives; Helena Business Woman's Suffrage Club Papers and Montana Suffrage Club Papers, MHS; T. A. Larson, "Montana Women and the Battle for the Ballot," *Montana The Magazine of Western History,* 23 (January 1973), 25–41; Harold Tascher, *Maggie and Montana: The Story of Maggie Smith Hathaway* (New York, 1954); Doris Buck Ward, "The Winning of Woman Suffrage in Montana," (master's thesis, Montana State University, Bozeman, 1974), particularly on the early history of Montana's suffrage movement; and Belle Fligelman Winestine, "Mother was Shocked," *Montana The Magazine of Western History,* 24 (July 1974), 70–79.

The author's sources on the antiwar movements in the first half of the century, particularly the 1920 and 1930s, include Selig Adler, "The War Guilt Question and American Disillusionment, 1918–1928," *Journal of Modern History,* 23 (March 1951); Charles Chatfield, ed., *Peace Movements in America* (New York, 1973); Marie

Louise Degen, *The History of the Woman's Peace Party* (Baltimore, Md., 1939), 145; Dorothy Detzer, *Appointment on the Hill* (New York, 1948); Claudius O. Johnson, *Borah of Idaho* (Nyack, N.Y., 1936); Frederick J. Libby, *To End War: the Story of the National Council for the Prevention of War* (Nyack, N.Y., 1969); and Mrs. Pope Hill's scrapbook on Jeannette Rankin, Rankin Collection, University of Georgia, Athens.

For an example of press coverage near the time of Jeannette's vote against World War II, see E. Evans, "Woman Against War," *Scribners' Commentary,* November 1941.

The author's complete bibliography is included in her original manuscript, "Fighting Pacifist: Jeannette Rankin and Her Times," a copy of which is at MSU, along with her clipping files, correspondence, and other research material.

Index

Since this is a biography, information about Jeannette Rankin is found throughout the book. Thus, readers are advised to look in the index under specific topics as well as the Jeannette Rankin subject entry for information about Jeannette, whose name is abbreviated as "JR" in this index. Page numbers in *italics* indicate photographs.